WOMEN /

With a doctorate in Indian history and culture from Georgetown University, Washington, DC, Vera Hildebrand is a senior research fellow at the Nordic Institute of Asian Studies at University of Copenhagen, Denmark. Previously, she taught at Harvard University and University of Copenhagen. She is the co-editor of *At Home in the World: A Window on Contemporary Indian Literature* (2002).

For *Women at War*, she travelled to Malaysia, India, Singapore, the United States, Great Britain and Japan to identify and interview all surviving soldiers of the Rani of Jhansi Regiment (RJR) of the Indian National Army, as well as male Indian and Japanese soldiers who had worked with RJR in World War II in Burma.

WOMEN

AT

WAR

SUBHAS CHANDRA BOSE
AND THE
RANI OF JHANSI REGIMENT

VERA HILDEBRAND

HarperCollins *Publishers* India

First published in India in 2016 by
HarperCollins *Publishers* India

P-ISBN: 978-93-5264-068-3
E-ISBN: 978-93-5264-069-0

2 4 6 8 10 9 7 5 3 1

HarperCollins *Publishers*
A-75, Sector 57, Noida, Uttar Pradesh 201301, India
1 London Bridge Street, London, SE1 9GF, United Kingdom
Hazelton Lanes, 55 Avenue Road, Suite 2900, Toronto, Ontario M5R 3L2
and 1995 Markham Road, Scarborough, Ontario M1B 5M8, Canada
25 Ryde Road, Pymble, Sydney, NSW 2073, Australia
195 Broadway, New York, NY 10007, USA

Typeset in 11.5/14 Perpetua STD by
R. Ajith Kumar

Printed and bound at
Thomson Press (India) Ltd.

Dedicated to
my husband Robert Blackwill
and
the courageous members of the Rani of Jhansi Regiment

CONTENTS

CONTENTS

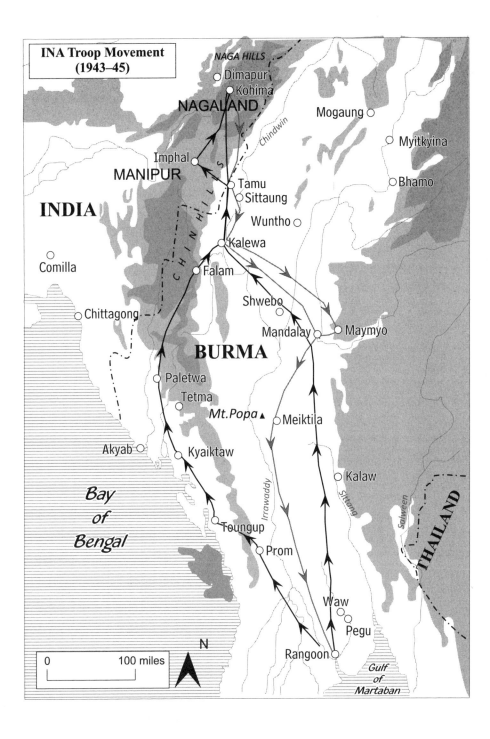

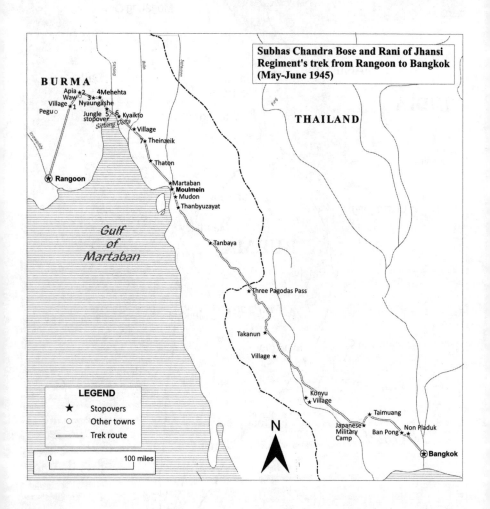

Subhas Chandra Bose and Rani of Jhansi
Regiment's trek from Rangoon to Bangkok
(May–June 1945)

INTRODUCTION

THE RANI OF JHANSI REGIMENT

AMONG THE MORE IMPROBABLE events of the Asia-Pacific theatre in World War II was the creation in Singapore in 1943 of a corps of female Indian combat soldiers, the Rani of Jhansi Regiment (RJR). In addition to the fighters, the women in the RJR included a small contingent of weapons-trained nurses. They were called Ranis and served under Subhas Chandra Bose in the Indian National Army (INA), also named the Azad Hind Fauj, the Army of Free India. This army in exile consisting of fifty thousand Indian men and women was formed in cooperation with the Japanese army, joining the Axis powers to liberate India from British colonial rule. The Ranis in the INA were deployed in the Burma campaign during the final stages of WWII. Because the creation of an Indian all-female regiment of combat soldiers was a radical military innovation in 1943, and because the role of women in today's broader context of Indian culture has become a prevalent and pressing issue, the extensive testimony of the surviving veterans of this unit is timely and urgent. More than seven decades later, the history of these brave women soldiers is little known, their extraordinary service and the role played by Subhas Chandra Bose having remained largely unexplored.

Five broad developments converged in the summer of 1943 to facilitate the creation of the Rani of Jhansi Regiment. First, since the

Bengali Renaissance movement in the nineteenth century, the perception of Indian women had evolved in positive ways, and in recent decades Mohandas Gandhi's (1869–1948) efforts to mobilize Indian women for the independence movement had furthered that trend. Aspects of life in the Indian communities in Malaya, Singapore and Burma caused this progressive shift in the status of Indian women to become more manifest in diaspora communities than among Indians residing on the Indian mainland. Second, again centred in Bengal and antithetical to Gandhi's passive resistance, the use of force, including by women, became a prominent instrument in the hands of dissidents who were fighting for Indian independence. Third, the charismatic Bengali nationalist Subhas Chandra Bose (1897–1945), the most prominent leader promoting armed rebellion against the British Raj, matured to hold advanced views for his time on gender issues. Fourth, the shockingly rapid defeat of the British by the Japanese in Burma, Malaya and Singapore in early 1942 had shaken the myth of imperial invincibility and fanned the embers of Indian nationalism in the South-East Asian diaspora, away from daily oppressive colonial realities in India. And fifth, tens of thousands of Indian prisoners of war held by the Japanese army in Malaya combined with this intensified Indian nationalism, led Bose to conclude that the best chance for the military liberation of India was an invasion across the Indo-Burma border.

The confluence of these disparate factors inspired Bose to recruit women from the Indian diaspora. And the women dared to exploit the opportunity to enlist in the Rani of Jhansi Regiment. The central themes of this book comprise the details of this alignment of social and political forces and their materialization in the establishment, recruitment, training and deployment to Burma of these fighting women.

Bose named the Rani of Jhansi Regiment after Rani Lakshmibai of Jhansi, the Indian heroine who died on the battlefield fighting against the British during the 1857 Indian rebellion. As Lakshmi Swaminathan Sahgal (1914–2012), the commander of the unit, explained in an interview with me in Kanpur, in January 2008, 'Netaji [Subhas Chandra Bose] told us that he chose the name "Rani of Jhansi" for the Regiment because he had read an article by an Englishman, who after the Mutiny in 1857 wrote that "if there had been a thousand women like the Rani, we could never have conquered India".'[1]

In the years since the RJR surrender in 1945, the story of Subhas Chandra Bose and the Rani Regiment of female combatants, as signature symbols of both the national fight for independence and of Indian women's struggle for gender equality, has taken on the aspect of myth. My interviews with the veteran Ranis together with archival research comprise the evidence that separates the myth of the Bengali hero and his jungle warrior maidens from historical fact, and this resulting book presents an accurate narrative of the Ranis.[2] The facts are nearly as impressive as the myth.

The Rani of Jhansi infantry and nursing units of the INA consisted entirely of civilian volunteers lacking any prior military training. They were recruited from traditional Indian families of the diasporas in Singapore, Malaya and Burma. The number of women in the Rani Regiment as reported by the press and even by historians has been as high as five thousand. Through new research, this book establishes the accurate number. Almost none of these new soldiers had been engaged in political activity before joining the Rani Regiment. They were deeply devoted to Bose's nationalist cause, went through vigorous military training before they were deployed to north central Burma in 1944 when the INA, in concert with the Japanese 15th Army, fought the Allied forces in an attempt to cross the border from Burma into the Indian state of Manipur at the city of Imphal.

'Combat infantry' denotes soldiers in uniform serving in an organized fighting force trained to engage in ground attack. The RJR may be the first all-female infantry combat unit within an established army. Being the first women to sign up for infantry combat duty was a matter of pride for the Ranis, and for Bose it was important that these path-breaking female soldiers were Indian. Although fable and history are replete with stories of female warriors from Queen Vishpala of the Rig Veda to the Amazons of Greek mythology to the current Kurdish Peshmerga Force, most of these ancient and legendary female warriors fought alone or with bands of soldiers to protect their homes. The historical Rani of Jhansi was a widow who belonged to the last category.

This strict definition of combat soldiers excludes resistance fighters and guerrillas. Hundreds of thousands of women fought in World War II and served in the British, the German, and in the American armies, but they were not in all-female infantry units and were not sent into the battle zones.[3] It was different with the USSR forces. By 1943 the army of the Soviet Union included a million fighting women. The 586th Fighter Aviation Regiment, 587th Day Bomber Aviation Regiment and the 588th Night Bomber Regiment of the Soviet Air Force were all-female units of pilots and aircraft engineers, although they were not formally designated 'women's regiments'.[4]

A principal reason for the traditional exclusion of women from ground combat has been to prevent them from becoming prisoners of war and suffering rape. The Rani of Jhansi soldiers, fully expecting to engage in ground warfare, accepted the danger of being taken prisoners, but they made it clear to me that they had not considered the danger of rape. Innocent in this regard, they deployed to the steamy jungles of Burma determined to follow their hero to victory and to the liberation of India. This is their story.

ONE

SEARCHING FOR THE RANI OF JHANSI REGIMENT

THE ALL-FEMALE RANI OF Jhansi Regiment was created as part of the Indian National Army operating in the Burma campaign during the final stages of WWII. In the many tomes written on the South-East Asian theatre of war by mainstream scholars of India and the British Raj, the history of the RJR has remained largely unexplored. These serious historians, Indian and Western, all male, judged the addition of women into a standing army worth only a couple of lines, if that.

During their service, the women of the Regiment were known as Ranis. In 2008 when I began to interview the surviving Ranis, they were already old ladies, ranging in age from their late seventies to early nineties. They had moved about in the years after the end of the War and the independence of India, Burma, Singapore and Malaya; so locating and contacting these women was a challenging task. In several cases the only available information was the Rani's first name and the town where she had once lived. Thanks to computerized telephone directories in Malaysia and Singapore, it was possible in those countries to create lists of all residents with a particular name. Using various improvised criteria to winnow down the list, such as elimination of women whose employment seemed unlikely for individuals in the age group of the Ranis, I telephoned the rest. I was eventually able to locate every living Rani whose name I had acquired, a total of thirty, and I arranged to conduct comprehensive interviews with twenty-two Ranis living in Malaysia, Singapore, India and the United States. After visits and interviews with the first few Ranis, the process of locating other veterans became simpler as each Rani identified any others with whom she had kept in touch. A Christmas card from 1959, an invitation to a daughter's wedding or a photograph of a Rani with her small children – all treasures the recipients had kept safeguarded for decades – served as clues that prodded memories and enabled me to pick up the trail of other RJR veterans. I believe that in the period 2008–11, I tracked down all surviving Ranis, with the remotely possible exception of any who may have remained in Burma, now Myanmar.

My telephone call or visit to the home of a Rani to ask for an appointment for an interview was almost always answered with happy excitement. Usually I was welcomed into their homes and was offered both drink and food, sometimes staying overnight with the Rani and her family. Several Ranis now live with children and grandchildren. Just one Rani, Eva Jenny, said that she was uncomfortable inviting me home. She thought it might be too difficult to locate her house in Tanjung Malim, about sixty miles north of Kuala Lumpur, and arranged that we instead meet at her church nearby.[1] Only few of the women needed to be persuaded to participate in the study, but three Ranis whom I located declined to be interviewed because they had come to regret their participation in the War. I did, however, in all three cases, speak to their sisters who had also served as Ranis. Generally, when no one answered the telephone at what I thought was the likely home of a Rani, I went to the location and enquired with the neighbours. In most instances, with the generous help of neighbours, shopkeepers and tradesmen, I found the Rani, but at other times I learned from relatives, friends or neighbours that she had died.

All but four of the Rani interviews were conducted in English. Other than these four exceptions, the Ranis spoke fluent English either as their first or as their second language. For two interviews that were not conducted in English, a professional Tamil interpreter translated consecutively questions and answers. In the case of a third informant who spoke only Tamil, the Rani's lively nineteen-year-old granddaughter acted as translator. In the fourth case, because the Rani was shy about speaking English, her younger sister, who was an English teacher, translated from Bengali. As the interview progressed, however, the Rani constantly improved upon the precision of her sister's translation.

Except for those sessions requiring translators, the Rani and I would sit apart from other people during the interview. Many of the Ranis lived in small quarters, and family members and servants could listen in; sometimes a daughter or a granddaughter commented or asked questions from other rooms. Several Ranis were interviewed more than once; I spoke with some over several days. I took photographs of each Rani who agreed to my doing so, and I received permission to publish the photographs as well as their testimony and life stories.

In this book, a Rani is initially referred to by her first name, her maiden name, and if she used the name of her husband then also her married name. Subsequently, the Ranis are identified by their first names because in the interviews that is how they referred to each other. The commander of the unit, Lakshmi Swaminathan Sahgal, MD, is generally referred to as 'Captain Lakshmi', which is what she was called during her service in the Regiment and as a prominent public figure in India after the War.

Stressing that participation was completely voluntary, I explained that I wanted to interview every surviving Rani about her experiences while serving as a soldier in the Rani of Jhansi Regiment in the Indian National Army, as well as her life before she enlisted. I said that my research would result in a book on the RJR. Before proceeding, each Rani gave her recorded permission for me to publish her responses. I recorded all interviews using a digital recorder placed in full view of the Rani.

Both before the interview and after, the Rani was invited to ask whatever questions she or her family might have. Each Rani received my full contact information, home address, email address and telephone numbers in case she wanted to add or change any of the information given.

One daughter, Subhashini Sahgal Ali, has subsequently written to enquire when the book will be published.

I had prepared in advance a series of questions that I asked each Rani about herself, her family, her education and her time in the army. My questionnaire was constructed according to standard guidelines for semi-structured cultural anthropological research interviews. An important aim was to make the interviewee feel comfortable in telling her story. The first questions established name, birthdate, birthplace, religion and where the Rani grew up. Next I asked about her parents, siblings and education. I then invited each woman to recount how she joined the RJR, focusing on her reasons for enlisting and the reactions of friends and family.

The third phase of this initial interview was the Rani's account of her training in the INA camps and whether she was deployed in Burma. The final section focused on her assessment as to whether her participation and that of the other members of the RJR made a difference in the way Indian women were perceived, and of the significance to the freedom struggle and to herself of her participation in the Regiment.

In our second and successive interviews, I used open-ended questions designed to elicit more details about the war experience and to determine whether the Ranis thought that they were different from other Indian women who had lived more conventional lives. I quickly learned that the Ranis sometimes, before answering, reflected much longer than people in the United States and Scandinavia, and that allowing them time to remember and consider produced important results.

I did not show the questionnaire to the Ranis because I did not want to lead their responses or make them feel bound by my text. The questions were not asked in the same order in each case so as not to interrupt the subject's train of thought; my objective was for each Rani to tell the story as she remembered it with as much detail as possible. I did, however, check that all points had been covered before I ended the interview.

Those Ranis who had held special positions in the INA or appeared to be better informed about various aspects of the Regiment were interviewed several times. In general, the Rani would first recount the story of her time in the INA as she most likely had told it many times over the decades, but as the interview progressed, and especially when I returned for a second or a third interview session, the process seemed to jog her memory and she would expand on her account as she remembered more of the experiences. At our first meeting, most Ranis told stories of their most exciting and frightening experiences, while at later sessions they focused more on everyday events and daily routine as well as on the details of their professional and personal relationships with other Ranis.

All in all, I interviewed twenty-two Ranis in India (Kanpur, New Delhi, Mumbai, Kolkata and Jamshedpur), in Malaysia (Kuala Lumpur, Ipoh, Tanjung Malim, Seremban and Penang), in Singapore, and in the United States (Baldwin, NY).[2] These twenty-two Ranis had between them nine sisters who were also Ranis and served together with them in the camps in Singapore and Burma.

In addition to the Ranis, I located and interviewed Kunizuka Ishiyo, the Japanese soldier who served as the Hindustan-Japanese translator for the Ranis and who had accompanied them on the retreat from upper Burma to Bangkok at the end of the War. At the time of our interview, Kunizuka was living in Kobe, Japan.[3] This ninety-six-year-old energetic veteran had vivid memories of 'the beautiful girls', and asked if Captain 'Lakshmi was still as exceptionally good-looking?'. Kunizuka-san was most eager to talk, and urged me to visit him at his cottage in the countryside, but because in our long telephone conversation he was not interested in expanding beyond the topic of how attractive the Ranis were, I did not go to Kobe.[4]

In New Delhi I also interviewed Captain S.S. Yadava, a retired male INA soldier born in 1920 in Jhajjar district, Haryana. As a havildar, sergeant, in the British Army, he was taken prisoner after the Singapore surrender. From the POW camp he immediately joined the INA and his first assignment was to protect a wooden bridge in southern Burma that the Japanese Army was constructing using British POWs as labour. In 1944 Yadava was transferred to Rangoon to serve as manager of the building where Bose worked. This was a job he loved because it allowed him close contact with Netaji, and here he also observed and admired the Ranis' contribution to the war. After retirement as a school teacher, Yadava dedicated several decades of his life to helping all INA veterans, including many Ranis, get the pensions to which they were entitled.

The Oral History Centre at the Singapore National Archives interviewed several former INA soldiers for a project on the Japanese occupation of Singapore. These interviews provide excellent information about the individual soldier's experience as well as observations regarding Bose and the Ranis in Singapore and Burma. P.K. Lakshmi Nair, aka Sheila Fernandez, was the only Rani among the INA soldiers interviewed for the Singapore Project.[5] From her daughter, I learned that Lakshmi Nair had died several years earlier, but because the Singapore Oral History Project interviewer asked insightful questions and received useful responses, I have incorporated some of that information.

Few original documents pertaining to the INA survived because on 22 April 1945, following the string of setbacks that led to the INA and Japanese surrender, Bose ordered all internal INA documents destroyed.[6] In 1946 British Intelligence estimated that a mere 5% or so of the original mass of documents had been salvaged and that 'it seems fairly certain that such documents as are now in our hands will remain the only historical record of the birth, life and death of the INA'.[7] In view of this inauspicious assessment by British Intelligence of the availability of material, it seemed particularly important to locate all extant documents, and I exhaustively searched archival collections for documents relating to the RJR in India, Britain, Singapore, Japan and Malaysia.

The Netaji Research Bureau housed in the Bose family home on Elgin Road in Kolkata holds all extant Bose letters and other papers, but on my several visits access to view any unpublished material or catalogues of holdings was denied.

The Private Papers Section of the National Archives of India in New Delhi keeps the Indian National Army Papers and the Indian Independence League Papers. These two collections yielded much valuable information.[8] Previously secret and top-secret Indian government files relating to Subhas Chandra Bose were declassified and transferred to the National Archives of India in December 2015. More documents are added each month. These files have so far produced no relevant new information.

In November 2010, the British Library opened access to the INA Interrogation Reports (IRs) produced by the Combined Services Detailed Interrogation Centre (India), (CSDIC[I]), a branch of the British Intelligence Service set up by the imperial defence department to interrogate captured and defecting INA soldiers.[9] The unit was in operation in Singapore and Burma from 1942 until the spring of 1946 searching for information on Bose, the INA and the Ranis. This book on Bose and the RJR is the first to incorporate and assess data from the CSDIC(I) reports.

Before the CSDIC(I) reports were finally located and made available, several historians had noted that thousands of interrogations of INA deserters and prisoners of war had been carried out by British Intelligence, but the fate of these documents was unknown.[10] From the outset of my research on the Rani of Jhansi Regiment, I considered it important to locate the interrogation reports as I hoped that they would be an important addition to the small store of otherwise available information about the Regiment.

After a long and fruitless search of several British, Indian and Singaporian archives to establish if the IRs were still extant, I found at the British Library in London several top-secret messages dated 1947. These exchanges among high-ranking officers of the British defence department's India Command mentioned the IRs. Two letters written at the end of November 1947, on the eve of his departure from India, by Field Marshal Claude Auchinleck, reveal the problem faced by the British officers of what to do with these interrogation reports. One letter said the documents could not be destroyed because the British government required them to 'be available to refute distorted claims or allegations made against us in connection with the INA, ... and the papers therefore should obviously be preserved with some care'.[11] Another letter dated a few days later followed up on that point, reporting that these top-secret documents had been dispatched to London. The letter added that the defence department's India Command officers 'don't want the two Dominion Governments here to know (for obvious reasons) that we have sent Home at this juncture papers in connection with the INA'.[12] Given that the official total number of these INA interrogations was 23,266, the shipment of these top-secret papers must have been large enough to make it unlikely they would simply slip through the bureaucratic cracks and disappear.[13]

Nonetheless, it remains unclear exactly what happened to the original INA interrogation reports and the mystery is now unlikely ever to be solved.[14] Leonard Gordon, the author of a detailed and reliable history of Bose, said that Colonel C. Hugh Toye, who was head of the British Intelligence Operations in Burma during WWII and in Singapore after the war, told him that Toye had obtained permission to copy the interrogation reports, and had placed all the copies in a large personal trunk that was shipped back to England.[15] A penciled note in the margin of the letter tallying the number of prisoners of war records stated that these papers ought to be returned after Toye, the chief of British Intelligence Service, had had copies made for his book. Gordon believed that Toye had deposited the copies with the India Office at the British Library.[16] At first my several intense searches of the British Library Holdings failed to find any Interrogation Reports of any INA members at the British Library. It appeared that if Toye's copies had been received, they were apparently lost. Indeed, I was repeatedly told by senior British Library officials that these documents were not and had never been part of the Library's collections.

When my search for the Interrogation Reports seemed to have reached its frustrating conclusion, and just before I was about to give up and leave the UK, a Library employee, calling herself or himself 'Freulein X' and who had seen the records of my earlier searches, sent me an anonymous email stressing that Toye's copies did indeed exist in the Library archives. In fact, this informant reported that there were twelve packages named 'INA Reports' in storage, marked with a red label saying 'Closed Collection. Not to be issued or retrieved.'[17] Freulein X insisted that I not try to identify her/him and not reveal that she/he had contacted me. Armed with that crucial new information, and without revealing what I knew from my source, I was able to convince chief curator Dr Antonia Moon of India Office Records to search all storage areas. The Interrogation Reports were finally discovered and made available to me as the first researcher to access them.

The contents of these boxes were clearly Toye's copies. He maintained a lifelong fascination with Bose and the INA; handwritten comments on the documents correspond to marginal additions and corrections in an unpublished, typed manuscript of a book on Bose, 'Subhas Pasha', that Toye authored.[18] Clearly, not all twenty-three thousand reports were in the rediscovered storage in the British Library archives, and the whereabouts of the original documents from which Toye made his copies remain unknown. In his introduction to the papers, Toye reveals that after 'all reports connected with the INA had been examined by a Board of Officers in May-June [1946], 60% were destroyed. Of the remaining 40% ... their subsequent fate is not known.'[19] Therefore, it seems that the recovered British Library collection comprises duplicates of what Toye judged to be the most pertinent Interrogation Reports and the most interesting Weekly Intelligence Summaries from the British Intelligence files in Singapore.[20]

Although one cannot trust that intelligence obtained from only one side in a war will present a complete and accurate picture of the conflict, it is fortunate that the British have a penchant for creating and preserving records. Because INA officers succeeded in destroying all documents on hand in Rangoon before retreating ahead of the Allied forces, information gathered by British intelligence officers and by interrogators debriefing INA deserters and captives is of great importance to historians writing on the RJR and the INA.

As most Ranis lived in Malaya before they joined the RJR, it is surprising that the National Archives of Malaysia asserted that no material pertaining to the Regiment is held there. It is fortunate that the Oral History Centre at the National Archives of Singapore possesses a rich collection of photographs and oral life histories of Singapore residents living there during the Japanese occupation. The Singapore National Archives holds various newspapers from the time the Japanese ruled with numerous stories about the Rani of Jhansi Regiment. The Centre of South Asia Studies, University of Cambridge, also holds several oral history interviews pertaining to the INA, Bose, and the Indian freedom movement. One long session with Subbier Appadurai Ayer (1898–1980), the minister for publicity and propaganda for the Azad Hind government, was especially useful because of his close relationship with Bose and his role as protector of the Ranis on their retreat from Rangoon to Bangkok.[21]

In Tokyo, even with the most generous and expert assistance of Professor Yoneo Ishii, an extensive search failed to produce any documents pertaining to the RJR at the Japan Centre for Asian Historical Records in the National Archives of Japan of which Ishii was director general.

At a meeting in Kyoto in June 2009 Professor Nobuko Nagasaki of Ryokoku University told me about her book, *Shiryōshū indo kokumingun kankeisha kikigaki*, a collection of interviews in which Japanese soldiers recounted their experiences with the Indian National Army in Burma during World War II.[22] The interviews had not yielded much information about the Ranis, but Professor Nagasaki provided me with contact information that allowed me to interview the Japanese translator who had accompanied the Ranis from Rangoon. Searches of the National Archives of the Union of Myanmar and the National Library of Myanmar failed to produce any account of the RJR presence in Burma.

Five Ranis, Janaki Thevar Athinahappan, Asha Bharati Sahay Choudhry, Aruna Ganguli Chattopadhya, Eva Jenny Murty Jothi and Dhanam Lakshmi Suppiah Ratnam, lent me their long unpublished voluminous diaries and memoirs of their time in the Regiment and gave me permission to copy and use these writings. These unpublished records are especially valuable for providing new detailed accounts of the mission and of the daily routine in the Rani camps.

The Bose family in Kolkata administers the Netaji Research Bureau, established to further Bose studies. Sugata Bose, a member of the Lok Sabha representing the Jadavpur constituency, West Bengal, and also Indian Gardiner Professor of Oceanic History and Affairs at Harvard University, is currently at the helm of the Research Bureau which continues to publish and update Bose's works.[23] The Research Bureau also issues *The Oracle*, a journal dedicated to the study of Bose, in which five Ranis – Lakshmi Swaminathan Sahgal, Manwati Panday Arya, Maya Ganguly Banerjee, Shanti Bhowmick Majumdar and Janaki Thevar Athinahappan – have contributed their views of Bose's abilities as commander-in-chief of the INA and guardian of the women's regiment.[24] Rasammah Navarednam Bhupalan herself wrote the third chapter, 'The Rani of Jhansi Regiment: A Will for Freedom' of the biography on her life by Aruna Gopinath.[25]

Like almost every published work on Bose, Rani Manwati Panday Arya's biography, *Patriot:The Unique Indian Leader Netaji Subhas Chandra Bose;A New Personalised Biography by One Who Worked for Netaji* (2007), expresses the writer's deep admiration of the man and his nationalistic zeal.[26] Manwati's book, one of the last written by someone who knew him, focuses on Bose's objectives for the RJR and his hopes for future generations of women in liberated India. In terms of substance, however, Manwati's contribution is hagiographic rather than historical.

After the War, Captain Lakshmi became the voice of the Regiment, travelling around India to speak about Bose and the Regiment.[27] Her autobiography, *A Revolutionary Life – Memoirs of a Political Activist* (1997), describes the creation and history of the RJR, providing information about the process of recruitment, the volunteers and their family backgrounds, training routines and daily life in the Rani camps, and the Regiment's service in Burma.[28] As we shall see subsequently, her memory of events does not always agree with other Ranis' recollections of the same occurrences or with the evidence of the newly discovered archival material.

In sum, despite numerous blind alleys and fruitless searches, my interviews with the surviving Ranis and my archival research uncovered significant new information on the Rani of Jhansi Regiment, which provides a fresh and more accurate perspective on these extraordinary women and their place in Indian and world history.

TWO

HISTORY OF INDIAN WOMEN IN INDIA AND THE DIASPORAS

AS THE RANIS SOUGHT to go to war to liberate their homeland, they were hardly building on a congenial past with respect to the role of women in Indian society. Scholarly discussions of the status of Indian women in the century prior to Independence in 1947 generally begin with a nostalgic invocation of some ancient quasi-mythical period, a golden age of gender equity. Historian Manmohan Kaur writes, 'Women in ancient India occupied a dignified place. ... All the high avenues of learning were open to women.'[1] According to Jai Narain Sharma, political scientist and professor at Panjab University, 'In Vedic times, women had freedom of movement, education, religious rights, equal opportunities with the men of those far-off times, as is found in the internal evidence of the literature of that era.'[2] Annie Besant, a British socialist and an early women's rights activist, assures us, 'The position of women in the ancient Aryan civilization was a very noble one.'[3] Both male and female writers on the status of Indian women at the time of the independence struggle and the concurrent nascent women's movement have pointed to women's putative elevated status in ancient epochs, perhaps as assurance to their readers that gender equity was not a mere fantasy, and that Indian women were indeed worth bringing out of their 'deplorable state of ignorance, illiteracy, superstition and physical seclusion'.[4] There is, to my knowledge, no definitive historical evidence for any of the claims of a glorious Indian past culture in which women were respected members of society or lived on an equal footing with men.

Numerous explanations have been proposed for the subsequent erosion of the position of women in India. Some cultural historians simply assert that the status of women fell due to their own biological limitations! Others trace the degradation of women to the introduction of specific customs. Polygamy inevitably lowered the status of women,[5] as did the fact that aristocratic Aryan families kept female slaves.[6] Another custom that reduced the value of women was the offering of little girls to serve in the temples. These unfortunates, known as *muralis* or devadasis, were the common property of the priests and often ended their lives as street prostitutes.[7]

When Muslim invaders threatened the safety of women, Hindu society adopted various restrictive means 'to protect the honour of their women'. One was the enforced seclusion of women in purdah.[8] Female infanticide, child marriage, sati (widow burning) and resistance to educating females were consolidated as 'traditional' elements of Hindu culture on the pretext of protecting the weaker sex against invaders and foreign occupiers.[9] A different theory attributes the diminished standing of Indian women to the influence of other religions: 'With the advent of asceticism in Buddhism and Jainism, the position of women in society began to deteriorate. Under the patriarchal Indian society, a woman's place became so miserable that she began to be treated like a chattel to be gifted away by the husband.'[10]

In *The Discovery of India* (1946), which Jawaharlal Nehru (1889–1964) wrote during his imprisonment for seditious activities, the author contemplates the problem of women's inferior status. 'The legal position of women, according to Manu, the earliest exponent of the law, was definitely bad. They were always dependent on somebody – on the father, the husband, or the son. Almost they were treated, in law, as chattels [sic].'[11] Nehru was referring to *Manu Samhita*, a collection of writings by many authors, composed more than two thousand years ago, around the beginning of the Common Era.[12]

In these ancient texts, Manu, progenitor of humankind, lays out detailed rules, dharma, for all aspects of conduct, including how women should be treated and how they should behave. Manu denies women any degree of independence or free will: 'In childhood a woman should be under her father's control, in youth under her husband's, and when her husband is dead, under her son's.'[13] These strictures impacted all Indian culture and society and still influenced the lives of Hindu women in the 1940s as young Indian women contemplated joining the Ranis of the INA.

As late as the beginning of the twentieth century, Hindu girls, especially Brahmins, were married while still young in accordance with the Laws of Manu: 'A thirty-year-old man should marry a twelve-year-old girl who charms his heart, and a man of twenty-four an eight-year-old girl.'[14] When a girl was married, it was ostensibly the duty of her in-law family to protect her, both physically and morally. In good families, the girl would not be used as a sexual partner until puberty, but that ideal was often ignored. Child marriage had the collateral effect that girls were often widowed before they reached maturity. That child marriage is still part of Indian culture in 2016 is demonstrated by a very successful soap opera, *Balika Vadhu*, 'Child Bride'. It is one of India's longest running TV shows, and was broadcast every day all over India, subtitled in several languages.[15]

The Bengali philosopher Ishwar Chandra Vidyasagar (1820–1891) led the campaign to legalize widow remarriage, which came into force in 1856.[16] Of course, neither social reformers nor the police could make widow marriage socially acceptable. Even in the 1940s, a widow continued to be regarded as eternally married to her deceased husband, and second marriages were rare among the upper castes. If a woman did marry again, she forfeited any inheritance from her husband's property. Furthermore, the guardianship of her children from that marriage would also be granted to the blood relatives of her deceased husband.[17] One of the members of the RJR, Akilandam Vairavapillai confirmed that those customs still prevailed in 1942. Married at age sixteen, one year later she was widowed while pregnant, and her husband's family, by right of law, claimed her daughter at birth. Akilandam never remarried and has had no connection with her only child since giving birth to her. [18]

Many Indian men of the period saw the changes advocated by social reformers as proof that India was becoming westernized and that its Hindu identity was endangered. The case of prominent Indian nationalist, journal editor and member of the Indian National Congress (INC), Bal Gangadhar Tilak (1856–1920) illustrates how difficult it was to change any aspect of the systemic oppression of women. Tilak, who earned the honorary title Lokmanya, meaning 'beloved of the people', was a prominent exponent of swaraj or self-rule for India, dedicating his life to the freedom struggle. Yet, as a social conservative he also fought against the passage of the Age of Consent Act of 1891, which raised the age of marriage consent from ten to twelve years. Tilak opposed child marriage, but he did not want the Raj to make rules that might undermine orthodox Hinduism.

Another convention that limited the standing of women in Indian society was purdah, a severe restriction on the physical liberty of women confining her to her home. For religious and social reasons, purdah was widely practised among Indian Muslims and was also prevalent among upper-caste Hindus in northern India and somewhat less stringently in the South-East Asian diaspora. The result was that upper- and middle-class women were cut off from participation in the social, political, economic and organized religious life of their community. They almost never left their homes, passing their lives cloistered in zenanas, the inner rooms set aside for women. [19] The lack of sunlight also contributed to women's health problems. In the close quarters of the zenana, tuberculosis thrived. [20] The tradition was less common in rural villages among peasants because women in those settings played an essential part in keeping the family fed and housed, especially by working the fields.

Under these circumstances it is not surprising that education for Indian girls, and especially the rural poor, was virtually non-existent. In 1907, Gandhi placed the blame on Indian men: 'That India is very backward in the education of women is a fact that cannot be denied. ... We can see that Indian men have deliberately kept their [sic] women backward.' [21] Indeed, many Indian men believed that the education of women was of no value

or was even detrimental to society. In 1947, at Independence, the mean
literacy rate for Indian women had increased to only 8 per cent and was
still among the lowest in the world.[22]

The heated and divisive early debates about the status of women, carried
out by men only, lost some steam before the end of the nineteenth century
when the public's attention turned towards the politics of nationalism.
Issues about gender that might seriously impede internal Hindu solidarity
were often tabled, political activists focused instead on the British
oppressors, and a small number of Indian women began to emerge in public
settings. Despite the strong social and religious constraints still hampering
women's activities, women from all parts of India and the South-East Asian
diaspora formed female-only social, political and religious associations with
nationalist themes.[23] Some of these developed into full-fledged women's
movement organizations, and historically it is impossible to disentangle
the women's liberation front from the concurrent anti-colonial struggle
in tracing the path by which women began to emerge from the oppressive
hold of the patriarchal traditions.[24]

Unsurprisingly, the great majority of these early female leaders came
from urban, educated families and had either fathers or husbands who
were politically active.[25] This was also true of a large number of the young
women who became Ranis. Remarkably, however, an even greater number
of illiterate, impoverished plantation labourers also joined the RJR.[26]

Many of the early activists for women's liberation experienced their first
public action in connection with the swadeshi (self-sufficiency) movement
(1905–11).[27] Nationalist Bengali politicians urged Indians to boycott
British goods and become economically self-sufficient, which meant using
only local products. Even timid and traditional women were able to join
this form of protest without violating their duties as housebound wife and
mother. The movement gained momentum, and women across the country
began to take a more conspicuous part in the boycott as they tossed their
foreign cloth on to bonfires in the streets, wrote petitions and attended
rallies. The experience of expressing their opinions in public was thrilling
and gave some of them the courage to also defy social taboos.

A final, decisively important factor in mitigating the religious and societal constraints upon women was Gandhi's 1915 return to India with the avowed goal of freeing India by non-violent means through his Satyagraha movement.[28] Beyond ending colonial occupation, Gandhi's stated objectives included the amelioration of the status of women. Gandhi immediately began to travel around India and made several visits to Burma and Malaya, speaking at conferences, universities, libraries, and wherever he could find an audience, urging women to join the struggle for Indian independence. Again and again Gandhi proclaimed, 'So long as women in India do not take equal part with men in the affairs of the world and in religious and political matters, we shall not see India's star rising.'[29]

Gandhi's entrance on the Indian national stage quickly led to increased involvement by women in the independence movement. They were attracted by his charismatic personality and his apparent sincerity. Gandhi astutely took care to balance his promotion of women's revolutionary activism against the danger of threatening the masculinity of Indian men.[30] He called for women to conform to the female archetype of humility and submission, urging his female audiences to aspire to the ideal embodied by Sita, long-suffering wife of Rama, protagonist of the epic Ramayana. He praised the Indian woman's capacity for self-abnegation and self-sacrifice: 'Silent and dignified suffering is the badge of her sex.'[31] When he asked for funds to support the struggle, women responded generously.

Women's participation in the Indian independence effort in the 1920s and '30s expanded in stages. Swadeshi, Gandhi's arrival and the non-cooperation movement precipitated the second step towards engagement in the freedom struggle for women. During this period, hundreds of thousands of women in India, mostly from the middle-class, joined the political crusade and abandoned forever the confines of purdah. When in 1920 the Indian National Congress ratified a resolution to support non-cooperation with the Raj, this wave of women joined the protest marches and responded to Gandhi's plea to spin, weave, wear and sell khadi, homespun and handwoven cotton cloth. They also picketed liquor stores as well as shops selling foreign-made cloth.

Founded in 1885, the Indian National Congress grew into the largest political party in India and the major power behind the fight for independence. A small and energetic group of women were involved from the beginning, but issues relating to women's status and education were not discussed at the annual meetings until Gandhi became a leading figure in the organization following World War I. Gandhi encouraged women to take part, and social problems also became standard items on the agenda. [32]

In a new development, significant numbers of women began to be arrested and jailed by the British during this period. There are no accurate statistics regarding how many women joined in the freedom struggle and in what capacity, but Government of India records list convictions of women for civil disobedience in the early 1930s. The total number of female incarcerations for all of India in 1932, a year with a high level of protest activity, came to 3,196. The number of women who were arrested for protesting was far greater, but the jails could not accommodate everyone taken into custody. [33] Most detainees were middle-class women who, having surmounted the religious and social impediments enumerated above, were jailed for their efforts.

Historians have speculated why Gandhi's call for women to engage was so effective and resulted in such dramatic changes in the behaviour of traditional young women. [34] Fathers who had been protecting their daughters' virtue and husbands who expected their wives to view them as gods experienced profound turmoil in their everyday lives. Political upheaval generates social transformation, and it is unlikely that this shift in the lives of women would have taken place but for India's revolutionary political environment. On the lighter side, poignant scenes occasionally occurred when women left purdah for the first time in their lives to join the protest marches. At the end of the day, after the demonstrations were over, they had no idea how to get home and had to wait for a son or a husband to fetch them. [35]

Gandhi's non-violent ideology was another factor that led women to feel it was acceptable for them to leave their traditional isolation. He conferred spiritual status on Satyagraha, the non-violent freedom fight, so that the struggle for Indian independence could also be experienced as religious service. Gandhi observed, 'In this non-violent campaign, although our weapons are small they are very powerful since they have in them the power of God.'[36] However, unlike Buddhism and Jainism, Hinduism neither demands ahimsa, 'non-violence', nor bans *himsa*, 'violence'. As one scholar observes, 'A general right to life is to be found in India as rarely as a general ban on killing.'[37] In particular, Gandhi's insistence on non-violence failed to persuade both the Bengali freedom fighters and Bose's many followers, among them the young women of the Rani of Jhansi Regiment.

Bengal, Bose's home territory in the eastern part of the Indian subcontinent, had traditionally been a political tinderbox. As Gandhi kept promising that swaraj was imminent, impatient young Bengalis established secret societies and militias. Since the turn of the century, groups of young men and a few women, mostly students who belonged to the Brahmin and Kshatriya castes, formed terrorist organizations committed to insurrectionary activities.[38] Weapons for their 'actions' as the members called their terrorists attacks, were funded by robberies and dacoity, gang robbery, and some were purchased from German weapons exporters.[39] When captured after a botched action, one of the revolutionaries confessed to the Home Department interrogator that they had expected eventually to raise a revolutionary army of fifty thousand men.[40] Bose was sympathetic to the ideas of the violent revolutionary groups with whom he shared a common background, and most likely the Raj suspected him of involvement with young Bengali revolutionaries. It is known that he had contacts inside these cells, certainly through the former headmaster and Bose's mentor at Ravenshaw College, Cuttack, Beni Madhav Das, and his daughters Kalyani and Bina. Since Bose was never accused, evidently the Raj police did not have positive evidence that he actively supported any terrorist cell or encouraged any acts of violence during this period.

In the 1930s, a few women, mostly young students, managed to overcome male reluctance to allow them to join violent revolutionary groups. Kalyani Das organized the Chhatri Sangha, an early women's group, which quickly grew to have one hundred and twenty-five students meeting several times a week to train lathi fighting, battling with the same long bamboo sticks police used to maintain order.[41] Das stresses that the women 'came not because their brothers were party members or anything, they came because the time was ripe for the movement, student movement.'[42]

The Bengali political leader Sarala Debi Ghoshal Chaudhurani (1872–1945) did not take part physically in the armed attacks against the British, but she donated funds for revolutionary groups and *akhadas*, physical culture clubs where young men trained in martial arts in preparation for militant action.[43] Other women transmitted secret messages, concealed ammunition, prepared explosives, hid revolutionaries in their homes and even pretended to be the wives of the male revolutionaries.[44]

The successful raid on the Chittagong Armoury in 1930 led by Bengali freedom fighter Surya Sen (1894–1934) included two Bengali women: Kalpana Dutt (1913–95) and Preetilata Waddedar (1911–32), in a cadre of sixty-six rebels.[45] Following that attack, Dutt lived underground disguised as a man until she was captured in 1934. Given a life sentence, she spent six years in prison. Two years after the Chittagong attack, Waddedar, the second female raider, led an assault on the Pahartali European Club in Chittagong, in which an elderly European woman was killed. Waddedar, the bomb thrower, was wounded herself, and as her comrades fled to safety she chose martyrdom by taking potassium cyanide.[46]

Several young women planned and implemented their own violent protests. At her college graduation ceremony, Bina Das (1911–86), daughter of Bose's mentor Beni Madhav Das, drew a revolver and attempted to assassinate Sir Stanley Jackson, the governor of Bengal, as he was handing her the diploma. She missed and was arrested. Two girls, fourteen-year-old Suniti Chowdhury and fifteen-year-old Shanti Ghosh asked Bose for his autograph and were inspired by his words which later also electrified the Ranis: 'To preserve your honour, take up arms yourselves, Ye mothers.'[47] Shortly thereafter, in December 1931, they shot the district magistrate of Comilla at point-blank range and were angry when they were only given prison sentences for the assassination. Hearing the news that she was saved from execution, Suniti told her attorney that she and Shanti had wanted to become martyrs for Indian freedom: 'Better to die like a hero than to live like a horse in a stable.'[48] Shanti and Suniti so impressed Bose that in his speech at the opening of the RJR training camp more than ten years later, he praised the courage of these two girls and often mentioned them as models worthy of emulation.[49]

When male revolutionaries, such as Surya Sen and Bhagat Singh, were convicted of murder, they were hanged, but the prospect of violent public protest led the Raj instead to imprison female fighters. For a time, girls who were arrested for obstructing the police actions would be collected in vans, driven far outside the city and dropped off. The British hoped that the long return walk would teach them not to take part in the struggle against the Empire, but the measure failed because sympathizers followed the police vans in taxis and private cars and drove the girls back home.[50]

Some scholars have remarked on the incongruousness of Indian women participating in violent actions against the British or anyone else. But others have countered that these women might have been motivated by the example of Ramayana's Sita as a model for self-sacrifice. Or they might have seen themselves as followers of Kali or Durga, both important Hindu goddesses associated with martial action. Kali destroyed evil before embarking on creative ventures. Preetilata Waddedar, the bomb thrower, expressed frustration that it was socially unacceptable for women to use force to end British colonial occupation of India. The Ranis would have agreed with the message in her suicide letter:

> I wonder why there should be any distinction between males and females in a fight for the cause of country's freedom. If our brothers can join a fight for the cause of motherland, why can't the sisters? Instances are not rare that the Rajput ladies of hallowed memory fought bravely in the battlefields and did not hesitate to kill their country's enemies. The pages of history are replete with high admiration for the historic exploits of these distinguished ladies. Then why should we, the modern Indian women, be deprived of joining this noble fight to redeem our country from foreign domination? If sisters can stand side by side with the brothers in a *Satyagraha* movement, why are they not so entitled in a revolutionary movement? ... Females are determined that they will no more lag behind, but they will stand side by side with their brothers in any activities, however dangerous or difficult.[51]

In 1943, eleven years after Waddedar's prophetic farewell, women finally had a chance to serve as soldiers in an Indian independence army.

Millennia earlier, as evidenced by legend and place names, the geographic locations of Burma and Malaya between the coasts of India and China have made them attractive sites for settlement by Indian traders and other seafarers since prehistoric days.[52] Waves of Indian migrant workers and merchants travelled back and forth for centuries. Emigration from India to Malaya, Burma and other British colonies was encouraged and strongly supported first by the East Asia Company and after 1866 by the Raj, because the colonial Government of India needed labour in order to exploit the rich South-East Asian resources for the Empire. All geographic regions and the major languages of the subcontinent were represented, although Pathans, Bengalis, Punjabis and Gujaratis combined constituted a much smaller proportion than Tamils.[53] Indian ethnic and religious groups among the people who formed the Indian communities in Burma and Malaya included Hindus, Muslims, Gurkhas, Sikhs, Parsis and Jains. In Burma, Tamils constituted 43 per cent of Indians,[54] and in Malaya roughly 90 per cent were South Indians – Tamil, Telugu and Malayali.[55] In Burma, Indian emigration grew rapidly after 1852, when the Irrawaddy delta was annexed in the Second Anglo-Burmese war by the East Asia Company, which built dykes and began to grow rice in this fertile part of the country.[56]

In 1866 Britain made Burma a province of India, and Rangoon, the capital of Burma, grew into a city with more Indian inhabitants than Burmese. By 1941, 69 per cent of the Burmese labour force was Indian, while a scant 7 per cent of the total population of the country was Indian.[57]

Indians in Burma formed three classes. The intellectuals, consisting of educators, public administrators and lawyers, held highly skilled positions in the government as well as in the private sector. The second large group comprised wealthy businessmen who controlled trade and commerce. The third and largest group was industrial labourers, who worked in the tin mines, rice mills and factories. People from each region in India brought their special skills and trades with them to Burma. Most government clerks were Bengalis holding positions similar to those they had held in Calcutta and the Gujaratis were traders in Burma as they had been in India.[58] People coming from the United Provinces, now Uttar Pradesh, farmed and sold eatables, raised cattle and established dairies.[59] With Indian labour and financing, Burma had become the world's largest rice producer by the end of the nineteenth century.[60] Menial work was provided primarily by Tamils arriving from Madras and Orissa.[61] In Burma, the Indian coolie was the cheapest labour, living in squalor, poverty and degradation, exploited and despised while fulfilling many of the essential tasks that allowed the country to function.[62]

Among Indian businessmen, Chettiars were the bankers and financiers in Burma, just as they had been in Chettinad, Madras. The first Chettiar firm is believed to have opened in Moulmein in 1850.[63] By 1929, the total number of Chettiar businesses in Burma was over 1,100. Chettiars held a near monopoly as moneylenders, and through foreclosures, they acquired large landholdings. The Chettiars made loans to farmers, many of whom failed, losing their land to the Chettiars who then hired cheap labour to run the farms. Indians of all backgrounds in Burma were the subjects of vilification deriving from antagonism towards the Chettiar moneylenders.[64]

Grand-scale Indian emigration to Malaya began a little earlier than in Burma. Already in the 1830s, Tamils and Telugus came to the coffee and sugar plantations as indentured labourers.[65] Until the Japanese invasion in 1941, a constant stream of new Indian workers arrived after being recruited for the rubber plantations in Malaya in order to satisfy the worldwide demand for rubber. By 1947, almost 600,000 of the inhabitants of Malaya, just over 10 per cent, were Indian.[66]

The Indian workforce in Malaya consisted largely of unskilled labourers most of whom worked on farms or in tin mines. Some of the men arrived under the indenture system sponsored by the Raj. Rubber estate owners invented their own manner of recruiting, the *kangani* system, to get even cheaper labour. Indian kanganis, plantation workers, were hired by estate owners and managers on a commission basis to go back to India to procure more labourers.[67] At signing, new labourers were advanced a sum to be repaid in instalments. The system was designed so that the worker never was able to pay off his debt with his earnings and thus was effectively enslaved. As in Burma, although on a smaller scale, Chettiar bankers and moneylenders also followed the British colonizers into Malaya.

After the 1857 uprising in India, the Raj identified Sikhs and Gurkhas as 'martial races' among the peoples of India. The British had developed the theory that some racial or ethnic groups were biologically and culturally predisposed to fight, and the Sikhs and Gurkhas were proud of this manly reputation.[68] In Malaya the Sikhs, who originally came from Punjab between 1860 and 1870 to serve as guards at the tin mines in the state of Perak, gradually assumed many of the jobs as policemen and armed guards, similar to the positions they had held back home. Many Sikhs joined the INA; they were former British Indian Army soldiers as well as locally recruited volunteers. After Hindus, Sikh women constituted the second largest group in the Rani Regiment.[69]

In Burma racial tensions had been brewing since the 1930s, due in part to the Indian community's insistence on remaining culturally, economically and politically separate from the native inhabitants.[70] Anti-Indian riots became more frequent, and after January 1942, when the Japanese army progressed northwards expelling British forces in Burma across the mountains into India, Indian businessmen and Chettiar bankers were left unprotected from the Burmese. During the first five months of 1942, between 400,000 and 500,000 Indians tried to escape to India. A few were able to leave by air, some fled by boat, but most were forced to trek overland, scaling mountains 5,000 to 8,000 feet high, with no food supply or shelter.

Rani Aruna Ganguli remembers that just days after the first Japanese bombers destroyed large areas of Rangoon, her elder sister and brother-in-law fled to India. In the course of the following week their Indian neighbourhood in Kamayut, a middle-class Rangoon suburb, was deserted. Every morning another house was left empty. Refugees departed without announcing their intentions to leave, or mentioning if they got tickets. People simply left their homes and friends behind and headed for Calcutta.[71] Thousands of Indians died in the attempt to reach India, many of them killed by the Burmese as they trudged along narrow jungle paths to cross into Assam.[72] Hardly any official records were kept of these incidents, and estimates of the number of fatalities along the road vary from about half of all refugees, that is as many as 250,000, to a more conservative 100,000 dead.[73] Bose's Azad Hind government later attempted to claim property abandoned by fleeing Indians for the Government of India in exile, but by then the Japanese had taken control of it and refused to part with it.[74]

An estimated 400,000 Indians chose to remain in Burma after the Japanese invasion, and it is from these Indian nationalist families the Burma-born Ranis came.[75] One of the officers of the Rani of Jhansi Regiment, Manwati Panday, grew up in a large family of Indian nationalists and active members of the Indian Independence League (IIL), a political organization of Indian expatriates dedicated to win independence for their homeland. Her father and his brothers were all Indian freedom fighters living in Burma.[76]

Only a small proportion of Indians living in Burma and Malaya at the beginning of the twentieth century were descendants of long-time residents. This tendency was reinforced because Indians came to Burma and Malaya principally to work and make money, not to live permanently.[77] Among the long-settled Indians in Rangoon were the Mehtas, wealthy Jain jewellers from Gujarat. Mrs Lilavati Chhaganlal Mehta and her two daughters Neelam and Rama were among the first to join the Ranis in Burma. Indians continued to maintain close contact with their extended families in the villages back home and sought also to retain their traditional values and customs. Men and women alike had a strong sense of belonging to the Indian culture established in their adopted country. Every subgroup of Indians in the diasporas, from wealthy bankers to the penniless menial workers, maintained its Indian culture and loyalty to the homeland.[78] In their new country Indians lived emotionally and culturally distant but economically entwined with the indigenous people, while remaining psychologically bonded to their mother country.[79] In Malaya, the Indian labourers frequently lived in isolated Indian communities on the large rubber plantations or other estates, where they had little interaction with indigenous Malays.

The cultural factors that circumscribed the lives of women in India also impinged on the lives of Indian women abroad. Indian emigrants felt strongly that they remained members of their large joint families connected to their villages in India. It was therefore their ethical duty to send a large share of their wages to help support their families back home, and it was their moral duty to maintain their traditional codes of conduct while overseas.[80] Most nourished the dream, referred to by anthropologists as 'the myth of return', of earning enough money abroad to be able to buy land and resettle in their ancestral village.[81] In short, being raised in the Indian diasporas in Malaya and Burma before World War II meant growing up as an Indian.

About fifty Ranis were born, grew up and resided in Burma before joining the INA, but during my research I learned of no Rani who still lived there in 2008. All Burma-born Ranis repatriated to India, most to Calcutta. Attitudes towards Indians in Burma became increasingly intolerant after WWII and Burma's independence in 1948; some Indians chose to become Burmese citizens, and those that did not were expelled.[82] Four hundred thousand ethnic Indians are living in Burma today without Burmese citizenship and another 1.2 million Burmese citizens have Indian ancestry.[83] INA soldiers living in Burma have received monthly Freedom Fighters' Pension since 1972 when INA veterans became eligible for that pension, but no INA women were reported to be on the list of recipients in Burma. Captain Lakshmi explained, 'All the families of the Ranis left Burma after the War because the Burmese would not allow them to stay.'[84]

From 1925 until 1957, the year Malaysia became independent, 80 per cent of Indians who had emigrated to Malaya resettled in India.[85] That statistic, however, differs significantly from the findings of my study. Of the Ranis and their sisters, who were born in Malaya and Singapore, almost all stayed in independent Malaysia or Singapore. One exception was Rani Ponnammah Navarednam who after retirement moved to the United States to live with her daughter and her family. To the question why they did not move to independent India after having fought for their freedom, several Ranis explained that they belonged where they grew up, in the Indian communities in Malaysia. Akilandam was willing to both die and kill for India's freedom, but she never wanted to live there.[86] Janaki Bai added, 'In India we would be foreigners.'[87]

Records and data are sparse for Indian women living in Burma, Malaya and Singapore in the early decades of the twentieth century. According to Manwati Panday, a substantial majority of Indian women still observed purdah in Burma as late as in the 1940s.[88] During this period, women made up between twenty-five and forty-five percent of the Indian labour force in Malaya, working primarily on the rubber plantations.[89] Some of the female plantation workers had immigrated on their own, but generally women became labourers because they were spouses or daughters of male plantation workers. Unskilled labour was poorly paid, and on average female rubber tappers and weeders received 20 per cent less than men for the same work.[90] These young women lived within the plantation in barracks; they had no privacy, little medical care and less education. It was common practice that the plantation managers demanded their 'right' to have sexual relations with the young women in their employment.

Nearly all Malayan plantation workers were South Indian Tamils – dark-skinned, low-caste and uneducated. They were treated poorly not only by their adoptive communities but also by other Indians.[91] Beyond the usual excuses for discrimination, there was a health issue – the Tamils' poor diet, lack of standard hygiene and ignorance of disease resulted in frequent cases of plague and smallpox which led other Indians to shun them out of fear of contagion.[92]

The illiteracy rate among female plantation labourers was very high, a factor that contributed to their bondage. In 1923 estate owners were by law obliged to provide schooling for the children of plantation workers, but they intentionally undermined the effectiveness of the schools. Teachers were unqualified and attendance was not compulsory. Boys received somewhat more education than girls, but children aged ten and older were offered employment rather than education.[93] By the end of WWII, 41 per cent of Indian females in Malaya aged ten and older were wage earners.[94] Also in the cities, the literacy rate for Indian women was much lower than that for men.

For female workers on tropical estates, life was as harsh as it was for their sisters on Indian farms.[95] Nevertheless, the shortage of women in the immigrant communities and the increase in the number of women being employed outside the home led to a slow improvement in the position of Indian women in the diasporas. Despite the resistance to assimilation, the evolution in Indian family structure reshaped women's self-perception and the role they envisioned for themselves in society. One of the reasons for this change was that the male:female ratio on the plantations in Malaya was 5:3.[96] Because women were in demand as wives, parents did not feel obliged to secure marriage partners for their daughters at an early age. As a result, infant marriage was practised only rarely among Indians in Malaya. All the same, by age fifteen almost all women were married.[97]

Malaya, where most Ranis were recruited, presented far better employment opportunities for women than did India. Palm oil and rubber plantations required female workers both for their labour as well as to balance the male:female ratio as required by law.[98] These agricultural jobs were poorly paid, low-prestige positions, demanding little training and no education. Nevertheless, dependence on the earning power of the women to sustain the family undermined the husband's authority, although in most respects male dominance was unchallenged.[99] Often enough, the estate owners abetted this state of affairs by disbursing a woman's wages to her husband and not to her.[100]

Female labourers continued to be responsible for running the household and especially for raising children. The burden on women was aggravated by the fact that conventional joint families were not common in the diaspora because so few Indians settled permanently. Plantation workers were given housing, allowing young people to form nuclear families; as a result, young brides had no one to share the household chores. On the other hand, they did not have to deal with despotic mothers-in-law. Another factor contributing to the loosening of tradition in diaspora was that, because of the shortage of women, Indian women in Malaya were able to remarry and sati was not practised.[101]

In sum, although diaspora society presented daunting barriers — religious, societal, psychological and, of course, physical — to women's participation in India's struggle for independence, to say nothing of combat service in a military unit, these impediments were probably less formidable in Malaya and Burma than in India itself. The diminished social rigidity constraining Indian women in the diaspora, combined with the persistence of loyalty to Mother India, enhanced significantly the effectiveness of RJR recruitment efforts among expatriate women.[102] Whatever the restrictive societal inhibitions that dominated Indian life in the diaspora, the Ranis meant to go to war against the British and to liberate their mother country, and Subhas Chandra Bose was determined to make that happen.

THREE

SUBHAS CHANDRA BOSE – A MAN NOT OF HIS TIME

SUBHAS CHANDRA BOSE IS as controversial in death as he was in life – loved and admired by some, reviled and despised by others. His reputation as a nationalist champion of the freedom that he never experienced and staunch promoter of women's rights is recognized by most Indians and outside observers, but opinions on the morality and efficacy of his tactics differ greatly, as do views on whether his efforts had any positive results for the Indian people. In order to understand Bose's contribution both to Indian nationalism and to the advancement of equality for women, including the creation of the RJR, it is necessary to examine his background – the cultural, religious and geographic roots that nurtured his dedication to the cause of Indian independence and the power of women.

By all accounts, Bose was an exceptionally gifted person. Dilip Kumar Roy, who became Bose's best friend, introduced Bose to his new middle school classmates: 'In our Cuttack Ravenshaw School there is a jewel of a boy, Subhash, son of Janakinath Bose.' He continued, 'Thus it began – my adoration of Subhash.'[1] General Shah Nawaz Khan of INA too was awed when he met Bose – 'one of the greatest men India has ever produced.

... I must frankly confess that from the moment I came into personal contact with him he exercised a strange influence over me.'[2] Similarly, Subbier Appadurai Ayer, who came to South-East Asia as Reuters special correspondent, enthused, 'I worship Netaji. To me, he is India's savior; and alive or dead, he will tenderly watch over the well-being and happiness of Free India. ... This man of destiny hastened India's freedom by at least ten years.'[3] To the youngest Rani, twelve-year old Anjuli Bhowmick, 'Netaji was like a god.'[4]

Bose had an extraordinary gift for oratory. He was able to so captivate an audience that few walked away, even during a torrential downpour.[5] That was the case, for example, in Singapore on 9 July 1943, when Bose publicly announced his plan for the Rani of Jhansi Regiment.[6] Bose was drenched, refusing an umbrella because there were not enough umbrellas for everyone. Bose's speeches were delivered in either English or Hindustani.[7] Although observers praised his elegant and simple Hindustani, his spellbound audiences in Singapore, Malaya and Burma were primarily Tamil speakers who would not have understood Bose's Hindustani, no matter how elegant or simple.

Like Mohandas Gandhi, Bose understood the importance of creating an effective public persona, and, like Gandhi, he was accomplished at staging and branding himself. Gandhi's increasingly humble garb and demeanour were intended to demonstrate his identification with the Indian peasant. Bose crafted a quite different image: he affected the trappings of European dictators of the era, particularly Hitler and Mussolini. He donned military uniforms and appeared in large open automobiles.[8] Seen with Indian eyes, as for example those of Bose's contemporary, the diminutive, well-known Bengali writer Nirad C. Chaudhuri (1897–1999), 'he was also physically impressive, being both tall, well-built and handsome. ... Besides, he was very fair, and without a fair complexion nobody is regarded as handsome in India.'[9] In photos, Bose does look taller than most other Indians. His passport states that he measured 5'11", but judging from his uniform, which is still on display in the family house on Elgin Road in Kolkata, he was probably 5'9". The Ranis also found Bose physically attractive.

In India individuals who are admired are often given honorific titles.

Jawaharlal Nehru was known as Pandit meaning 'scholar', and Mohandas Gandhi is still revered as Mahatma, the Great Soul. Today, Bose is rarely mentioned by his given name. In fact, referring to Bose by his proper name alone generally is an indication that the speaker has a negative political opinion of the man. Not one Rani with whom I spoke called him Bose. Rather, he was Netaji, 'Respected Leader'.

On Bose's second evening in Singapore in July 1943, his aide-de-camp, Abid Hassan, told some of the INA officers, 'Bose should be referred to and addressed only as Netaji – Leader.'[10] Several people, who knew him at the time, including Captain Lakshmi, claimed that Bose had objected to the moniker, but lost that battle.[11] For Hitler's propaganda minister Joseph Goebbels (1897–1945), there was no ambiguity as to why Bose called himself Netaji, 'He has set up his organization exactly according to Nazi models and gives himself the designation "Führer".'[12] Goebbels's interpretation is, of course, not in any way proof of Bose's actual political orientation.

As a controversial politician Bose certainly had his detractors. Adam von Trott zu Solz (1909–44), the Oxford-educated Rhodes scholar who served as Hitler's liaison officer to Bose in Germany, disliked him intensely, although Bose was not aware of this.[13] Trott told his wife Clarita that while Bose was brilliant, it was hard to work with him because of his cold and stand-offish personality.[14] Nirad C. Chaudhuri, who served as secretary to Bose's elder brother Sarat Bose (1889–1950), penned the most colourful criticism of Bose. Impugning every aspect of Bose's character, Chaudhuri disparaged his patriotism as extremist, his lofty goals as delusions, his zeal as irrationally inflamed by his hatred of British rule, his judgement as craven and demented, especially with regard to his 1945 attempted escape to Russia and consequent death in an airplane crash on the island of Formosa, and his morals as debased by a 'commonplace entanglement' with his German secretary.[15] Throughout his adult life, Bose triggered such passionate reactions among both his ardent supporters and those who believed he was a menace to India.

So who was Subhas Chandra Bose, creator and patron of the Rani of Jhansi Regiment? What propelled this man through his extraordinary life and what influenced his political ideas? What led to the nationalist passion of the charismatic leader who engaged thousands of Indian soldiers in a doomed jungle war in Burma from which thousands failed to return? What made him a champion of women's rights?

Bose was born in 1897 into an affluent, upper-class family in Cuttack, a city about two hundred fifty miles south-west of Calcutta, Bengal.[16] In his autobiography, he stresses that his family belonged to the Kshatriya or the warrior caste and that its history could be traced back for roughly twenty-seven generations.[17] Bose's father, Janakinath Bose (1860–1934), a prominent attorney preoccupied with his work as government pleader and public prosecutor, left the upbringing of his children to his wife. Prabhabati Bose (1869–1943) gave birth to fourteen children in twenty-one years, liked to sleep late, enjoyed two-hour daily baths, took long naps, and managed the household servants.[18] The daily lives of Janakinath and Prabhabati Bose followed the usual pattern of life in wealthy Bengali families, which left little time for either parent to give the children much individual attention.

In his autobiography, *An Indian Pilgrim*, Bose introduces himself as 'the sixth son and the ninth child of my parents'.[19] 'The earliest recollection I have of myself,' he confides, 'is that I used to feel like a thoroughly insignificant being.'[20] That Bose endured psychological pain in early childhood is palpable throughout the book. The first and second sons in a traditional Indian family carry the hopes and expectations for the new generation, as well as the obligation to perform the last rites at the funerals of his parents. The sixth son enjoyed no special place or attention, and young Bose felt unloved by his parents. 'To be overawed by my parents was not the only tragedy. The presence of so many elder brothers and sisters seemed to relegate me into utter insignificance.'[21] Bose lamented that he never had the individual intimate attention from his mother or father that would have been conducive to normal development of his personality; he envied children who were 'on friendly terms with their parents'.[22] Like most upper-class households at the beginning of the twentieth century, the Bose family employed ayahs or nannies to care for the children, but remarkably, young Subhas still felt close to no one in the household.[23]

Throughout his adult years, he remained shy and in some situations socially inept.

As a teenager, Bose gave substantial thought to finding or creating a suitable identity for himself. Before studying psychology, he developed a system of self-analysis, a 'practice of throwing a powerful searchlight on your own mind with a view to knowing yourself better', a discipline he exercised for the rest of his life.[24] He confided that one of his first insights resulting from his self-analysis was 'that there were ignoble impulses within me which masqueraded under a more presentable exterior'.[25] His next step was a conscious effort to change the ignoble or unworthy aspects of his personality, to conquer weaknesses of the mind. Clearly, Bose was striving from an early age to apply his powerful intellect to controlling himself, and, as much as possible, the world around him.

At the age of five, Bose began formal education at the English missionary school for boys attended by all his brothers and uncles. The school curriculum aimed at educating the children to become English gentry, and even as a small child Bose was aware of racial discrimination against Indians in the curriculum. The boys studied the geography of Great Britain, but not of India, the Bible but not Hinduism, Latin but not Sanskrit. Sensitive as he was, young Bose reacted to the bias against his culture and became an ardent Indian nationalist.[26]

When Bose was twelve, he transferred to an Indian school and the shift had a profound impact on his self-image. Although in the beginning only able to speak Bengali, but unable to read or write a word of his native language, Bose felt that he was among 'his own people' at the Ravenshaw Collegiate School in Cuttack. The new environment, he recalled, gave him a 'self-confidence which till then had been lacking and which is the *sine qua non* of all success in life'.[27] The teachers had high expectations for him, and his classmates respected him. As a mature man looking back, Bose mused, 'It is strange how your opinion of yourself can be influenced by what others think of you.'[28] Always competitive, he completed his first year as the student with the best grades in Bengali studies.[29] At Ravenshaw, headmaster Beni Madhav Das became an important mentor who taught Bose that 'in human life moral values should count more than anything else'.[30] Das's two daughters, Bina and Kalyani became prominent members of the young Bengali revolutionaries, and as a young politician Bose frequently sought advice from his old teacher.[31]

In 1916 a decisive event foreshadowed much of what was to occur in Bose's life, and suggested that his future was on a decidedly non-Gandhian trajectory as manifested later in the INA and the RJR. Elected to represent his class on the Students' Consultative Committee, Bose was nonetheless expelled from Presidency College in Calcutta, which he had joined in 1913.[32] Founded in 1817 as Hindu College, Presidency College, rechristened so in 1855, one of the oldest institutions of higher Western education in South and South-East Asia, was considered the most prestigious school in India. At the time, it was also the place where young nationalists found each other and began to protest against the Raj. The reason for Bose's 'rustication' was that he had participated in an 'argument of force and in the process [the teacher] was beaten black and blue'.[33] The incident, for weeks widely covered in the Indian press, provoked student strikes, and led to the temporary closing of the college, as well as to the suspension and subsequent retirement of the principal. This incident underscores the racial tensions in Bengal during the first decades of the twentieth century, tensions that contributed strongly to the Indian independence movement.

The teacher in question, history professor Edward Farley Oaten, was unpopular with the Indian students for his racist remarks. 'As the mission of Alexander the Great was to hellenise the barbarian people with whom he came into contact, the mission of the English here was to civilize the Indians,' was a particularly outrageous example of Oaten's jibes.[34]

When witnesses asserted that Bose had been one of the participants hitting Professor Oaten, he among other students was called to the principal's office. Bose subsequently recalled with satisfaction how the principal snarled at him, 'Bose, you are the most troublesome man in the College. I suspend you.'[35] At the time Bose neither denied nor admitted his participation in the incident. Twenty-one years later, in his autobiography, he also evaded a straightforward admission of guilt: 'Being an eye witness myself I can assert [that Mr O. was not attacked from the back] without fear of contradiction.'[36]

This incident, which Bose considered seminal for his personal development and career, is important in several respects. He had engaged in his first battle, and as he said, had experienced 'a feeling of supreme satisfaction, of joy that I had done the right thing, that I had stood up for our honour and self-respect and had sacrificed myself for a noble cause.'[37] It demonstrates that early in his teens Bose already saw himself and was seen by others as a leader, that he had found his political calling to fight against British dominance. Crucially, it shows that Bose, unlike Gandhi, was ready to use physical force to avenge what he judged an insult to Indian national pride.

The event also sheds light on Bose's moral stance. 'I had established a precedent for myself from which I could not easily depart in future. I had stood up with courage and composure in a crisis and fulfilled my duty. I had developed self-confidence as well as initiative, which was to stand me in good stead in future. I had a foretaste of leadership ... and of the martyrdom that it involves.'[38] As noted, Bose did not in fact admit that he had struck the teacher until decades later. A few years after the incident, Bose told his brother Sarat that he had learned that 'compromise is a bad thing' and that he regretted having 'denied any complicity in the [Oaten] affair. I was then labouring under a delusion that the end justifies the means.'[39] However, in 1937 when he retold the story in *The Indian Pilgrim*, Bose still did not admit to participating in the violent act. Apparently, his youthful insight of the importance of taking responsibility for his actions did not last.

When Bose absorbed the implications of being thrown out of school, he was distraught and appealed to the authorities to be allowed to enrol in another college. But even after his father and elder brother had exhausted all influential family and business connections, that permission was denied indefinitely. The brilliant student faced a future much diminished from his early expectations. Janakinath Bose refused to finance his son's studies abroad and instead demanded that he apply himself to removing the stain on his reputation at home. Bose complied, joining a group of friends who volunteered as practical nurses to aid impoverished cholera and smallpox patients near Cuttack. For a devout Hindu, exposing himself to a fatal or disfiguring infection may also have been experienced as the sort of selflessness taught in the Bhagavad Gita.[40] Bose tells of his great enjoyment at saving patients 'from the jaws of death'.[41]

Although he knew perfectly well the risks of becoming infected and of passing the infection on to others, Bose admits, 'in the matter of taking precautions, I was criminally negligent'.[42] He did not follow simple safety procedures to disinfect his clothes and kept his nursing activity a secret from his family. In so doing, Bose put his own life at risk as well as the lives of his family and servants. While working with the patients in advanced stages of smallpox, he kept wondering why he did not infect others or become ill himself.[43] This type of behaviour recurred in subsequent years and in much more consequential ways. For the rest of his life, he continuously took extreme chances with his own life and later with the lives of the INA soldiers, including the women of the RJR.

After a year's absence from college, Bose reapplied for permission to continue studying for his BA. He was admitted to Scottish Church College and graduated with first class honours in philosophy two years later. Bose had begun studying for an MA degree in experimental psychology when his father suggested that he go to England to prepare for the Indian Civil Service (ICS) entrance exams. The ICS was the civil service administration of the Government of India during the Raj. The entry requirements were considered extremely demanding and most ICS officers were British graduates from Oxford and Cambridge universities. In 1920 very few Indians had passed the exams.

Bose had twenty-four hours to decide on whether to follow this new career path. He wanted to go abroad, and, as he admitted to his best friend Hemanta Kumar Sarkar, his primary desire was to obtain a university degree in England.[44] Not wanting to miss an opportunity to travel, Bose told Hemanta that he had no hope of passing the very difficult exams, but should he succeed he would turn down the job because working for the Raj would 'mean giving up my goal in life'.[45] The Indian Civil Service certificate would guarantee a secure, highly prestigious and well-paid job, but it was a career in service of the hated colonial masters. Having arrived at Cambridge, Bose confided in his friend Dilip Kumar Roy that before leaving India, he had already taken a secret vow to decline the post if he passed the exam.[46]

In his autobiography, Bose tells how his father called in favours to secure a berth on a ship to England for his son; a distant relative in the Indian police procured his passport in record time; and his family undertook the high costs of tuition and travel.[47] Yet Bose curiously asserts, 'Relying entirely on my own resources and determined to try my luck in England, I set sail on the 15 September 1919.'[48] It is noteworthy that these lines were written not by the youthful Bose setting out in the world, but eighteen years later by the mature man who does not acknowledge that he had relied primarily on his family's resources and connections.

Arriving a few weeks into the term in October 1919, Bose was nevertheless accepted to Cambridge University to study for the ICS exam. Deciding not to waste any time, he worked hard and after nine months of study managed to graduate, fourth among all candidates. Bose's success in the difficult exams was such important news that it was published in the Indian newspapers. Bose informed his parents by cable and then decided that he would use the next seven months to discover whether he really wanted to take the highly coveted position.

After time for reflection and despite his father's stern disapproval, Bose did what no Indian had done before: he rejected the offer to join the ICS.[49] He had decided as he had already shared with Hemanta Sarkar five years earlier and prior to his years of study abroad, 'I am realizing more and more as time passes that I have a definite mission to fulfil in life and for which I have been born, and I am not to drift in the current of popular opinion.'[50] In a series of letters to his elder brother Sarat Bose, he argued his case with the skill of a seasoned politician. Entering the British imperial bureaucracy would not be fulfilling, and he could be more useful to his country if he were not working for the Raj.[51] Although he was clearly aware that his decision was causing significant distress and embarrassment to his father, Bose claimed that by rejecting the ICS he was making a sacrifice not only on his own but also on behalf of his family.[52] With a master's degree in philosophy from Cambridge University and the fame of having turned down the ICS, Bose returned to India.

FOUR

BOSE AND GANDHI AT ODDS OVER THE FREEDOM STRUGGLE

THE SHIP BRINGING THE new Cambridge University graduate back to his country anchored in Bombay on 16 July 1921, and Bose began his life's mission that same afternoon in a life-altering meeting with Mohandas Gandhi. Bose arrived eager to meet the most influential politician in India, the man who had launched a massive non-cooperation campaign and promised self-rule within a year.[1] Having studied the works of revolutionary leaders and the histories of revolutions in other parts of the world, the fledgling politician wanted to get a clear understanding of Gandhi's plan of action. He expected to learn the details, the successive stages that would lead to 'the ultimate seizure of power from the foreign bureaucracy'.[2] Finding Gandhi's answers at best too idealistic, young Bose, already a political realist, had the temerity to ask the head of the Congress party, 'How could the Mahatma promise "Swaraj" (that is, Home Rule) within one year?' as Gandhi had been doing since the Nagpur Congress held six months earlier.[3]

With the realization that Gandhi's strategy for winning swaraj was principally one of faith and not of action, Bose concluded that Gandhi and he could not agree on a common path to freedom and that Gandhi's ideology would never deliver independence for India. Bose left the meeting 'depressed and disappointed' but with the powerful spur of opposition to Gandhi's methods that would impel him for the rest of his life.[4] The outcome of this encounter eventually resulted in the creation of the INA and the Rani of Jhansi Regiment, the first all-female infantry combat regiment.

The Ranis would become Bose's devoted disciples which would have a profound influence on their lives and on their perceptions of the legitimate role of women in Indian society. Thus, examining the ever-growing conflict between these two pre-eminent figures of Indian independence provides a necessary backdrop to the story of the RJR.

Bose joined the Indian National Congress to carry out the work he now believed to be his destiny, and quickly worked his way up the Congress party ladder. In his private letters over the years, he referred more and more often to Gandhi as the 'Dictator' and assiduously publicized Gandhi's many 'Himalayan blunders' – instances where a capricious decision by Gandhi undermined the work prepared by other Congress members.[5] The chasm between the political philosophies of the two men was wide and fundamental, and it was never bridged as the two politicians constantly found themselves opposite players on both the practical and the philosophic sides of the issues facing the independence movement.

As noted, perhaps the most critical difference between the two men concerned the morality of violent action. Bose thought it unlikely that the British would leave India without a military defeat, and the Mahatma regarded any form of violence, physical or mental, unacceptable.[6] The fact that the two men were of different generations, Gandhi being older by almost thirty years, accentuated the contrast: Gandhi's free India would remain a village-based agricultural society with women in the kitchen, the bedroom and the fields, while Bose wanted India to develop into a modern industrial economy where women would play an active professional role.

In Bengal especially, devotees of the Hindu cult of Bharat Mata, Mother India, believed that India, the country, was sacred, a goddess, and that all Indians were her children whose duty it was to protect the sacred land

no matter how demanding the necessary sacrifice.[7] In Varanasi a temple
is dedicated to Bharat Mata, and the slogan of the modern Indian Army
is 'Bharat Mata ki Jai', Victory to Mother India. As Bose explained, 'The
spiritual quest of Bengal has always been voiced through the cult of the
Mother. Be it God or be it motherland – whatever we have worshipped
we have done so in the image of the Mother.'[8] Bose shared his grief over
'the miseries of our lovely India' with his friend Dilip Kumar Roy, a poet
and musician, who commented, 'He struck the note of a mystic deifying
a peninsula into a Goddess.'[9]

Worship of Bharat Mata specifically as the goddess Kali is but one
violent tradition among many.[10] In the Hindu tradition, Kali's domain was
the battlefield and the goddess was invoked for success in war. From the
eighteenth century on, worship of the goddess Kali played an important role
in the spiritual life of Bengal, becoming notably more important after 1882,
when Bankim Chandra Chattopadhyay published his novel *Anandamath*.[11]
The author was a Bengali and the book was particularly popular in Bengal.
The novel, set in the late eighteenth century and based on the historic
revolt of Hindus against their Muslim rulers during the famine in Bengal,
represents Kali as languishing in a desecrated state because her land was
occupied and her people enslaved. The novel became a political manifesto
for Indian nationalists and in the twentieth century, young revolutionaries
adopted the narrative in this mythopoetic best-seller as the prefiguration
of their own battle to rescue the Motherland. A poem, '*Vande Mataram*', 'I
praise thee, Mother', from the novel became a favourite song for the Ranis
and other freedom fighters. The song title became a popular and powerful
slogan 'Vande Mataram', which caused such patriotic fervour among
freedom-seeking Indians that its use was banned by the British.

For Bose, who was of the Kshatriya, warrior caste, this fusion of religion
and nationalism was the keystone of his general world view, and therefore
his politics. It was also at the root of his most profound differences with
Gandhi.[12] Bose was a man for whom religious pursuit was a pragmatic
necessity in every sphere of life; accordingly, he 'felt convinced that
spiritual enlightenment was necessary for effective national service'.[13]
In his private life he was devoted to the Supreme Being in the form of

the mother goddess Kali, and he sought the divine mother's blessing for all his important endeavours. Planning his escape from India in January 1941, Bose sent his niece Ila Bose to the Dakshineshwar Kali temple, an hour's travel away from Calcutta, to ask for the goddess's sanctions of the dangerous undertaking. A picture of Kali was hanging on the wall of his bedroom when Bose left India for the last time, fleeing to Germany.[14]

Bose shared the feeling expressed in *Anandamath* that his country and religion suffered as one. As a young teenager he asked his mother, Prabhabati Bose, 'Shall we continue to turn a deaf ear to the wailings of our nation? Our ancient religion is suffering the pangs of near death – does that not stir our hearts? How long can one sit with folded arms and watch this state of our country and religion? ... How many selfless sons of the Mother are prepared in this selfish age, to completely give up their personal interests and take the plunge for the Mother?'[15]

The concepts of Mother, Motherland and Durga/Kali for Bose came to resonate urgently with calls for nationalist service and sacrifice. Describing his happiness at celebrating puja at the annual festival of the Mother Goddess, Bose wrote, 'In Durga we see Mother, Motherland and the Universe all in One. She is at once Mother, Motherland and the Universal Spirit.'[16] The conviction that the RJR arose as a manifestation of the mother/warrior goddess was shared by many of the INA soldiers. One officer in the INA, Colonel Gurbaksh Singh Dhillon expressed the sentiment clearly: 'Within a few days of his arrival in the East, Netaji gave us a Vanguard – the Rani of Jhansi Regiment. We felt that the valour of the Goddess Durga had reincarnated in the daughters of Mother India. They manifested the blessings of the Goddess and power of her Shakti.'[17]

Bose continued to mobilize for the freedom struggle certain demographic segments that had not received much attention from the old-school Congress leaders. He was the politician for the young, for students and for women. In 1929, at age thirty-two, he personally identified with these deprived sectors of the population and travelled around India to speak at youth conferences. Bose's aim was to ignite in the young men and women of India an idealism that he believed would achieve results in the stagnated freedom struggle. Stressing that in all civilizations change had originated with the young, he shared his views of the objectives and ideals for which they ought to strive. One was his dream of a society in which 'women will be free and will enjoy equal rights with men', but will also accept equal responsibility to work 'side by side with men' to serve their society.[18]

As an Indian nationalist who never veered from his objective of complete independence for India, Bose wanted a nation rid of all foreign domination and tried quite pragmatically to forge a coalition of all militant factions among his countrymen in order to win that freedom. At the same time, he was less clear as to how the future free India should be governed. In his speeches and in *The Indian Struggle*, Bose affiliated himself at various times with an array of systems including communism, socialism and fascism.

In *The Indian Struggle*, Bose argued against a 1933 speech by Jawaharlal Nehru who at the time saw only two possible forms of government in the world, fascism and communism.[19] Given that choice, Nehru denounced fascism and said that no middle road between those two systems of government was possible. Bose declared Nehru wrong and claimed that India might well be the place where a historic synthesis of fascism and communism could occur.[20]

In an earlier speech accepting the position of mayor of Calcutta in September 1927, Bose outlined what the new corporation of Calcutta would work to achieve:

Free primary education; free medical relief for the poor; purer and cheaper food and milk supply; better sanitation in bustees [slums] and congested areas; housing of the poor; development of suburbs; improved transport facilities; and lastly greater efficiency of administration at a cheaper cost. ... I would say that we have here in this policy and programme a synthesis of what Modern Europe calls Socialism and Fascism. We have here the justice, the equality, the love, which is the basis of Socialism, and combined with that we have the efficiency and the discipline of Fascism as it stands in Europe today.[21]

As evidence of the feasibility of this synthesis, Bose observed that both systems were predicated on the supremacy of the state over the individual, and 'both believe in party rule. Both believe in the dictatorship of the party and in the ruthless suppression of all dissenting minorities.'[22] He called the new fusion *Samyavada*, 'an Indian word, which means literally "the doctrine of synthesis and equality",' and claimed that it would be India's task to work out this synthesis.[23]

Ten years later, in a 1938 interview with a London newspaper, Bose was confronted over his support of fascism as a form of government suitable for a free India. Bose explained that his political ideas had developed since he wrote *The Indian Struggle*. At the time he was writing, fascism had not yet begun 'its imperialist expedition' and then seemed to Bose to be merely an aggressive form of nationalism.[24] Far from endorsing fascism in its then current form, Bose explained, what he had 'really meant was that we in India wanted our national freedom, and having won it, we wanted to move in the direction of Socialism'.[25]

Subbier Appadurai Ayer, Bose's friend, admirer and a member of the Azad Hind cabinet, described Bose's method of arriving at a political decision: 'He convinced himself first of the wisdom of his move, the foolproof character of his planning, and the practicability of its execution.'[26] Bose next corrected all defects, and, being a 'stickler for democratic procedure', presented the matter to his cabinet and answered all questions; but in the end 'he had his own way every time'. So Ayer's conclusion was that Bose 'was a democrat at heart and a dictator in effect'.[27]

In the 1930s Bose became one the most important political figures in India. Only Gandhi and Nehru were better known and more highly respected throughout the country. In Bengal, Bose was the most eminent politician with no serious rivals. In this period, Bose continuously appealed to women to become actively involved in the Indian political struggle, believing that they had an important role to play in the modern independent India that he envisioned. During these years, Bose became more and more certain that only armed opposition would free India from

Britain's imperial yoke. Gandhi's non-violent approach, in Bose's view, had produced no meaningful movement towards independence. Instead, it had resulted in long prison terms for all of the Congress's leadership, including Bose. Unsurprisingly, these convictions of Bose exacerbated the rift between him and Gandhi.

By tradition over the years, a candidate for the presidency of the Congress party would succeed only with Gandhi's support. In the fall of 1937 when it was time for a Bengali to assume the presidency, despite Bose's political weaknesses within the upper reaches of Congress, Gandhi finally decided to support Bose, long the leading representative of the Bengali nationalist movement. But a few months into Bose's tenure, Gandhi was unable to moderate his disapproval of not only the new president's policies but also his inefficient management methods. Work in Congress that year was marked by deep divisions between the Gandhi faction and others in the INC.

Bose then decided, against Gandhi's vehement opposition, to run for a second one-year term. Contrary to all expectations and despite Gandhi's efforts to prevent it, Bose prevailed over Gandhi's candidate. Next, the Mahatma and his ahimsa supporters applied Gandhi's well-honed non-cooperation tactic and refused to join Bose's Congress Working Committee (CWC), making it impossible for Bose to turn his victory into policy and action.[28] In spite of his re-election, without a majority in the Working Committee, Bose in effect stood without a mandate to continue as the president of the Congress. Recognizing that no reconciliation was possible, Bose had to choose between open conflict within the Indian National Congress or resignation.

Feeling pressed, Bose confided in a February 1939 letter to his Austrian companion Emilie Schenkl (1910–96), whom we will later meet in detail, that he did not know what to do about the re-election and asked for her advice on how to proceed in the future.[29] Schenkl was no expert on Indian politics, and normally Bose did not trust her with even the simplest tasks, so one must assume that it was for emotional support that he turned to her regarding this crucial event in his life.[30] On 29 April 1939, Bose resigned the Congress presidency and reported to Emilie Schenkl, 'I have not lost anything by resigning.'[31]

He was mistaken. RabindranathTagore (1861–1941), Bengali humanist, intellectual and winner of the 1913 Nobel Prize in literature, warned Bose not to resign, not to 'commit this big mistake ... if you lose this favourable chance due to hesitation you will never get it back'.[32] Many commentators from across the political spectrum have concluded that Bose's resignation was unnecessary, a sign of weakness and psychological inflexibility.[33] It was not in Bose's nature to back away from a fight, but the responsibility for a continued struggle within the party and with Gandhi might have seemed intolerable. In any case, Bose had forever lost his chance to fundamentally influence the freedom fight from inside India.

Immediately following this dramatic political defeat, Bose created a new 'radical and progressive party within the Congress'.[34] He called it Forward Bloc and was joined by some four hundred Congress members whose chief reason to sign up was that they shared his disgruntlement with Gandhi. Rani Anjuli Bhowmick proudly told me that her father Dhirendra Chandra Bhowmick and her uncles Amulya, Haripada and Motilal Bhowmick were some of the many freedom fighters who joined Forward Bloc to support Bose. In the months following his resignation from the Indian National Congress presidency Bose travelled across India speaking to large crowds at hundreds of meetings, contrasting his conviction that armed struggle was the only means to eject the British from India with Gandhi's refusal to exploit Britain's vulnerability as the European crisis deepened.[35]

On 3 September 1939, when Britain declared war against Germany, Bose saw it as 'India's golden opportunity' to successfully confront its weakened oppressor. Bose's admiration of the capability and strict discipline of Hitler's army was reflected in the editorial 'A Word about Germany' he wrote seven months later. Describing the German occupation of Denmark as 'a picnic' and Norway as 'a cakewalk', Bose's conclusion was: 'Germany may be a fascist or an imperialist, ruthless or cruel, but one cannot help admiring these qualities of hers – how she plans in advance, prepares accordingly, works according to a timetable and strikes with lightning speed. Could not these qualities be utilized for promoting a nobler cause?'[36]

The outbreak of WWII in Europe also prompted Gandhi to react, but in complete opposition to his previous stance, shocking the Indian people by announcing in a press statement that India should cooperate with Britain in its hour of danger. [37] Nevertheless, in July 1940, as the Battle of Britain raged and the future of the United Kingdom hung in the balance, returning to his core values Gandhi wrote a letter 'To Every Briton':

> I want you to fight Nazism without arms, or, if I am to retain the military terminology, with non-violent arms. I would like you to lay down the arms you have as being useless for saving you or humanity. You will invite Herr Hitler and Signor Mussolini to take what they want of the countries you call your possessions. Let them take possession of your beautiful island, with your many beautiful buildings. You will give all these but neither your souls, nor your minds. If these gentlemen choose to occupy your homes, you will vacate them. If they do not give you free passage out, you will allow yourself, man, woman and child, to be slaughtered, but you will refuse allegiance to them. [38]

The responses of Bose and Gandhi to the news in Europe defined in stark terms the differences between the strategies they advocated and between the two men. In December 1940, before Bose's final departure from India, Gandhi cited their fundamental differences in methods. He pointed out that although their goals might appear to be the same, that similarity was apparent, not substantial. Gandhi concluded, '...we must sail in different boats.'[39] Gandhi, with no tolerance for Bose's militant intentions, advised the ailing revolutionary, 'You are irrepressible whether ill or well. Do get well before going in for fireworks.'[40]

Bose was arrested for the last time in June 1940.[41] Charged with violating the Defence of India Act, he expected to be kept in prison in Calcutta until the end of the War. By November 1940, Bose found jail intolerable, and he began a hunger strike to death. He publicly announced that he was taking this step after months of contemplation and sealed the plan with a vow on the sacred day of Kali Puja.[42] Just eight days later, he was released from prison in Calcutta by the British governor of Bengal, who feared that the hunger strike would end with Bose achieving his published wish for 'peaceful self-immolation at the altar of [his] cause'.[43]

Home again at the family compound on Elgin Road in Calcutta, the convalescent provocateur was kept under strict observation day and night by a large crew of guards and spies working for the Government of Bengal. Because he expected the Raj to rearrest him when his health had improved, Bose immediately began to plan his escape. On 17 January 1941, Bose in disguise left India for the last time. He arrived in Berlin on 2 April 1941 via a complicated and dangerous route across Afghanistan and through Moscow.

Bose spent the next two years in political limbo, living and travelling in Europe with Emilie Schenkl. He was welcomed as a leader among Indians in Germany and accepted by the Nazi government as an important Indian political figure. Hitler's Foreign Office provided Bose with lavish housing, a generous allowance, special food and wine, car, driver and extra gasoline, plus a staff to take care of the house and garden.

To further Bose's goals and those of Nazi Germany, the Free India Centre was established in Berlin as a hub for preparing and disseminating anti-Allied propaganda, including Bose's Azad Hind and Free India Radio broadcasts, transmitted by a powerful radio station in Holland. The broadcasts reached and inspired many Indians. John A. Thivi, an ethnic Indian freedom fighter in Malaya and future member of the INA, was 'thrilled to hear the voice of Subhas Babu' assuring the members of the newly formed Indian Independence League 'that he would come from the West to the East ... leading us on to victory'.[44]

The German Foreign Office and at times the Italian government agreed in principle to Bose's demand to raise an Indian army. The Free Indian Legion, consisting of prisoners of war, was to be sent to India as part of an Axis power expeditionary corps.[45] In the opinion of Rudolf Hartog, who was attached to the Legion as a translator, 'The story of the Indian Legion in Germany, in which former soldiers of the British

Indian Army volunteered to fight for the freedom of their country on the side of the Axis powers, is one of the strangest episodes of the Second World War.'[46]

Following a recruitment model later employed in establishing the INA in Singapore, the Indian Legion was composed of former Indian Army soldiers captured by the Italians in North Africa who had been given the choice of remaining prisoners of war or signing up to join the Legion. The mission for the Indian Legion in Europe was that when the invasion of India by land from Germany via Iran was possible, the Legion soldiers would fight the British inside India.[47] The role played by this corps of Indian soldiers was so far from serving any practical purpose that it could, according to WWII historian Milan Hauner, only be considered symbolic.[48]

In Germany, the Indian Legion volunteers, unlike the INA soldiers, had to swear allegiance not only to Bose but also to their Axis partner Hitler as the Supreme Commander of the Indian Legion. As a safeguard, Bose included in the agreement that the Legion could be deployed only against the British in an invasion of India.[49] In his stirring swearing-in speech to the soldiers, broadcast to India via Azad Hind Radio, Bose stressed, 'Freedom can never be had by begging. It has to be got by force. Its price is blood... We shall achieve freedom by paying its price... Throughout my life it was my ambition to equip an army that will capture freedom from the enemy.'[50]

Nevertheless, just two months after his arrival in Germany, Bose reconsidered the value of staying in Germany and asked for help to return to Asia. The German Foreign Office did not respond to his request. Bose had come to Germany to solicit Hitler's assistance against their common enemy to break the bonds of British imperialism, but ended up waiting more than a year for what turned out to be a single disappointing meeting with the Führer. In that encounter on 27 May 1942, Adolf Hitler refused to approve and publish an official German policy statement prepared by Bose supporting India's right to freedom.[51] Lowering the level of his request, Bose then asked for Germany's moral and diplomatic support.

Berlin and Tokyo had discussed the best ways for the Axis powers to use Bose, and Hitler advised Bose to go to Japan. The German leader offered to provide a submarine for Bose's travel back to Asia because movement by air would be too dangerous. Bose agreed to the plan which at the time, when Allied forces were bombing Germany, was regarded as the safest way for him to accept Japan's invitation to return to Asia.[52] His gamble was that Prime Minister Tojo Hideki (1884–1948) of Japan and the Japanese Army would be more willing than Hitler and Germany to give military support to the Indian liberation struggle.

FIVE

SUBHAS CHANDRA BOSE AND WOMEN

BOSE'S WRITINGS AS WELL as testimony from several of his friends demonstrate how Bose's complex view of women evolved as he matured towards the day in 1943 when he created the Rani of Jhansi Regiment. In his presidential address at a conference in Poona in 1928, he called for full participation in the political arena by women. [1] For his time this was a progressive demand, perhaps inspired by his stay in England, but it must be assumed that the cultural environment of his upbringing, his family and his own sexuality formed his fundamental outlook on women. While Bengali society was increasingly receptive to the idea of female education, Bose was raised in a family in which the males were highly educated and the females not at all. Despite his espousal of certain path-breaking modern theories, Bose often responded with traditional paternalistic Indian prejudices in his relationships with women.

Subhas's father, Janakinath Bose grew up in the period known as the Bengali Renaissance, during which Bengali society experienced a general moral and cultural awakening. Calcutta was the Indian hub of education, culture, politics and science where self-critical examination and enlightenment came together, ostensibly reflecting a desire to combine the best from Western civilization with the best of the East.

English-speaking schoolmasters, lawyers, doctors and government civil servants formed the first substantial middle-class in India, the bhadralok.[2] Bhadralok is a Bengali term denoting gentlefolk or people of means and education and culture.

Like other upper-class Bengalis of the period, the Bose family was intellectually progressive and culturally conservative. When Janakinath Bose married in 1880 at the age of twenty, he was a westernized liberal thinker; nonetheless, Prabhabati, the bride chosen by his family according to custom, was only eleven years old.[3] Prabhabati Bose, an orthodox Hindu, was in charge of the religious upbringing of her children. Like most Bengalis, she practised the Shakta form of Hinduism and taught her children to worship the Mother Goddess in the form of Durga or Kali.[4] The Bose youngsters, who were all required to attend puja, religious service, grew up with the traditional Bengali Hindu customs of their mother and also their father's more modern beliefs.[5]

This modernizing trend in Bengal affected the roles of the *bhadramahila*,[6] as the new middle-class women were known. Some local schools were created on the model of the English girls' schools; girls and young women were exposed to the contemporary ideas of Europe, particularly those of Great Britain. Magazines were run and edited by 'ladies only', copying the European fashion of women writing biographies and autobiographies. These publications introduced Bengali women to the concepts of 'emancipation of women' and may eventually have led them to take a greater interest in political affairs.[7]

The bhadralok during Bose's childhood years agreed that educated mothers would produce enlightened offspring and that, as wives, informed women would make better company and partners for their husbands.[8] While only a tiny fraction of the female population of middle-class Bengal was literate at the beginning of the nineteenth century, a hundred years later school attendance had become an almost normal part of a modern urban girl's daily life. The six Bose daughters, however, were still slated for early marriage rather than school.[9]

Janakinath Bose was a highly educated man who prided himself on speaking perfect English with the right intonation and whose passion was English literature. Prabhabati Bose, however, was barely literate in Bengali and spoke no English.[10] It was in this evolving Bengali cultural context that Subhas Chandra Bose developed his revolutionary ideas about military resistance to British colonial rule and the radical role of women in that endeavour.

According to Bose, his mother, Prabhabati Bose, was a redoubtable figure. 'No doubt she ruled the roost and, where family affairs were concerned, hers was usually the last word.'[11] Bose felt that his mother showed bias in favour of some of her children. As a boy, Bose ached for attention but did not get nearly enough.[12] In a letter to his friend Hemanta Sarkar in 1914, he comments on the notion that a mother's love is immeasurable: 'My dear friend, I do not rate maternal love so highly. ... Compared to the love I have tasted in this life, the ocean of love I find myself in, mother's love is like a puddle.'[13]

During his difficult teenage years, Bose wrote many letters to his mother asking for attention, pleading with her to engage in his life: What profession should he choose to make her proud and happy? Would it please her if he became a vegetarian? He wrote in emotional turmoil begging her to listen to him, to help him understand motherly love and his love of India.[14] We do not know how she replied, if she responded at all.

When Prabhabati Bose failed to give her son Subhas the mothering he craved, he sought and found substitutes. While studying in England, he met Mrs J. Dharmavir, an English-born cosmopolitan married to an Indian doctor, who remained a lifelong friend. The Dharmavirs welcomed Bose and Dilip Roy into their family; Bose addressed Mrs Dharmavir as didi, elder sister, and felt at home. He was moved when Mrs Dharmavir offered him 'a penny for [his] thought'. As he wrote wistfully, 'It is not always that we find somebody who is eager to know what we think and feel.'[15] He had often shared his feelings with Hemanta, his brother Sarat, and Dilip Roy, but this was the first time he had experienced tenderness, compassion and understanding from a woman. In 1937 when Bose needed five months of rest and recovery after a year and a half in prison, he was cared for by the Dharmavirs at their hill station cottage in Dalhousie, Himachal Pradesh in northern India.[16]

Chittaranjan Das (1870–1925), known as Deshbandhu, 'Friend of the Country', was the most important Bengali politician at the time and became Bose's political father and mentor. Basanti Devi (1880–1974), the wife of Deshbandhu Das, was also a woman who listened and soothed, and Bose found in her another mother surrogate. Bose addressed Basanti Devi as 'Mother' and their relationship was so close that Prabhabati Bose was heard telling her, 'You are the real mother, I am just the nurse.'[17] At times Bose's faith in the power of Basanti Devi's blessings took on an almost religious quality. In a state of exhaustion, he sent a plea for spiritual help, 'Still I pray – do bless me on this particular day; there is some other significance in such blessings. Mother, I am an absolutely unworthy and useless son. Your love is taking me towards full manhood. Mother, bless me so that in lives to come I may have the good fortune of having a mother like you. ... You are the only refuge of this helpless person ... tell me the path I should take in future.'[18] Even taking into account Bose's penchant for occasional excess in his personal style, the intensity of this letter is remarkable.

In addition to finding an emotional and political home with the Das family, Bose shared quarters with his brother Sarat, his wife Bivabati and their eight children across the street from the main Bose family compound on Elgin Road in Calcutta. Bivabati Bose, just one year older than Bose, became his confidante and friend. Together with her husband, Bivabati helped with Bose's many needs, including financing his endeavours, as his political work did not produce a steady income sufficient to support his lifestyle.

Bose related to these three married older women as if he were a son or younger brother, and not one young Indian woman is noted as friend or potential romantic interest. Krishna Bose in her article on the women in Bose's life claims that Deshbandhu Das and Basanti Devi received many offers of marriage for Bose from the fathers of hopeful young women, but Bose never considered any proposal.[19]

In 1937 Bose spent a month at a health resort in Bad Gastein, Austria, writing his autobiography, *The Indian Pilgrim*. Sexuality is an important theme in this exhaustive review of his first twenty-five years. Bose details his struggle as a teenager to control his overpowering sex drive, which he considered unnatural and immoral. Always in search of pragmatic solutions to problems, Bose studied Swami Vivekananda and Ramakrishna, his spiritual teacher, and in their philosophy he found 'a basis on which to reconstruct his moral and practical life'. Bose would follow the gurus' demand, he sought to completely transcend sex and to become 'impervious to the sex-appeal of others' so that all his reactions would be non-sexual. By employing a method of conquering sexual lust, 'whereby to a man every woman would appear as mother, ... he could feel as an innocent child feels in the presence of its mother'.[20] In 1914 during his tumultuous adolescence, Bose left home for several months without telling anyone that he was leaving or where he was going. Together with Hemanta Kumar Sarkar, his best friend, Bose went in search of spiritual enlightenment and to find a guru.[21] After their return to their families, Bose and Hemanta wrote to each other daily because Bose's family barred Hemanta from visiting the ailing Bose. Some of Bose's letters, even when 'suitably edited' by the Bose family reveal a passionate relationship.[22] The Netaji Research Bureau holds an unknown number of still unpublished letters from Bose to Hemanta Sarkar, but their correspondence as published by Sarkar is unambiguous, and reveals Bose's feverishly self-subjugating love for Hemanta.[23]

It appears that growing-up Bose did not have personal relationships with Indian women of his own age, other than his nieces and other family members. As a young adult in Britain in 1919–21, Bose may have grown more comfortable with his sexuality, but his efforts at self-control may have contributed to his avoidance of associations with unmarried young Indian women. Bose's best friend for many years, Dilip Kumar Roy, describes him, as 'a pure character. No girl had ever dared to darken with her shadow even the shadow of his shadow.'[24] At Cambridge University Bose stood completely apart from the other young Indian men. Unlike his compatriots, he tolerated no bawdy language or sexual jokes and avoided any contact with young women. In the many pages of his book on his friendship with Bose, Roy elaborates on Bose's lack of positive emotional response to any female other than one or two of his nieces.[25] 'Cocottes and flirts ... he regarded as beneath contempt' and 'he never talked of women, far less mixed with them.'[26] Bose advised his friends at Cambridge: 'Never court the company of women – no playing with fire if you please.'[27] As an adult looking back, Roy realized that Bose's aloofness did not originate in strength; rather his behaviour was self-protective because he feared to be intimate.[28]

Despite his assertion in 1937 that it was an easy decision to devote his life to a noble cause, Bose found that 'it required an unceasing effort, ... which continues till today, to suppress or sublimate the sex-instinct'.[29] Although he had studied psychology, Bose seems unaware of, or dismisses, Sigmund Freud's *Theory of Sexuality*. Still in 1943 he demanded that the INA instructors of the Ranis apply Ramakrishna's moral principle in their relationship with the young women.

The issue of sexuality became more pressing as the traditional time for marriage loomed. Bose's parents arranged marriages for their elder sons Satish and Sarat when they were twenty-two and twenty years old, but for Subhas marriage was deferred due to his prolonged academic career. When Subhas Bose had passed the ICS exams in 1920, he was twenty-four, and he brought up the topic of marriage in a letter to his brother Sarat. Defending his decision not to enter the ICS, Bose assures, 'I am not going to marry – hence considerations of worldly prudence will not deter me from taking a particular line of action if I believe that to be intrinsically right. ... If the match-makers come to trouble you again, you can ask them straight away to take a right about turn and march off.'[30]

Although he admitted that his struggle to suppress his sexual urges was unremitting even as he penned his memoir in 1937, Bose and Emilie Schenkl, his Austrian companion, were actually living together at the time.[31] In a footnote to a discussion about the universal value of exerting great energy to conquer the sex drive, Bose admits, 'As I have gradually turned from a purely spiritual ideal to a life of social service, my views on sex have undergone transformation.'[32] Along the way Bose apparently judged it more ethical to apply the utilitarian principle, as he expressed it, 'the greatest good [for] the greatest number' by committing his entire psychic energy to his Indian liberation rather than to control his own sex drive.[33] In November 1942, Bose and Schenkl became the parents of a daughter.

After the end of the war, a brief letter from Bose to his brother Sarat written in Berlin on 8 February 1943, a day before Bose boarded the submarine for Japan, shocked those who knew Bose well. The note read: 'I have married here and I have a daughter.'[34] Until then family, friends and political colleagues had all believed that Bose had dedicated his life entirely to winning India's independence and that he would remain celibate until liberation was achieved. In 2008, Aruna repeated what almost every Rani said: 'We all knew that he would not marry until India was free.' The Ranis saw Bose as an ascetic warrior.[35]

A letter to a friend written in Vienna in 1933 illustrates the total commitment that everyone assumed Bose had made: 'Every moment there is only one thought, only one effort, one *sadhana* that is consuming me all the time – by what means, mobilizing what kind of power, by what method can this half-awake nation attain self-fulfillment and be victorious. … Where I have taken my stand today, I am alone, friendless.'[36]

A year later, in June 1934 Bose hired Emilie Schenkl in Vienna to work as his secretary while he was writing *The Indian Struggle*. From 1934 until 1942, the two worked and travelled together during Bose's visits to Europe, and corresponded regularly when he journeyed alone or returned to India. Emilie Schenkl told her daughter Anita that Bose and she had married secretly in a Hindu ceremony, but Anita Pfaff is not sure if that actually occurred.[37] In various interviews, Schenkl gave conflicting dates for when that alleged event took place, and the truth remains uncertain. No witnesses were present, and even A.C.N. Nambiar, a close friend of both Bose and Schenkl, learned of the purported marriage only after the war.[38] Historian and biographer of the Bose brothers, Leonard Gordon's careful search of Austrian and German archives failed to produce any record of the marriage.[39] After the death of Bose, Schenkl remained single, and her daughter was baptized Anita Schenkl.[40]

One can hypothesize that Bose staged a private marriage ceremony in an effort to assure Emilie of his love and commitment because he feared the political fallout should his marriage to a non-Indian woman become public knowledge. Although they may not have married officially, the 1943 Berlin letter to Sarat Bose quoted above demonstrates that Bose wanted Emilie

Schenkl and Anita to be known as his wife and daughter.[41] Emilie Schenkl
had always realized that she was not the first or the most important love
of Bose's life. Early in their relationship he had warned her, in a heartfelt
and conflicted letter, 'I must leave you and go back to my first love – my
country. ... Do not blame me for not loving you more. I have given what
I had – how can I give more? ... You are the first woman I have loved.'[42]

In January 1941 when Bose returned to Europe, he lived together
with Emilie Schenkl in Berlin. Eighteen months later, Bose was urgently
awaiting finalization of logistics for his transfer to Japan and onward to
Singapore to take command of the INA. The plans entailed his departure
prior to the birth of his child.[43] However, Bose's stay in Germany was
extended several times because the Japanese were unable to arrange safe
transport. So, although he was not in Vienna with Emilie Schenkl when
their daughter was born on 29 November 1942, Bose saw them both
before he left for Asia. According to Nambiar, Bose, staunch proponent of
gender equity, nonetheless expressed profound disappointment on learning
that his firstborn was a girl.[44] Apparently, Bose's intellectual and political
commitment to equality of the sexes clashed with his more conventional
Indian male outlook.

Captain Lakshmi thought that she was the one person that Bose had told
of his relationship with Emilie Schenkl in Germany, and that he believed
that his marriage to a foreigner would be difficult for the people of India
to accept. Captain Lakshmi explained why Bose's reasoning might have
been correct: 'People in India have the funny notion that their leader should
be superhuman and not have any ordinary normal feelings like wanting
to have a wife and raising a family. The whole of India is their family and
they should be content with that.'[45]

From the novel *Anandamath*, the 'cruel laws' for qualifying as a true
freedom fighter were engraved in the public mind: 'He alone is worthy
of this duty who has renounced everything for the sake of Mother India.
The man whose heart is tied with the strings of human attachment is
like a kite that is tied to the reel; it cannot fly high or far from the earth
below. ... We forget our higher duties in the moment we look at our
wives and children.'[46] Bose was different. His heartstrings did not prevent

him from flying away and devote his life to the fight for Mother India. In the interviews, the Ranis bore out Bose's foreboding about reactions to his marriage. Although several Ranis had seen newspaper photographs of Anita Pfaff, who bears a strong resemblance to her father, they refused to believe that he had married or fathered a child. That his rumoured wife was a foreigner was even more unbelievable.

Two accounts from the Ranis, one second-hand from Asha Sahay and the other from Captain Lakshmi, both emphasize that Bose's dilemma was not that he missed his child and her mother who were left behind in war-torn Europe and that he worried about them, but that by getting involved with a non-Indian woman, he might have compromised his political future.[47]

Bose left Emilie Schenkl and his infant daughter in Vienna in 1943 without arranging for financial or other support. From the time of Bose's departure on the submarine in February 1943 until August 1945, the day when she heard news of his death on the radio, Schenkl received two letters from him. These letters were confiscated by British Intelligence when Schenkl was searched and interrogated and unfortunately they must be assumed to be no longer extant.[48] Devastated at the news of Bose's death, Emilie Schenkl contemplated suicide but reconsidered because of her responsibility to her daughter.[49] The relationship with Bose had never been easy, and in a letter to Bose on 28 January 1937, she laments, 'Sometimes I wonder, what for I live at all. There is rather no sense in going on living and still, one is too much of a coward to throw away life.'[50] After the death of Bose, Schenkl guarded her privacy with dignity. She refused financial assistance offered by the Bose family when they learned of her relationship with Bose, and she declined invitations to come to India, but she did meet with members of the Bose family in her own home in Vienna.[51] Recently declassified Indian government documents revealed that Emilie Schenkl accepted an Indian government stipend of Rs 6,000 per annum for her daughter, but refused a widow's pension for herself. She worked as a telephone operator, and raised her daughter by herself.[52]

When Bose joined the Indian National Congress in 1921, he was assigned a variety of jobs by Chittaranjan Das; one of them was as organizer of non-cooperation activities and demonstrations. To make a political statement, Das encouraged his wife Basanti Devi and his sister, Urmila Devi, to go out to agitate for the use of khadi instead of British machine-made cloth. At age twenty-four, Bose's instinct and upbringing still led him to protect women, and he argued that women should not be permitted to demonstrate in public 'as long as there was a single man left'.[53] These two prominent women ignored Bose's concerns, joined the protesters and were duly arrested. As a result of a huge public outcry over Mrs Das's arrest, the women were released the same night; the nationalists were pleased with the political impact of Basanti Devi's courageous action.

This event occurred in 1921 just after Bose had returned to India from two years at Cambridge, where he had met accomplished women like Sarojini Naidu (1879–1949), the poet and nationalist activist. Bose was surprised but also proud and happy on behalf of his mother country: 'I could see that even today a woman of India had such erudition, inspiration, qualities and character that she could face the Western world and express herself.'[54] Meeting several other gifted, intelligent Indian women in England gave Bose additional reason to dream and work for a liberated India: 'I have come to believe that the country which has women of such high ideals, cannot but make progress.'[55] He became convinced that women should serve as an additional force in the freedom struggle.

Bose's view of the potential of women developed quickly, and already in the early 1920s his ideas differed markedly from those of other Indian politicians, except for Gandhi. At this time, Gandhi and Bose, encouraged women to leave purdah, Bose advocating 'a society in which the woman will be free and will enjoy equal rights with man and take upon her all civic and political responsibilities.'[56] He argued that the first important step was for women to become engaged in the political process with the goal of changing women's position in society to full emancipation and genuine equality.[57]

Several young and well-educated Bengali women joined Bose to implement his ideas. One woman, Leela Nag (1900–1970) began in 1922 by serving as secretary of All Bengal Association, an organization formed to change public opinion in favour of women's suffrage, and continued to work with Bose on several other projects until he left for Germany.[58]

All-female political groups such as Deepali Sangha, Chhatri Sangha and Bengal Revolutionary Movement were dedicated to improving the status of women, but became 'feeder' organizations for more radical associations because the members were well educated, idealistic and already motivated for revolutionary activities.[59] These former terrorists and politically active young women agreed about the role played by Bose: 'If there were a living figure who encouraged their activities, it was Subhas Chandra Bose.'[60] The female revolutionaries considered Bose the greatest exponent for women's rights in Bengal; in return, they staunchly supported Bose's projects.

Lotika Ghose, a graduate of Calcutta University and the niece of freedom fighter Aurobindo Ghose (1872–1950), had worked on her own to mobilize Indian women for political work when in 1928 she was invited to meet with Bose at his private residence at Elgin Road, Calcutta.[61] He wanted her to join the Congress, but she refused because she did not believe that the country's freedom could be won by purely non-violent methods. Bose agreed but told her that for now they had to go with Gandhi because there was no other politician who could unite the whole country.[62] In 1928, with the strong encouragement of Bose, Lotika established the Mahila Rashtriya Sangha, the National Association of Women, to propagate his revolutionary ideas about the role of women.[63] In spite of having written to her son that she preferred 'the ideal for which Mahatma Gandhi stands', Bose's mother, Prabhabati Bose agreed to serve as the first president of the society.[64] Popularly known as Colonel Lotika, Ghose was the organization's first secretary, and in 1928 she commanded Bose's first group of uniformed women, the Bengal Volunteers.[65]

Bose understood that full emancipation of women could not be achieved merely by picketing toddy shops and weaving khadi. Looking for capable women to fill upper-level political positions, he pleaded with Chittaranjan Das's widow, Basanti Devi, to continue her husband's work. He used powerful arguments to persuade her: her grief over her husband would lessen; her husband would have wanted her to fill the void left by him; and her non-participation was an injustice to the youth of Bengal who counted on her. He tried to persuade her that religion was not a valid reason to resign from political life. 'Mother,' he wrote, 'today our house is on fire. When the house is on fire, even a woman observing purdah has to take courage in both hands and come out on the street. She has to work as hard as a man to save her child, to protect valuable property from fire. Does that detract from her prestige or grace?'[66] Mrs Das was not stirred to action by Bose's appeals. Nor was he more successful in persuading his sister-in-law, Bivabati. Throughout their lives, Sarat Bose helped as his younger brother's campaign manager, lawyer, benefactor and advisor in all matters, but he refused to allow his wife to join the freedom fight, and she did not disobey her husband.[67]

In 1938, while he was president of the Congress party, Bose wrote to a woman, Amita Purkayastha, who had asked how she could best serve her country; his answer encapsulated his position on women which was reflected in the members of the RJR.[68] The missive began with a complaint on the dearth of female partisans willing to accept the freedom struggle as a personal mission. Some women would begin national service, he wrote, but after a short while they would leave, their enthusiasm dampened as domestic duties called them away. Bose urged Purkayastha that in order to be useful to the country, she must make more than a half-hearted commitment; she must adopt the mission as the principal aim of her life. The next step would be to join the Congress party in order to win the country's independence: 'To achieve independence is not merely man's job. It is also woman's job.' As a woman Amita could do what men could not, Bose insisted. She could awaken the women of India.

Bose stressed that if women, who constitute half of society, did not engage, India would not progress. His prescription was that women must be made 'strong and brave' and educating women would forge that transformation. Part of the education should be vocational training so as to enable poor women to earn money. Bose argued that younger women should also train to build up their strength and learn self-defence.

Unlike earlier reformers, who sought to change the social landscape by very modestly constraining the traditional prerogatives of males to decide the lives of women, Gandhi and Bose engaged Indian women directly. They urged them to join the freedom movement and in that way to liberate themselves. Both men said that after independence, they expected women to take an active role in politics. Gandhi, however, never made a serious effort to include women in his own political work, and although he was always accompanied by women, he had no women among his closest political advisors. In contrast, in his government in exile, Bose created a department for women and appointed Lakshmi Swaminathan to serve as minister for women's affairs in the Azad Hind government.

Although both twentieth-century reformers emphasized the importance of education of women as an essential means of elevating women's inferior status, Gandhi and Bose differed significantly as to how that education should be acquired and what its aims should be. In Gandhi's free India, women would be responsible for raising the children and running the household, but he thought it a depraved world where women would seek employment outside the home. For that reason, he argued, education for girls should be separate and distinct from that of boys, and it should be geared primarily to producing the best possible housewives and mothers.[69] Bose, on the other hand, wanted girls to be educated in all subjects in the same way as boys so as to produce self-supporting women able to participate in the new nation's politics, education, business and social life. Within his own family, Bose fought to assure that his nieces would have the opportunity to get the education they desired.[70] While Bose's plan for women broke the old patriarchal hold on women and encouraged them to become more like women in Europe, Gandhi's more conservative plan aimed to confine women within the domestic sphere.

The two politicians agreed that the traditional exaltation of female fecundity compromised not only the educational opportunities available to women but also their health and longevity and even their ability to leave the physical confines of their homes. Both advocated for smaller families. Their ideas for limiting the Indian birth rate were, however, quite distinct. Gandhi was fiercely against any means of birth control. He found it immoral and sinful, declaring somewhat disingenuously, 'The [sexual] union is meant not for pleasure but for bringing forth progeny. And union is a crime when the desire for progeny is absent.'[71] Instead, he proposed, an agreement between husband and wife to maintain abstinence would eliminate the need for contraceptives. Bose did not agree with Gandhi

that a vow of celibacy, *brahmacharya*, and self-control were reliable means
of controlling the rapidly expanding population of India. He, therefore,
considered other birth control measures a necessity. He shocked his
contemporaries by urging the development of scientific methods of birth
control.[72] Even more radically, he recognized that some women might
prefer not to marry, particularly as new professional opportunities for
self-support became available.[73] He argued that having many children at
an early age prevented women from obtaining an education that would
allow them to enter the modern world and provide for themselves.[74]

Both politicians wanted women to leave the confines of their houses
in order to strengthen India's freedom struggle, but the two men differed
fundamentally in their visions for women's roles in that fight. Given his
blanket opposition to violence, Gandhi could not accept female military
service. Beyond that scruple, he felt that training women to handle weapons
would constitute a complete break with the traditional role of Indian
women as mothers and housewives. The historical Rani of Jhansi is shown
in sculptures and drawings mounted on her horse, sword in hand with her
child swaddled to her back. The historical fact that the child was ten years
of age in 1857 and therefore would not have been carried by his mother
is disregarded, for in order to be accepted as a heroine Rani Lakshmibai
needed to be shown also as a mother.[75] A woman brandishing a sword would
not be considered a normal woman, because women were supposed to be
passive and willing to sacrifice themselves; killing others was not a human
female characteristic. In short, while Gandhi's notions of the proper place
of Indian women were essentially a variant of the traditional patriarchal
views. Bose had an entirely different view. For him, Rani Lakshmibai was
the archetypal Indian hero. He insisted that women should embrace and be
accorded full gender equality, including serving as soldiers in the fight for
independence.[76] The establishment of the RJR was a direct consequence
of Bose's revolutionary conviction, and my interviews with the Ranis
confirmed that they too had adopted the very practical manifestation of
this principle – life as infantry soldiers in the INA.

SIX

THE INDIAN FREEDOM MOVEMENT IN MALAYA AND BURMA PRIOR TO THE ARRIVAL OF BOSE

IN A MOVE THAT was eventually going to set the stage for the Ranis to enlist and prepare for battle, on 8 December 1941, the Japanese 25th Army invaded Malaya. The attack was timed to coincide with a cascade of dramatic strikes at Pearl Harbor, the Philippines, Wake Island, Guam, Thailand, Shanghai and Midway Islands, followed by the landing of troops near Singapore and the invasions of Burma and Hong Kong. Masters in jungle warfare and, equally important, equipped with accurate maps, the Japanese troops advanced rapidly south through Malaya, quickly conquering the entire Malay Peninsula.

On 15 February 1942, Japanese forces sacked the reputedly impregnable British fortress of Singapore. The fall of this 'Gibraltar in the Far East' was considered the most calamitous defeat in British military history. Lieutenant General Arthur Percival of the British Indian Army surrendered unconditionally, turning over eighty thousand soldiers, including forty-five or fifty thousand Indians.[1] It was from these prisoners of war that the Indian National Army (INA) was constituted in 1942. Information gleaned by British Intelligence in June 1942 from a Bangkok conference between Indian nationalists and the Japanese government revealed that the Japanese wanted to make it appear to the world that the creation of the Indian Independence League and the INA was a spontaneous movement originating with Indian nationalist organizations in Thailand, Burma and Malaya, and that it was linked with Gandhi and the Congress party.[2]

In the years between the two world wars, educated Indians in both Burma and Malaya formed dozens of associations and clubs. Each association attracted its own kind of membership. Some clubs catered to particular professions such as businessmen or members of a certain caste. Other associations brought together Indians originating from a particular geographical region in India. People gathered at the clubs or associations to celebrate religious holidays and festivals, replacing to some extent the extended family events back home. For the most part, these organizations were established to provide a venue for socializing and other recreational activities, rather than to implement political agendas.

At the same time, the social clubs were well positioned to serve as vehicles for the promotion of outside activities. Prominent members of the Indian National Congress, including Nehru and Gandhi, visited Malaya and Burma in the decades before World War II in order to confer with expatriate Indian business and social leaders. Lokmanya Tilak, the father of the Indian independence movement, was imprisoned by the British for sedition and sentenced to spend six years in a Mandalay jail from 1908 to 1914. Bose was arrested and imprisoned in Burma from 1924 to 1927. Both men spent their days writing and meeting with political associates continuously urging Indians to fight for independence. Rani Manwati Panday expressed the belief in our interview that for her family and many other Indians in Burma, the imprisonment of these two prominent freedom fighters played an important role in keeping the nationalist political agenda alive.[3] As a result, the Indian elite in South-East Asia felt politically connected and informed about the independence movement in India. Dr P. J. Mehta, grandfather of Rani Rama Mehta, was a friend of Gandhi's. The Mehta family hosted Gandhi on his visits to Rangoon, helped funding Gandhi's political work, and remained closely connected to the freedom movement.[4] Rama in her late eighties was still working as a Japanese-language tourist guide in Mumbai. She climbed the steep stairs and with deep reverence showed me Gandhi's modest room in Mani Bhavan, now a museum.[5] She has fond memories as a little girl of sitting on Gandhi's lap, when he visited her childhood home in Rangoon. Although brought up as a Jain, as a political realist Rama supported Netaji's army of freedom fighters because she considered it more effective than Gandhi's passive resistance.

The Central Indian Associations of Malaya and the Young Men's Indian Association were gathering places for Indian men who supported the independence movement, and in 1929 these organizations merged to form the Indian Independence League (IIL).[6] Until the Japanese occupation, upper- and middle-class Indian women in Malaya and Burma were generally housebound and not active in the organizations, but the invasion changed the level of political engagement for the entire Indian population of Malaya, and women found that their skills were also useful in a variety of positions within the IIL. Historian Virginia Dancz describes the 'political awakening of Indian women' in Malaya as one of the more remarkable effects of the war.[7]

Before the outbreak of war in the Pacific, Japan had seeded Singapore and the Malay Peninsula with Japanese operatives working in a variety of intelligence-gathering positions. Japanese nationals, who owned many of the photo shops in small towns across Malaya, systematically photographed roads, railroads and military installations. Japanese fishermen drew maps of the coastal areas, and Japanese businessmen in Singapore monitored construction of the British naval base.[8] In addition, the Japanese had established the organizational framework for what would become the INA and also the independence armies in Malaya and Burma.[9] Concurrently, they supported the construction of the IIL, which later came to serve as the civil administration for the Indian freedom struggle in South-East Asia.[10]

In September 1941 the Japanese government sent newly promoted Major Fujiwara Iwaichi (1908–86) of the Japanese Army Intelligence Unit to Thailand to network with groups of anti-British Indians living in Malaya and to facilitate collaboration with prominent Indian nationalists.[11] A military intelligence officer trained at the Imperial Army's Nakano School, Fujiwara worked through the IIL, which had by then established regional offices across Malaya, Singapore and Burma.[12] Colonel Suzuki Keiji was the intelligence agent tasked with organizing collaborators in Burma.[13] These two intelligence operatives were highly skilled propagandists and were able to convince many Indians of Tokyo's genuine commitment to the cause of Indian independence. Some Indians were even led to believe that Japan had attacked the British primarily in order to bring self-rule to the subcontinent.[14] Based on her interviews with Fujiwara, American historian Joyce Lebra argues persuasively that the INA recruits who fought and died in Burma to liberate their homeland had been cruelly deceived by the imperial Japanese. After the end of the war, Fujiwara acknowledged Japan's cynical exploitation of the Indian desire for independence to expedite their military takeover of South-East Asia and eventually of India itself.[15]

When the Japanese army entered South-East Asia, Indians and Europeans fled Malaya, Singapore and Burma in great numbers, but the Indians who stayed experienced a new sense of cultural cohesion. Many became actively involved in nationalist politics. Indians joined the IIL not only because they supported the liberation of India from Britain's colonial yoke, but also because Japanese soldiers were instructed not to harass members of that organization. As sixteen-year old Rani Aruna Ganguli experienced the developing nationalist spirit, 'S.E. Asia Indians joined the Indian Independence League in an organized way. Gradually village after village, cities after cities all Indians came to be one. They joined INA or IIL.'[16]

An IIL membership card (in Japanese *angkyosho*, 'family registration') identified the holder as Indian.[17] This was an important document because Japanese occupation troops had difficulty distinguishing among the diverse ethnic groups populating Malaya. Japan was at war with China and Japanese soldiers treated the Chinese inhabitants of Malaya and Singapore with extreme cruelty, so it was vital to be able to identify oneself as Indian. The identity card also allowed the member to obtain rations of rice, sugar and cigarettes, a privilege that was sufficient as incentive to motivate nearly every Indian family to join.[18] With its large membership, the IIL would provide the ideological and bureaucratic backbone for Bose's movement when the time came to mobilize Indians in Singapore, Malaya and Burma on behalf of Indian liberation and the INA. The families of several of the Ranis interviewed for this study were enthusiastic IIL members who urged their daughters to enlist in the RJR.

The Japanese initiative to mobilize Indians in the South Asian diasporas was vigorously promoted by Indian nationalist Rash Behari Bose (1886–1945).[19] Since fleeing from Bengal in 1915, Rash Behari, based in Tokyo, had continued his struggle to oust the British from India in close collaboration with the Japanese government. Instrumental in creating both the INA and the IIL, he was elected president of the IIL in 1942.

As Japan expelled the British from Malaya, Singapore and Burma in 1941, it sought to persuade the Indians of the defeated British Indian Army to join a new army, an army consisting only of Indian soldiers, the Indian National Army. Fujiwara's preparations had progressed as planned and prisoner of war camps stood ready for the surrendering Indians. As the victorious Japanese army advanced south along the Malay Peninsula, the beaten soldiers of the British Indian Army were detained in Ipoh, Penang and elsewhere along the invasion route and transferred to the waiting POW camps.

When the defeated Indian soldiers emerged from the jungle, Japanese aircraft bombarded them with propaganda leaflets assuring 'the coloured races of their immediate liberation and beseeching them to join hands in that mighty undertaking'.[20] The aim was to appeal to the honour, dignity and self-respect of all Asians in general, and Indians in particular. Japanese propaganda was peppered with ingratiating catchphrases such as 'Asia for Asians', 'Kick out the white-devils from the East' and 'India for the Indian'.[21] Once the prisoners were interned in camps, the Japanese wardens applied harsher means of persuasion to convince the Indian soldiers to take up arms against their former comrades in the British Indian Army.

One captured Indian officer who believed the Japanese promises was Captain Mohan Singh (1909–84), a Sikh from a small village in northern Punjab. In December 1941, chosen by Fujiwara, Captain Mohan Singh became the first general of the INA. A patriotic Indian, Singh did not find it difficult to divert his allegiance from the British Indian Army. In his view, he was no longer serving as a mercenary for the British; instead, he was simply making common cause with the Japanese to fight for the future independence of his own country.[22]

Following the British surrender on 15 February 1942, all Indian soldiers, sepoys (foot soldiers) and officers were ordered to muster in Farrer Park in central Singapore.[23] At 2 p.m. on 17 February the assembled prisoners of war numbered about 40,000. British officers were separated out and sent to the POW camp near Changi Prison in east Singapore. Indian Army officer, Colonel J.C. Hunt, then told the Indian troops that they would be handed over to the Japanese government, and that they were to obey the orders of their Japanese officers or face severe consequences. Mohan Singh and Fujiwara stood next to the British officer to receive the nominal rolls of the Indian captives.[24] Fujiwara brought all men to attention and announced, 'I, on behalf of the Japanese Government, now hand you over to G.O.C. (General Officer Commanding) Captain Mohan Singh who shall have powers of life and death over you.'[25]

Taking over the microphone and switching from English to Hindi, Singh explained to the assembled soldiers that if they joined the INA and cooperated with the Japanese, the two armies, Japanese and INA, would together liberate India. A great number of prisoners immediately and joyfully joined the INA. One factor contributing to Mohan Singh's success in recruiting prisoners of war to join the INA was that the defeated Indian soldiers felt deeply betrayed by their British officers. As the Indian foot soldiers saw it, the officers had abandoned them in the jungle while trying to save themselves from capture by the Japanese.

Many Indian soldiers, among them a large number of officers, remained unpersuaded by Singh's vision for the future. Captain Shah Nawaz Khan expressed a common sentiment of the Indian officers who found the situation completely against what they had learned at Dehradun and Sandhurst. They were now being 'handed over like cattle' to an Indian officer of inferior status than they, and who was just as much a POW as they.[26] Many officers thus declined the opportunity to evade the expected cruel Japanese POW treatment because they doubted the honesty of the Japanese promises of freedom for India and did not trust Mohan Singh to stand up to the Japanese and manage negotiations.[27] When Dr Lakshmi Swaminathan, who lived and worked in Singapore, heard about the INA, she volunteered as a medical doctor, but the bluff refusal from Mohan Singh was that he was not having any women in his army![28] In July 1943 when Bose took command of the INA, many of these well-educated and experienced Indian Army officers changed their minds and pledged allegiance to the new Indian National Army and Bose recruited Dr Swaminathan.

From the outset, the association between Japan and the Indian independence movement was an uneasy alliance. The various nationalist groups in South-East Asia disagreed about what level of involvement with the Japanese was strategically sound. In Thailand, with an Indian population of about 40,000 of mostly small businessmen, the Thai-Bharat Cultural Lodge served the same function as the IIL in Malaya and Burma.[29] These Thai-Bharat nationalists had become especially suspicious of the way Japan's plans for South-East Asia were evolving, and they feared that they would end up Bunraku puppets in the hands of the new imperialists.[30]

In March 1942, on behalf of the Japanese government, Rash Behari Bose invited Indian delegates from all parts of Asia to a conference in Tokyo for a discussion of the future of collaboration between the Indian nationalists and Japan.[31] Prior to the Tokyo conference, representatives of the various Indian groups met in Singapore to coordinate the proposals they would present at the conference. In addition to internal divisions over the nature of the Japanese–Indian alliance, the delegates faced chilling news on the home front, as Jawaharlal Nehru published a warning that Indians residing outside India who interfered in Indian politics would be considered traitors. In response to Nehru's statement, the Indian nationalists resolved to ask the Indian National Congress to approve their cooperation with Japan in pursuit of Indian liberation.[32] Unsurprisingly, that approval was never granted.

Mohan Singh was one of the delegates chosen to represent the INA at the conference. He suggested to the South-East Asian nationalists that they request Subhas Chandra Bose to accept leadership of the entire independence movement. That suggestion won unanimous support. Many Indian nationalists distrusted Rash Behari and other Indian nationalists who had lived for many years in Japan. They feared that these expatriates had lost their Indian perspective and had been coopted by the Japanese. Mehervan Singh, an INA soldier, mentions that Rash Behari's little green Japanese soldier's cap irritated many people who saw it as a clear symbol of his sympathies.[33] Damodaran, son of K. Kesavan, an INA soldier from Singapore observed:

> At the early stages during the time [of] Rash Behari Bose not many people gave any weight to the [INA], because everybody knew he was more of a Japanese than of an Indian even though he was a freedom fighter those days. But still not many people believed that he could do much. We thought he will be something like the tool in the hands of the Japanese. But when Netaji came, the feeling was different.[34]

An Indian whose allegiance was only to India was needed, and Bose met that qualification. In the judgement of Damodaran and the vast majority of the Indian expatriates, 'Bose was just in line with Nehru and Gandhi and all; a top real nationalist. And so we all had great faith in Netaji's leadership. And he was a real, a potential leader and he was a real revolutionary.' On 17 April 1942, the Japanese Ministries of War, Navy and Foreign Affairs decided to bring Bose to Tokyo so that they could evaluate his usefulness to their purposes.[35]

In the meantime, until Bose took over as the new leader of the INA, Mohan Singh plunged ahead with preparations. According to his memoirs, Singh 'launched an all-out campaign to recondition the brains of the Indian soldiers by inculcating in them a spirit of patriotism and self-confidence. We appealed to their sense of honour, dignity and love of the motherland.'[36] The propaganda efforts were largely successful, and eventually Mohan Singh convinced 30,000 Indian soldiers to join the INA.[37] Nevertheless, in total 20,000 captured British Indian Army men chose to stay out of the first INA, remaining prisoners of war because they suspected that 'the Japanese were going to utilize [the INA] for their own selfish ends'.[38]

As Mohan Singh worked to assemble the INA, his efforts were hampered by increasing demands for various kinds of labour imposed by the Japanese on Indian soldiers. Singh found the exploitation of his men for non-military purposes unacceptable.[39] He thought that he had reached a firm agreement with the Japanese army and government about the proper role of the INA in their joint effort to oust the British from India via Burma. At what Mohan Singh in his memoirs refers to as 'the turning point', Singh realized that the Japanese did not share his intentions and enthusiasm for the creation of a large and robust INA, with the IIL functioning as a well-organized Indian provisional government. The Japanese, he wrote, 'wanted the army and the organization to be just a showpiece and a convenient puppet, but not a strong and powerful reality which may become a problem for them later on and thwart their secret designs on India'.[40]

After months of frustrating negotiations with the Japanese, Singh finally understood that he had been deceived from the outset. Realizing that the Japanese plans for the INA were for Japan's benefit only and that India's next occupier might well be Japan, he finally rebelled. In December 1942, Mohan Singh was arrested by the Japanese military administration under orders from the president of the IIL. His last defiant act was to formally dissolve the INA, an action the Japanese claimed exceeded his authority and violated the discipline of the army.[41] The Japanese insisted that they had removed Singh as INA commander because of his 'grave and unpardonable crime of suspecting and challenging the Japanese Government's sincerity regarding India's freedom'.[42] Mohan Singh spent the rest of the war in various Japanese prisons and was still incarcerated at Changi in eastern Singapore when Bose arrived in July 1943 to revive the INA.

SEVEN

BOSE IN SOUTH-EAST ASIA

JUST BEFORE DAWN ON 9 February 1943, Subhas Chandra Bose and his aide-de-camp Abid Hasan boarded German submarine U-180 in Kiel, Germany, to return to South-East Asia.[1] Bose's departure followed months of planning for his safe passage by the Japanese and German governments. It was another step forward in Bose's mission to conquer India with an Indian army raised abroad, a grand strategy that Bose had begun to develop in Calcutta three years earlier. The alliance with the Japanese was, as Bose saw it, based on the principle 'the enemy of my enemy is my friend'.[2] If the plan succeeded, Bose as the new head of the IIL and the INA would cross the Indo-Burma frontier together with the Japanese army, drive the British out of India and liberate his homeland.

Despite months of planning, the voyage from Europe to the Far East was a reckless gamble. The Japanese government gauged the chances of Bose's safe arrival in Asia at just 5 per cent, and they told him as much before his departure.[3] The exact number of fatalities among German soldiers in submarines during WWII is not available, but it probably exceeded 75 per cent. That Bose undertook the journey despite the danger shows the level of risk he was willing to accept in order to command an Indian liberation army. On 28 April, in the rough seas east of Madagascar, Bose and Abid

Hasan experienced a dramatic and dangerous transfer to the Japanese submarine I-29; on 6 May they reached the Sabang Island naval base off the northern tip of Sumatra. From Sumatra, Bose was transported to Tokyo in a small Japanese combat aircraft for negotiations with Prime Minister General Tojo Hideki before continuing on to Singapore. In Tokyo Bose was greeted by Indian freedom fighters in exile, among them Rash Behari Bose, but General Tojo kept him waiting for an audience.

On 10 June the two men met, and Bose received Tojo's permission to travel to Singapore to become the new commander of the INA. At the Japanese Imperial Diet on 16 June 1943, Tojo declared: 'Japan is firmly resolved to extend all means in order to help to expel and eliminate from India the Anglo-Saxon influences which are the enemy of the Indian people, and enable India to achieve full independence in the true sense of the term.' The agreement, he said, would 'live in history for all time'.[4] *Syonan Shimbun,* the Japanese-controlled English language newspaper in Singapore, published a supporting story a few days later, under the front-page headline 'Chandra Bose Coming to Nampo to Take Active Part in Indian Independence Move'. Nampo refers to Singapore, the 'southern region' of the Japanese-occupied areas. According to the account, 'Nippon has offered that assistance and has given India and the world the sacred pledge that the full independence of India, in the true sense of the term, is Nippon's one and only aim as far as India is concerned.'

Because the tides of war were turning against Tokyo, the Japanese war machine welcomed collaboration with Bose, leader of the nationalist Indian freedom movement outside India, as leverage to provoke political turmoil for Britain inside India. For Bose the alliance with Japan meant an end to the search for the partnership he needed to fulfil his dream of an Indian army engaging the British on Indian territory.

It would have been uncharacteristically naive for Bose entirely to trust the Japanese to leave India once the British Raj had been driven out. There was no rational basis for him to believe that Tokyo, after an enormously expensive campaign in Burma, would renounce all India's vast natural resources, so badly needed for Japan's industrial development. Although Bose's public speeches all expressed complete confidence in Japanese goodwill, Shah Nawaz Khan, who eventually came to hold the rank of a general in the INA, reported that Bose often reminded his men of the dangers of complacency:

> In the question of the independence of one's country one could trust no one and, as long as we were weak we would always be exploited. ... He said that we should ask for no safeguards from the Japanese, our surest safeguard must be our own strength, and if on going into India, we found that the Japanese wished to replace the British, we should turn round and fight them too.[5]

But to believe that Indian freedom fighters and nationalists, who for a century had failed to budge the British colonizers, would be able to wrest the spoils of war from a victorious Japanese army was perhaps overly optimistic.

Another perspective on Bose's collaboration with the Japanese comes from poet and yogi Dilip Kumar Roy. A friend and admirer since early childhood, Roy became convinced that Bose's dreams had been thwarted so many times that in the end Bose simply abandoned reality and joined the Japanese notwithstanding the manifest dangers.[6] 'Otherwise,' Roy observes, 'I do not think he would have even dreamed of joining hands with the Devil's disciples in order to wrest phantom laurels from reluctant hands of Destiny.'[7] Roy concludes magnanimously that Bose must have been guided by 'his unbending will-power and faith in idealism which, to the likes of us, often seemed too mythical to be true'.[8]

When Bose arrived in Singapore on 2 July 1943, the Japanese had already established both the IIL, which now was prepared to serve as the bureaucratic branch of Azad Hind, the provisional government, as well as the INA.[9] On 4 July 1943, standing in front of a crowd of ecstatic Indians with huge Japanese and Indian national flags as backdrop, Bose accepted leadership of the Indian independence movement in East Asia from Rash Behari Bose.[10]

Joining Bose in Singapore for the transfer ceremonies, General Tojo was apparently impressed with Bose's leadership qualities and gave the go-ahead for the designation of Azad Hind as the Provisional Government of Free India, with Bose serving as head of state; he further promised that Japan would transfer the Andaman and Nicobar Islands, located in the Bay of Bengal, to the newly created government in exile. However, after the much-publicized pledge of the islands, Japan showed extreme reluctance to cede formal sovereignty, which perhaps alerted Bose to future problems.[11] As it turned out, Japan never intended to transfer the administration of the islands. The formal handover happened on 21 October 1943, but the ceremony was pure propaganda, and in any case, under international law Japan did not have the right to transfer sovereignty of the islands.[12]

As a matter of fact, the Azad Hind itself possessed no sovereign authority under international law. In addition, as head of government and commander of the Azad Hind Fauj, Bose operated under direct Japanese control. The Azad Hind cabinet had no power, and Azad Hind held no territory. Still, for his monumental venture, Bose considered the estimated one-and-a-half million people who thought of themselves as ethnic Indians then living in South-East Asia to be citizens of his provisional government in exile.[13] It appears that Bose may have exaggerated the number of expatriate Indians as well as the anticipated overwhelming support for his ideas from them both in the form of taxes and service as soldiers.

Why cannot three million Indians, backed by a powerful movement at home, hope to throw the British out of India, when the aid of powerful Japan is readily available?[14]

... I stand here today representing the Provisional Government of Azad Hind which has absolute right over your lives and properties. ... Legally speaking, there is no private property when a country is in a state of war. The government has absolute right over the lives and properties of its people during such emergencies. ... Your lives and your properties do not belong to you; they belong to India and India alone.[15]

The Japanese army had agreed to supply war material to the INA, and Bose agreed to refuse assistance from other parties.[16] In many instances whole families joined the INA: the husband enlisting in the INA, the wife in the RJR, and the children in one of the several training camps for boys and girls. These families transferred all their possessions to the Azad Hind government to become 'fakirs', or ascetics. Shah Nawaz writes that a total of twenty crore (two hundred million) rupees was raised from East Asian Indian families and deposited in the Azad Hind Bank in Rangoon.[17]

Bose tolerated no freeloaders, demanding absolute allegiance from every Indian in Singapore, Malaya and Burma. Indians who did not belong to the IIL would not be considered true Indians; their homes would be ineligible for protection from Japanese raids and other benefits granted to members of the IIL.[18] British Intelligence reports indicate that many Indians, who refused to pay more than an absolute minimum, were turned over to the Kempeitai, the Japanese military police, accused of being anti-Japanese and pro-British.[19] The notorious brutality of the Kempeitai was known and feared in all Japanese-occupied areas. Bose appointed General Amil Chandra Chatterji (died 1954) of the INA in his capacity as the Azad Hind minister of finance to be in charge of collection of funds. Several sources, including Captain Lakshmi, called General Chatterji an 'evil genius', a 'cruel brute', and asserted that 'arrests and torture of various Indians was entirely due to Chatterji'.[20] Captain Lakshmi said: 'Chatterji was regarded by Bose as a necessary bureaucrat in an otherwise revolutionary movement.'[21] Anand Mohan Sahay was considered extremely good at procuring funds, especially from his homestead around Dacca, Bengal (now Dhaka in Bangladesh). His fund-raising methods were known as 'squeezing ceremony' during which wealthy Indians who were considered to have paid too little were handcuffed, slapped 'in typical Japanese fashion' and humiliated until they paid up.[22] It is unlikely that reports of this behaviour did not reach Bose, but Toye credits him with at least not directly sanctioning torture.[23]

With these varied and strong incentives by June 1944, 2,30,000 Indians in Malaya had sworn allegiance to the Azad Hind by joining the IIL.[24] Bose's speeches grew ever more fiery. He wanted to inflame his fellow Indians to follow him with an intensity that matched his own:

We Indians do not hate the enemy enough. If you want your countrymen to rise to heights of superhuman courage and heroism you must teach them – not only to love their country – but also to hate their enemy.

Therefore, I call for blood. It is only the blood of the enemy that can avenge his crimes of the past. But we can take blood only if we are prepared to give blood. Consequently, our programme for the future is to give blood. The blood of our heroes in this war will wash away our sins of the past. The blood of our heroes will be the price of our liberty. The blood of our heroes – their heroism and their bravery – will secure for the Indian people the revenge that they demand of their British tyrants and oppressors.[25]

On 5 July 1943, the day after he accepted the leadership of the IIL, wearing starched khaki uniform with jodhpurs and gleaming knee-high boots, Bose reviewed the INA for the first time and told the officers and jawans: 'Today is the proudest day of my life.'[26] He urged them to join him in the invasion that would allow them to raise the flag of free India over the Red Fort of Delhi. Bose changed the name of the Indian National Army to Azad Hind Fauj and announced the new battle cry for the army: 'Chalo Delhi, Chalo Delhi.'[27] The expression Chalo Delhi, 'onwards to Delhi', is a slight modification of Dilli Chalo, a battle cry with the same meaning used in the Uprising of 1857.

Perhaps out of modesty, or more likely political acumen, Bose did not affect a traditional military rank such as general. Instead, having little formal knowledge of warfare, he preferred to be addressed as Supreme Commander of the INA, a civil post.[28] Nevertheless, Bose made all decisions concerning every aspect of the INA, often overruling his senior military command.[29] For the rest of his life, no matter how hot the weather or how informal the occasion, Bose never again wore civilian clothes in public. He always dressed in a high-collared military uniform, albeit without any insignia of rank, and knee-high leather boots.[30]

When Subhas Chandra Bose took command of the Indian National Army and created the Rani of Jhansi Regiment, his qualifications as a military leader were by any standard minimal. In 1917, at age twenty-one,

Bose had responded to a recruiting campaign for the 49th Bengalees of the Indian Army, but his poor eyesight disqualified him and he was sent home 'heartbroken'.[31] Shortly thereafter, however, he was accepted into the Indian Defence Force (IDF) through his new school, Scottish Church College in Calcutta, where the military admission requirements were less demanding.[32]

Although he studied philosophy in college, Bose was delighted to spend four months in training camp, 'standing with a rifle on my shoulder taking orders from a British army officer'! This officer, Captain Gray, a rough Scotsman with what Bose characterized as 'a heart of gold', ably trained the awkward students and imparted to them a conviction of the importance of military service. The experience, Bose felt, 'gave me something which I needed or which I lacked. The feeling of strength and self-confidence grew still further.'[33]

At that time young Bose had, as noted earlier, just spent two years in limbo after his expulsion from Presidency College for assaulting a British professor who, in Bose's judgement, was disrespectful to his Indian students. It might seem incongruous that the rebellious young firebrand should be so eager to take orders from a British officer, but Bose took a different perspective. Parading with his rifle at Fort William, headquarters of the Indian Army in Calcutta, Bose imagined that he was reconquering his homeland. In uniform, he enjoyed attracting admiring attention from the people on the streets when his unit came marching through the city. With his weapon on his shoulder, Bose felt indomitable even though he was parading under the banner of the hated British Empire.[34] Later, in 1921, reconsidering his service in the Indian Defence Force, Bose expressed regret that he had sworn an oath of allegiance to the Raj, since there was no such commitment in his heart.[35]

After that initial arms training, Bose's next experience with martial affairs came several years later at the annual Indian National Congress meeting in 1928. In a replica of a general's full-dress uniform fashioned for the occasion by British tailors in Calcutta, complete with shoulder chains, Bose commanded a corps of uniformed volunteers, both male and female. Clearly, the ritual, uniform, discipline and structure of the military appealed to the mature Bose, just as they had in his student years.

When Bose resided in Germany during1941–43, hoping to return to Asia to take over command of the INA he plunged into the study of warfare. In an interview with B.R. Nanda, biographer of twentieth-century Indian politicians, Emilie Schenkl confirmed that Bose sought military knowledge wherever possible. In Berlin, he kept company with German generals and admirals in order to learn the art of war. [36] He also studied manuals on guerrilla warfare; the history of Ireland's anti-colonial struggle was a favourite topic. Bose saw the Sinn Fein as a prefiguration of the Indian movement and had been delighted to meet with President Eamon de Valera (1882–1975) for a long interview in London in January 1938. [37] As became evident on the battlefields of northern Burma, such book learning, interviews with foreign notables and social fraternization with Nazi flag officers constituted a poor substitute for formal military education and actual combat experience.

For several months following his inauguration, Bose raced around, visiting Singapore, Malaya, Thailand, Burma and Japan raising funds and recruiting soldiers, making full use of the airplane that General Tojo had placed at his disposal for travel. [38] To Bose's chagrin, Tojo turned down his request for an Indian pilot and crew. Instead a Japanese–Hindi translator joined the staff, probably to keep Tojo informed of Bose's conversations while en route. Bose insisted on displaying his national colours on the aircraft and substituted his own emblem, the Indian tricolour banner with the springing tiger, for Japan's rising sun.

Inactive since Mohan Singh's imprisonment in December 1942, the INA had dwindled by July 1943 from 30,000 to only 8,000 men. [39] Some officers had requested and had been granted separation; a few had attempted sabotage against their Japanese captors, and some had deserted. [40] During the interregnum, the Japanese had sent thousands of INA soldiers, once again prisoners of war, to build bridges, roads and airfields all over South-East Asia. [41] The Japanese government refused Bose's request for the return of these soldiers, initially leaving the Second INA much smaller than the First. [42]

With Bose invested as head of the new INA, however, the number of soldiers quickly rebounded from 8,000 to 20,000 as former INA men rejoined and successful appeals for civilian volunteers in Singapore and Malaya drew fresh recruits.[43] Bose's goal for the INA was a troop strength of 50,000, and General Chatterji asserts that this objective was achieved during 1943. The INA had three active divisions, each 10,000 strong. Another 20,000 civilians were recruited and trained, but not deployed to Burma.[44] Seeing that his army and provisional government were developing satisfactorily, on 5 January 1944, Bose transferred the advance headquarters of the provisional government from Singapore to Rangoon to be closer to the Japanese army control centre.

Those officers of the INA with a rank of battalion commander and above had served as officers in the British Indian Army. Some of them had been educated at the Indian Military Academy at Dehradun and others at Sandhurst.[45] Only a few officers of lower rank (platoon and company commanders) had had any officers' training at all. Mohan Singh, as the commander of the First INA, had promoted men directly from sepoy to officer.[46]

This lack of well-trained officers also had an impact on the Rani regiment, because soldiers who lacked adequate battlefield skills themselves were assigned the responsibility to instruct the Ranis in jungle warfare and to teach RJR officers how to command their troops in combat. One instructor, thirty-one-year-old Kannappa Muthia (POW L3698), in July 1945 told British interrogators that his occupation was instructor of weapons handling for the Ranis in Burma. A 'petty' business owner and a recruiter for the IIL before the war, L3698 Muthia's only prior military experience had been a three-week stint as a Tamil-Hindi interpreter attached to the Gandhi Brigade of the INA.[47] Obtaining a medical certificate stating that he was unfit for active service, he taught weapons handling to the 'Madrassi girls' from early August 1944 until 23 April 1945, when the last contingent of Ranis began their retreat.[48] Described in the IR by British Military Intelligence officer Captain Rashid Yusuf Ali as 'a shifty and unprepossessing type', this instructor was probably not an unusual example of the INA's deficiency in military expertise; nonetheless all Ranis, including Captain Lakshmi, praised their instructors and were confident that they had received excellent training.

Consequently, while it was an accomplishment for Bose to re-establish the INA so quickly, he did not produce a well-trained or well-commanded army. Major Hugh Toye (1917–2012) was head of British Military Intelligence in Singapore at the end of the war and his report on Bose is positive on the whole, but he blames him as the commander of the INA for unreasonably expecting an assemblage of raw recruits to somehow transform itself into a first-class army despite a dearth of professional officers.[49] In his memoirs, General Mohan Singh, the former leader of the INA, expresses his scepticism regarding Bose's competence as a military commander.[50] In December 1943 while the Japanese were holding Singh in Changi Prison, Singapore, Bose arranged to meet him. Singh recalled his surprise at Bose's self-confidence when Bose told him how he expected that 'the moment [Bose] entered India, there would be a general revolt in the country. The Indian Army would desert the British and join him.'[51] Singh added wistfully, '[Bose] thought that he had generated a great fighting spirit in the rank and file of the INA.'[52] Regarding the last point, the opportunity for Bose to confirm that Indian soldiers serving in the Allied forces would lay down their weapons never came.

The Japanese 15th Army had successfully occupied all of Burma by the end of May 1942, but by July 1943 the Emperor's string of victories during the early years of the war had come to an end. Bose had received reports that the Japanese army was losing in the Pacific, and therefore he wanted the INA to join the war as quickly as possible. Immediately after his arrival in Singapore, Bose met with Field Marshal Count Terauchi Hisaichi (1879–1946), commander of the Japanese armies in South-East Asia. Negotiations about the role of the INA in the joint invasion of India began, but agreement was delayed because the Japanese generals were unable to settle on a plan for the next move of the Imperial Japanese Army in Burma.

General Mutaguchi Renya (1888–1966) who had taken over command of the Japanese 15th Army in Burma, was anxious to forestall a British recapture of Burma across the mountains and the Chindwin river, and he proposed therefore to launch attacks on Kohima in the state of Nagaland and Imphal in Manipur, two Indian cities located just a few miles beyond the Indo-Burma frontier.[53] Other Japanese generals had deep reservations about Mutaguchi's plan, but after repeated delays Tojo finally signed off on it.[54] Mutaguchi's headquarters had moved to Maymyo, a lovely hill station with a pleasant climate, almost 400 miles north of Rangoon, but still 300 miles in a direct line from the intended battle sites at Imphal and Kohima. In the spring of 1944, Bose also relocated his INA command centre to Maymyo.[55]

Bose was pleased with the proposed strategy, believing that speed was of the essence for success in this military campaign.[56] In exuberant expectation of victory, Bose asked his Calcutta collaborators, members of the Bengal Volunteer Group, to plan routes for the influx of arms across the border to Burma from Manipur. Members of this underground group were later proud to report that they also worked to fulfil Bose's proactive demands and had acquired the necessary military intelligence with particulars about the strength and deployment of Anglo-American forces, their arms and air strength. The optimistic Volunteer Group had also recruited men who stood ready to engage in guerrilla warfare in Bengal coinciding with the entry of INA into India.[57] Bose expected a warm welcome for the INA in Bengal, and as we shall see later in detail, wanted the Ranis in Burma fully trained and ready to lead the INA troops on to Indian soil. Confident that the rest of India would quickly rise up, Bose readied plans to establish a civil government in India quickly and smoothly.

The first contingent of INA soldiers, the Subhas Brigade under the command of Shah Nawaz Khan, arrived for action in Burma in January 1944. The INA men left Singapore for Rangoon ready and eager for jungle combat, but at the end of the 1,200-mile journey, much of it on foot, and after two months on the road they were in poor health and so emaciated that they were unfit for battle. The INA soldiers carried on average a load of eighty pounds and still easily advanced 25 miles a day. Shah Nawaz found it extraordinary that the distance Indian soldiers travelled in two days took their Japanese companions five days to cover, and, therefore, they often unnecessarily delayed the arrival of the INA fighters.[58]

INA deployment to north-western Burma was again postponed because the Japanese commanders and Bose disagreed on the role of the INA in the upcoming campaign.[59] Bose insisted, 'The first drop of blood to be shed on Indian soil should be that of a member of the I.N.A.'[60] Japanese commander-in-chief in Burma, General Kawabe Masakazu (1886–1965) wanted small squads of INA soldiers attached to each invading Japanese division to serve as spies and guides. Bose, however, insisted that his army serve as a cohesive unit.[61] Fujiwara, who liked Bose and wanted his quest to be successful, later told Toye that he regretted to admit that Bose's skill in operational tactics was low. Bose was inclined to be idealistic and not realistic.[62]

On the basis of documents collected from fallen Japanese soldiers, Field Marshal William Joseph Slim (1891–1970) of the British 14th Army anticipated an attack on Imphal and Kohima by the Japanese army in mid-March, 1944.[63] General Mutaguchi, confident of an easy victory, finally launched the offensive exactly as described in the plans and as expected by the Allied commanders.

There is broad agreement among scholars that the INA arrived on the field of battle too late and too poorly equipped to have had any chance of making a positive difference in the outcome of the disastrous campaign.[64] Inadequate cooperation between the Japanese and the Indian officers also played an important role in the poor performance of the INA. In early April 1944, the Gandhi Brigade of the INA was marching towards Kohima and Imphal to join the First INA contingent, the Subhas Brigade, following the same route taken by the INA in January. Several days' march from the battlefront, they met Japanese troops who told them that the Indian forces were too late to participate in the decisive battle to cross the border into India, and that most likely Imphal would fall before they arrived.[65] The Japanese liaison officers travelling with the Gandhi Brigade were responsible for arranging transport and supplies, and they advised the Indians to leave all their heavy equipment behind. If they wanted to be among the first to enter India, they should advance each carrying only one blanket, a rifle and fifty rounds of ammunition. The Japanese assured the Indians that plenty of resources awaited them at Imphal. Every INA soldier wanted to participate in the assault on Imphal, so the brigade took that advice and rushed to the front.[66] On reaching Palel, 20 miles south-east of Imphal, they learned that Imphal had not fallen, and the poorly

equipped soldiers met intense fighting. General Shah Nawaz recalled, 'The
Gandhi Brigade was faced by powerful British forces and had to bear the
brunt of some of the heaviest fighting in that area without any artillery or
air support and with the additional disadvantage of having left behind at
Kalewa all their heavy equipment including machine guns, hand grenades
and entrenching tools.'[67]

Looking back, General Kawabe of the Japanese 15th Army regretted
sending the INA into a battle he knew they could not win, but the decision
was not up to him alone. As the commander of the Indian soldiers, Bose
insisted that as long as one man's hand could be raised to hold a weapon,
the fight must go on.[68] Informed on 12 July 1944 of the Japanese army's
imminent withdrawal from Imphal, Bose still refused to abandon hope
for the mission. Devastated, Bose ordered his men to stay on the Indian
frontier: they were not to withdraw south of Mandalay.[69] With no weapons,
ammunition, food or medical supplies, suffering from malnutrition,
malaria and dysentery during an extremely strong monsoon, the Indian
soldiers were struggling to survive on whatever they could scrounge up
in the jungle. Many died, some from battle wounds, more from starvation
and disease. In September 1944, Bose finally ordered his forces to fall
back, at which time practically every surviving male soldier of the INA
was infected with malaria.[70]

During the remaining year of the war following the abandonment of the
plan to invade India via Kohima and Imphal, the INA continued to retreat
southwards through Burma with huge losses and many desertions. Subhas
Chandra Bose's dream of conquering India had become a catastrophe.

EIGHT

CREATION AND MISSIONS OF THE RANI OF JHANSI REGIMENT

BOSE'S INA ADVENTURE AND the dreams of the Ranis was in the distant future when in 1928, as a prominent leader in the Indian National Congress, Bose was appointed General Officer Commanding (GOC) of the annual Congress session to be held in Calcutta. To maintain order at this massive event, Bose organized a corps of uniformed, but unarmed, guards, the Bengal Volunteers. The Government of India approved Bose's request that police not be posted along the route of the presidential procession, and further in response to Bose's warning that the British Raj would be responsible for any disturbance or deaths unless they let him 'take complete charge of law and order'.[1] Bose's volunteer force numbered about 2,000 young people, of whom 250 were the sort of committed and determined women who later became members of the RJR. They were recruited primarily from local colleges and associations, including several who were members of Bengali revolutionary and terrorist groups.[2] For months Bose invested considerable time and effort in supervising the training of these volunteers.

Lotika Ghose was appointed Officer Commanding in charge of the

women volunteers. According to her recollections, the participants were
'excited' and felt 'that something extremely serious was going on. An
armed revolution was being planned.' Bose contacted his friend Kalyani
Das to get names for possible recruits for the corps. Years later, Das,
Ghose and other women from the 1928 Bengal Volunteer force clearly
remembered the event and explicitly saw themselves as precursors of
the Rani of Jhansi Regiment.[3] Ghose believes that already when he was
organizing the women's section of the Bengal Volunteers, 'Netaji dreamed'
of the women's regiment of the INA.[4]

Coincidentally, the fourteen-year-old future Captain Lakshmi attended
the same Congress conference with her mother, and was thrilled to
witness 'the rebel and *enfant terrible* of the Congress, Subhas Chandra
Bose' commanding 'the parade like a seasoned military man'.[5] She was
particularly impressed by the women's wing, well drilled in parade
discipline and led by 'Colonel' Lotika Ghose.[6] 'They did not carry arms,'
observed the young Lakshmi, 'but the smartness and precision with which
they drilled would have done credit to any crack infantry unit.'[7] Gandhi,
the pacifist, naturally disliked the martial display with booted militants
strutting and saluting. He likened the whole spectacle to the Bertram
Mills Circus.[8]

In the '1970 Netaji Oration', Bose's aide-de-camp Abid Hasan Safrani
provided the earliest known report on the creation of the RJR.[9] Hasan
described Bose's 1943 submarine journey from Germany to Asia and
recounted a dramatic event that occurred while Bose 'was working
on a favourite subject, the formation of the Rani of Jhansi Regiment'.
Suddenly the submerged U-boat shook terribly and tilted. Hasan feared
that the submarine had sustained an incapacitating hit and that everybody
aboard was doomed. Bose, however, remained completely calm and
continued his dictation.[10] Using Hasan as a sounding board, Bose asked
him to list all possible arguments 'why our women would not respond
to his call to go with him to Burma in trousers and bush-shirts, rifle in
hand'.[11] Hasan answered after the submarine had stabilized, but does
not report his response. At other times the discussion of the women's
regiment was not whether the INA would include women soldiers,

'there was no doubt that they would come and join our army,' the point of disagreement was rather their uniform. Bose insisted 'he was going to put them into pantaloons and bush-shirts [sic] uniform'. Hasan was sure that South Indian women and Bengalis would be ready to die for Bose, take up arms, but never give up the sari. The Ranis accepted Bose's design with pride.[12] Hasan summarized, '[Bose], however, did not want [the women] to jump into flaming pyres,' committing sati, a ritual which at the time was still practised by some Indian women. Instead, Bose wanted his women to 'ride out into the field, sword in hand as the Rani of Jhansi did'.[13]

Indians learn much of their history orally, and over time the historical narrative is merged with mythology, heroic legend and folklore.[14] As he reflected on the RJR project during his four-month submarine voyage, Bose did not have to search through dusty forgotten annals to exhume Rani Lakshmibai to serve as a model for female combat soldiers. Since her death in battle during the 1857 Rebellion against the British forces, the historical Rani's valour had inspired novelists, poets and storytellers, both Indian and British.[15] She had become an emblem of the Indian nationalists' struggle for freedom and was seen as the embodiment of female Shakti, divine feminine power. '*Jhansi Ki Rani*' was a popular protest song of the freedom struggle in India. The refrain '*Khoob ladi mardani woh to Jhansi wali Rani thi*', 'Gallantly she fought like a man, the queen of Jhansi', must have resonated strongly among the young female volunteers. Bose and the women he aimed to recruit for his regiment were naturally familiar with the Rani of Jhansi, iconic heroine of Indian womanhood and Indian nationalism.

It was just a few days after his arrival in Singapore that Bose again addressed another huge audience, about 60,000 Indians in Singapore on 9 July 1943. In a speech 'Why I left Home and Homeland', Bose called for every able-bodied Indian to enlist in the INA and concluded with a stunning demand: 'I want also a unit of brave Indian women to form a "Death-defying Regiment" who will wield the sword, which the brave Rani of Jhansi wielded in India's First War of Independence in 1857.'[16]

Three days later Bose reiterated this theme at a meeting of Indian women held under the auspices of the Women's Section of the IIL. For this event Dr Lakshmi Swaminathan and the head of the IIL in Singapore, Attavar Yellappa (1912–45) organized a female guard of honour for Bose. With some difficulty twenty women were persuaded to train to present arms using Lee-Enfield 303 rifles borrowed from the INA. With no time to produce uniforms, the women wore white saris.[17] Bose was pleased. In his speech to the female audience praising the ways that women in India had already taken part in the freedom struggle, he emphasized their traditional mode of service: 'What is more there is no suffering which Indian women have not gladly and bravely shared along with our men in the course of several decades of our national struggle.'[18]

Inevitably, Bose's call for the creation of a female combat unit generated strong opposition, verging at times on contempt. While Bose appreciated the female guard that greeted him on 12 July 1943, the idea of women soldiers shocked the civilian Indians and had an even more profound effect on the male soldiers of the INA. Documented comments from male INA soldiers are few, but British interrogation reports obtained after the war contain two revealing accounts.

One evaluation of female combat soldiers came from a high-ranking officer in the INA, General Mohammad Zaman Kiani with corroboration from his wife, the physician Dr Nasira Kiani.[19] Educated at the prestigious Indian Military Academy at Dehradun and recipient of the gold medal as outstanding cadet of his year, Kiani was a professional soldier who, at the time of his surrender at the end of the war, had achieved the rank of Major General in the INA and served as chief of the general staff. When questioned about her knowledge of the INA, H1152 Dr Kiani explained to the interrogators that she had been pressed very hard by Lakshmi Swaminathan, a medical colleague in Singapore, to participate in the guard of honour and had only joined reluctantly. Dr Kiani said that her husband was astounded to see his wife standing with her rifle among the women presenting weapons to honour Bose and that he 'regarded her with the most extreme disapproval which he did not attempt to hide and [later] ordered her to sever all connections with the Regiment'.[20] Dr Kiani did not join the RJR.

In August 1945, General M.Z. Kiani (identified in British Intelligence reports as POW H1175) described his dismay at seeing his wife parading as a soldier and gave his view of the Rani of Jhansi Regiment.[21] As Kiani explained, Bose had not consulted any officers about creating a unit of female combat infantry. Plans for the Regiment as well as its training programme also seemed to be entirely Bose's own concept. When Kiani first heard of the RJR, it was not a Bose suggestion but already his decision. Although Kiani himself disapproved of the idea, he did not voice his objection because he had been informed that the purpose of the female soldiers was to serve as propaganda only, and not as a fighting unit. He stressed that he was so strongly opposed to the RJR that in October 1943, at the opening of the RJR Singapore camp, when he learned of his wife's role as a doctor for the unit, he ordered her to stop helping with medical exams of the new recruits and to have no further interaction with the Ranis. Dr Kiani did cease all further contact with the Regiment.

Soon after the war several INA soldiers penned memoirs in which they confirmed the presence of women in the INA, although they apparently did not all understand the RJR mission. General Chatterji attempted to show support for Bose's idea in his 1947 book on the campaign in Burma. Positive comments regarding Indian women in the military were apparently hard for him to generate; for five pages he praised Indian women as Sitas and Savitris, as devout worshipers of God, brilliant mathematicians, philosophers and poets, and as able nurturers of their children. It was only at the end of his observations that he tied these characteristics to the RJR:

> Bearing in mind all the factors mentioned above, it was but natural for Netaji to consider the establishment of a Women's Organization part of which would be a combatant unit in India's Independence Movement in South-east Asia. He accordingly conceived the idea of establishing a Women's Regiment and named it after the illustrious Rani of Jhansi.[22]

Mehervan Singh, a Sikh INA veteran, a much younger man than Chatterji, had a very different view of the Ranis whom he first encountered in 1943. As a contributor to the Oral History Project in Singapore, Singh was asked about the Ranis. When the interviewer prompted him, 'But culturally it is bad for the females to [be soldiers],' Singh interrupted:

> I will mention this, where Sikhs are concerned, there is no difference because Sikh history has it on record there were women soldiers even in the time of the Guru, two hundred, three hundred years ago. So why not in the 20th century? Please remember, that Rani of Jhansi herself fought in the battlefield. She was not a Sikh – she was a Rani of Central India. … Some people might have thought it funny, but I don't consider it out of the ordinary because the idea behind the mind of Subhas Chandra Bose in organising the Rani of Jhansi segment, I say, was fantastic.[23]

Singh repeats in his own words Bose's idea that the sight of the Ranis entering Indian territory would make the Indian soldiers on the British side lay down their weapons. He acknowledges that the Ranis' mission would not have been to 'fire artillery guns'. However, simply by parading as well-trained soldiers the 'Regiment would have become a fantastic asset because it would raise the spirit of the Indians in India on Indian soil.'[24] Captain S.S. Yadava of the INA, the only male soldier alive in 2008 I found to interview, worked together with the Ranis in Rangoon. He too gave his wholehearted endorsement of women soldiers.[25]

Unsurprisingly, not every INA soldier had such an enthusiastic view of the RJR. An undated British Interrogation Report summarizes a captured INA soldier, POW 897's assessment of his female colleagues:

> The women are employed for the most part as nurses in base hospitals at Rangoon and Singapore. A certain amount of purely propaganda military training is also carried out. The general reputation of these women in Burma and Malaya is bad.[26]

Much information about daily life in Singapore is available from the several Oral History Projects in the Singapore National Archives. Many citizens remembered the Ranis and their camp in the middle of the city as well as their marches with flags, weapons and loud singing of stirring patriotic songs. Some Indian men were unimpressed. Dr Kanichat Raghava Menon, former secretary of the IIL in Singapore, was a supporter of Gandhi and agreed with the Mahatma that the best weapon for the fight for Indian independence was ahimsa. He was therefore in total opposition to Bose's martial approach. [27] Dr Menon's political view was also expressed in his impressions of the Ranis:

> They formed the Women's Regiment, Rani of Jhansi Regiment. But it was mere show. I tell you, just a mere puppet show. And not a single woman knew how to wield a knife properly. They knew how to wield the kitchen knife, but not a knife in battle. ... They were undergoing regular training, military training. ... And some of them were taught to shoot. ... I'm sure no woman really meant to go into the battlefield and fight. ...That is just to show that even Indian women were very anxious of India's independence. That's it. They were not going to fight. I did not have any doubt. [28]

M. S. Varma, another Singapore resident, had known Captain Lakshmi since youth because their parents were friends. When asked about Lakshmi and the RJR, Varma did not mask his criticism of the idea of women as soldiers, 'Honestly, they were only decoration, that's all. No one expected much of womenfolk.'[29] Another person who disapproved of the RJR was retired librarian Vilasini Perumbulavil, whose cousin was one of those 'adventurous sorts' who had eagerly joined the Ranis. Perumbulavil did not believe that the Ranis would make good soldiers. 'The women's regiment wasn't much, it was just more propaganda. They could have done much better work doing something instead of carrying guns.'[30]

Dr Tan Ban Cheng contributed his story about life as a young Chinese boy in Singapore during the war. His chief resentment of the RJR was that most of the field where he and other boys played football was confiscated to give the female Indian soldiers a training camp. When the ball would occasionally go over the fence into the Ranis' camp, he asserts that they refused to return it and threatened to shoot the boys. More generally, Tan

Ban Cheng, who developed beriberi during the war, had little confidence in the Ranis' patriotism and surmised they had probably signed up 'because it was a way to get a good meal each day'.[31]

Despite such widespread scepticism among the Indian male population, Bose was not deterred. To Indians everywhere Bose's compelling message was '*Tum mujhe khoon do, main tumhe azadi doonga*', 'Give me your blood and I promise you freedom'.[32] The need for ultimate sacrifice on behalf of the noble cause was a recurrent theme, but Bose concentrated especially on Indian women's traditional willingness to sacrifice themselves; he sought to inculcate in them the belief that 'the price of freedom is suffering, sacrifice and struggle'.[33] In his appeal to women to become combat soldiers, Bose repeatedly assured his audience: 'I know what our women are capable of, and, therefore, I say without the slightest exaggeration that there is no work, there is no sacrifice and there is no suffering which our sisters are not capable of.'[34] The Ranis understood Bose's words literally, concretely, and sixty-five years later, in our interviews, they still expressed the belief that Bose had promised each of them personally that if they were willing to sacrifice their lives, India would be free. Janaki Thevar's eyes filled up with tears and her voice broke every time she repeated to me the narrative of the sacred bond that Bose had made with her.[35]

Again and again Bose in his speeches outlined the imagined armed deliverance of India: fully trained armed Ranis would be among the first INA soldiers crossing the border to free their country. When the British Indian Army sepoys fighting on the side of the Raj saw Indian women carrying weapons, willing to risk their lives to liberate their motherland, Bose was certain that they would lay down their weapons in shame and join the INA.

On 5 April 1945, a civilian woman with knowledge from inside the Rani camp in Burma surrendered to British authorities. Captive L2243, Rahmat Bibi Ma Khin U, a Burmese Muslim woman worked as a recruiter for the IIL in Mandalay and on the basis of her information the British officer surmised Bose's expressed purpose of the Regiment:

It is possible that it was formed by early enthusiasts actually to go to the front – not for actual fighting but in order to appeal to Indian Army soldiers to lay down their arms. Later the 'fighting group' was probably used for propaganda purposes in the rear areas while the 'nursing' group put in some really good and useful work.[36]

The Indian historian H.N. Pandit expanded on the theme of Bose sacrificing women on the battle front, claiming that Bose had actually selected a band of eighty women of the Ranis' regiment, and that the plan was for 'the girls to have fallen one by one under the eyes of the Indian soldiers of the British Indian Army. The sight would have shaken the British officers commanding the sepoys to their bones, and a widespread mutiny would have come...'[37]

That dramatic event did not happen, but in 1988 when Pandit wrote his history of the war, he made Bose's prospective sacrifice of eighty women sound tantalizingly realistic. Rani Rasammah told me that she was certain that she had heard Bose describe a scenario that did not differ much from Pandit's.[38] Rasammah's duty, as she understood it, was to train to be ready for the day when the male INA soldiers crossed the Indo-Burma frontier. At that moment, she expected Bose to order the armed Rani Regiment to advance into Bengal, where she assumed the Ranis would all immediately be killed. Rasammah confirmed that that had been her expectation for the RJR mission when she signed up. Janaki Thevar tearfully agreed completely.[39] Manwati Panday, with several other Ranis, expressed deep disappointment that this mass slaughter of the Rani Regiment just inside Mother India and the resulting honour of martyrdom did not materialize: 'When we joined the Ranis, we wanted to become martyrs for India. We would have been proud to be martyrs, and I am sorry that it did not happen.'[40]

Rani Mommata Gupta saw her role differently: 'Netaji did not want us to fight in Burma, but only fight after we came into India. He wanted the Rani of Jhansi Regiment to go first into India, lead the soldiers to show India what Indian girls could do. Netaji said that there was no difference between men and women, that women should think like men.'[41]

In a recruiting speech printed in *Young India*, 18 July 1943, Bose described the devastating moral impact the female soldiers would have on their misguided countrymen:

It is not merely the number of rifles you may carry or the number of shots you may fire which is important. Equally important is the moral effect of your brave example. I have no doubt in my mind that when our countrymen on the other side of the Frontier, whether they are civilians or whether they are in the British Indian Army, when our countrymen see you marching with rifles in hand, they will certainly come over and join you and take the rifles from you and carry on the fight which you will begin.[42]

In a recruiting speech a couple of weeks later, in August 1943, Captain Lakshmi, paraphrasing Bose, concisely expressed this same rationale for the use of female soldiers in the Indian battle for freedom:

This new regiment when formed will be composed not only of women soldiers but also of others who may be employed as first aid nurses, cooks, orderlies or special staff all serving in the front line. The regiment will not work behind the lines but right in front. When we come into contact with the Indian Army on the other side, the very presence of Indian women armed for the freedom fight will, I am sure, have a very great effect on the British-Indian Army and the moral effect of their presence right on the front line will be very great for those of the Indian National Army fighting side by side with them. [43]

It is interesting to compare these differing versions of the RJR mission. Bose expected the all-male British Indian Army troops to defect to the INA, relieve the Ranis of their weapons and take over the fight. Captain Lakshmi's prospect was far less paternalistic: she foresaw that the Regiment would continue to fight on the front line side by side together with the converted British Indian Army soldiers.

By Bose's design the Ranis were to promote two ideas: that women could be as proficient infantry soldiers as their male counterparts and that the new Indian woman would stand shoulder to shoulder with the men in all endeavours. The fit and smartly dressed young women would project those concepts by marching through Singapore and Rangoon singing patriotic songs, encouraging other young women to join the Regiment. As 'additional propaganda work', Bose sent a group of Ranis by train to the principal towns in Malaya, where they would parade 'carrying their rifles'.[44] Lakshmi Nair joined the Ranis at age fourteen and travelled widely in Malaya for this propaganda purpose. Describing herself, Lakshmi Nair said that she spoke three or four languages, was not afraid of anything and was very successful at attracting new recruits to the Regiment especially among the workers at the palm oil and rubber estates in upper Malaya.[45]

As noted above, many Singapore citizens voiced their negative view of female soldiers, but several admitted that they found that the Ranis looked quite professional in their uniforms. Indeed, much was made of the Ranis' impressive parade display – of their vigour, their starched uniforms and their crisp goose-steps – as if this was evidence that the women were highly trained combat soldiers ready to go to war.

These parade rituals also served to promote the myth of the reincarnate Rani of Jhansi out to reclaim her country. Whether consciously or intuitively, Bose may have intended that the repeated public performances would re-enact on city streets the sacred battleground of Jhansi. This compellingly stylized representation of female military prowess would lend credence and plausibility to the nationalist image of female warriors poised to redeem the honour of Mother India.

General Kiani's perception that the RJR was only intended to serve as a propaganda tool was shared by Dr S. Sen, Bose's physician. The doctor encouraged his two young daughters, Amba and Reba, to enlist because Bose had told him that the Ranis would serve only as symbols for the new Indian woman and never be in any danger.[46] Abdealli Motiwalla, a young Singapore supplier of stationery to the INA, was in almost daily contact with the RJR. His understanding was also that 'the Women's Army' was just for propaganda. 'I think there must be about four or five hundred only, not small, just enough for propaganda sake.'[47]

At an INA spy-training centre on Penang Island, Malaya, male INA
soldiers were trained to cross into India to infiltrate the British Indian
Army. The function of this Bahadur Group was to go behind enemy lines
in civilian clothing, and through casual conversation or employment as a
local citizen gain background information about the British army.[48] When
ready, the INA man would then discard his civilian clothes and report in
uniform to an Indian unit of the British army pretending to be a straggler
from another unit. After a short stay, having gathered intelligence and
attempted to subvert Indian prospects, he would return to the INA in
Burma with his findings.[49] This project of intelligence gathering was not
successful, for a large proportion of these trained intelligence officers did
not return from India but instead crossed over, defected and assisted the
Allies. To make matters worse, British Intelligence had insider informants at
the centre in Penang and was well informed of activities at the spy school.[50]

Although some Ranis talked about themselves as possible spies, research
for this study did not locate reliable and specific information about any
actual plans to train a Rani corps of infiltration agents. In a June 1944 letter
to Captain Satiavati Thevar, the commander of the Rani camp in Singapore,
Bose informed her that he had asked Colonel Bhonsle to 'arrange for
additional training for the Special Services Group' of the RJR. The issue
was whether to build an additional facility in Singapore for this purpose
or send the Special Services Group to Burma for training.[51] It is certain
that after the departure to Burma of the first group in late May 1944, no
other Ranis were transferred from Singapore to Rangoon. Of the Ranis
who remained in Singapore, Rani Dhanam said that she 'unlike her sister
Anjali' was not working for the secret service.[52] When questioned, Anjali
was not sure that she had done any secret service work. After passing the
officers, exam, Anjali was one of a small group of Ranis who learned the
Morse code. They were taken to a separate building for these lessons, but
the girls never used the training and no explanation was ever given why
they should master that skill. In any case, Anjali enjoyed herself: 'it was
fun, like being in camp.'[53]

Several Ranis said that they were specifically invited by Bose to join a
Secret Service (SS) corps. Ponnammah reported that Bose set up an SS unit

in Burma, which included both male and female soldiers. About 'thirty educated girls', she said, were invited to join to be trained as spies.[54] Shanti Bhowmick heard that Bose, accompanied by Colonel Habibur Rahman would come to the camp to personally interview Ranis looking for 'some smart and efficient girls for secret service training'.[55] The recruiting INA officers emphasized that becoming a Secret Service officer was voluntary, but members signed their names in blood to join.[56] Shanti was selected and felt very proud when together with other girls from the Regiment:

> We cut our own fingers a bit and with the blood oozing out of them, painted a *Tilak* mark (an auspicious sign) on the forehead of Netaji and also had signed our respective names with that blood on a piece of paper bearing the statement on oath, 'We shall sacrifice the last drop of our blood for the cause of our motherland.'[57]

Looking up at Bose, the girls saw that tears of joy were trickling down his cheeks.[58]

Rani Mommata recalled the names of two other Ranis, Pratima Sen and Maya Ganguli, who joined the SS with her.[59] Still enthusiastic about the project, Mommata proudly remembered, 'It was a great, great honour to be chosen to be an intelligence officer. We had separate classes.'[60] Anjuli Bhowmick was not asked to be a SS member, but was impressed when her sister Shanti was selected and told Anjuli that she signed her name in blood.[61]

In response to my question of what kind of intelligence work Bose wanted her to do, Mommata Gupta opened her mouth wide and pointed, 'Look at my teeth, there was a microfilm put inside. Look at my fourth tooth. They drilled a hole in my tooth and put microfilm in it and covered it up.'[62] Her duty, she said, was to get to India to deliver the film to an [unspecified] army officer. It seems unlikely that Mommata actually had a microfilm inserted in her premolar, and no other Ranis mentioned being asked to carry messages in this manner.

Nevertheless, in the spring of 1945, Manwati Panday from the Burma RJR contingent reported to Lieutenant Colonel Ehsan Qadir of INA that another INA officer, Biren Roy, had approached her for assistance. He wanted help to 'secure girls from the Rani of Jhansi Regt. to work as his secret agents'.[63] Roy was mobilizing a group he called 'more revolutionary than the INA'. In the expectation that by March 1945 Bose's military mission would have failed, Roy wanted to engage 'sincere and patriotic workers' to be ready to continue the freedom fight. Perhaps lively and beautiful young Mommata was also approached with a similar appeal to join Roy's secret group.[64] In addition, Biren Roy attempted to enlist the support of Captain Lakshmi for his scheme, and 'although she appreciated his penetrating analysis of men and affairs', she considered him impulsive and unstable and therefore deemed it impossible to carry out his proposed project and refused.[65]

When I asked the Ranis if anyone had warned them that their lives would be at risk if they went into Burma as part of the INA, they answered that INA officers had come to the camp in Burma to give them 'pep talks'. Two Ranis added that, in addition to the prospect of being killed by the enemy, there was another danger: they had also been asked to serve as 'Mata Haris' – female agents exchanging sex for secrets. Janaki Bai, an eighty-six-year-old dignified, retired schoolteacher, a Rajput woman, was the first to mention this:

> I remember one officer who said that we must even be prepared to be Mata Haris. Mata Hari, you know, sold her body. The thought was odious to me, but of course I did not show that. I do not think that any other Rani was willing to do that, and the situation never arose. But we were told in the pep talk that that would be required of us. Highly educated Indian officers who used to serve in the British army were the ones who told us that.[66]

Ponnammah told me the same story and added that another Rani, Papathy Thevar, Janaki Thevar's half-sister, was also asked to be ready to make that sacrifice for her motherland.[67] Neither Janaki Bai nor Ponnammah knew exactly what was entailed in serving as a Mata Hari, other than, presumably, the seduction of enemy soldiers in order to obtain secrets. In any event, they were never assigned any enemy soldier whom to seduce, and both women were relieved at never having to learn more about that instrument of military intelligence. Mommata strongly denied that these accounts could be true: 'No seducing. The Englishmen should be killed. No, no, we were not told to be Mata Haris.'[68]

Aside from Mommata, no Rani chosen for the Secret Service reported having had espionage training beyond a few separate classes, and none left camp for either training or actual secret service. With no other corroborating evidence from the Ranis, Captain Lakshmi or British Intelligence, it seems that special training of the Ranis as spies both in Burma and in Singapore was very limited if it occurred at all. The drama of the special interview with Bose and sealing the oath with their blood on his forehead, however, created a strong bond between Netaji and the young girls. Shanti Bhowmick was just fifteen.

New recruits to the Regiment could choose to become soldiers or nurses, although Bose primarily wanted fighters. Some nurses remained stationed in Singapore for the duration of the war; others worked in Rangoon and a small group went with Captain Lakshmi farther north to Maymyo.[69] Both in Burma and in Singapore the nurses took care of the wounded and sick soldiers who returned from the battle front, malnourished and suffering from malaria, cholera and dysentery. The nurses received their initial medical training at the INA base hospitals in Singapore and Rangoon. Before leaving for the hospital every morning dressed in their blue or white cotton uniforms and white caps, the nurses had to participate in the physical training programme required of all recruits.[70] In basic training they learned elementary weapons handling because Bose wanted to be sure that the Ranis remained a fighting force and did not primarily turn into a company of nurses.

NINE

CAPTAIN LAKSHMI, BOSE AND THE RECRUITMENT OF THE RJR

THE REALIZATION OF THE RJR depended in many different ways on Captain Lakshmi, as recruiter, role model, and caretaker of the recruits. After the war she laboured vigorously as publicist for Bose's ideals, striving to sustain the myth, the story and the reputation of the Rani of Jhansi Regiment. Lakshmi Swaminathan became Bose's first recruit for the RJR. He immediately identified her as a woman with the courage and ability to lead the Regiment and gave her the rank of captain in the INA. Shortly afterwards he also asked her to serve as the minister for women's affairs in the provisional government.[1] As commander of the RJR and member of the Azad Hind cabinet, she was eager and grateful for the opportunity to make a difference in the lives of women and to fight for Indian independence.

Lakshmi Swaminathan was born to Ammakutty and Subbarama Swaminathan in Madras on 24 October 1914, and died in Kanpur, India, 23 July 2012.[2] Although her legal surname at the time of her service in the INA was Rao, the family name of her estranged husband, she was generally known as Swaminathan, and people referred to her most often as 'Captain Lakshmi'. She lived an unusual life at a time of great change, taking advantage of the new opportunities for Indian women. Singapore resident Vilasini Perumbulavil knew Captain Lakshmi and her family because they came from the same village in India. Although Perumbulavil acknowledged that the Swaminathan family was accomplished and respected in the community, she distanced herself from Captain Lakshmi, whom she considered very pretty, but also a 'very modern, westernized lady who goes for ballroom dancing and all that'.[3]

Lakshmi's father was a prominent British-educated lawyer with a Harvard University PhD.[4] Her mother was fourteen years old and uneducated at the time of her betrothal to a man twenty-three years her senior. After their wedding, Swaminathan hired the best tutors for his wife, and Ammu Swaminathan soon became the most admired hostess in Madras and was the first woman to drive a car, to play tennis and to arrange theatre performances. The Swaminathan children were well educated and successful: Lakshmi became a medical doctor; her younger sister Mrinalini a famous classical Indian dancer, and her elder brother Govind, a lawyer.

In 1920 Subbarama Swaminathan was part of the defence team in the De la Haye murder trial, a spectacular criminal case tried in the Bombay High Court which drew media attention around the country.[5] The principal of a government school for boys was murdered and one of the students was accused of the crime. The purported motive was that the British principal, Mr De La Haye, had referred to the Indian students as 'barbarous Tamilians' or 'Tamil barbarians'.[6] The student was acquitted due to the utter lack of evidence, and Lakshmi tells a riveting story of how the incident changed her life at the age of six. Subbarama Swaminathan was publicly reviled by British friends and colleagues for having 'saved a native who had brutally murdered an innocent Englishman'.[7] Taking a stand against this racism, the Swaminathan family decided to speak Tamil and Malayalam instead of English, and the family no longer wore imported clothes.[8] Lakshmi stressed that the Swaminathans suddenly became patriotic Indian nationalists.

After the death of her husband in 1930, Ammu Swaminathan joined the Indian National Congress and, working with her friend Margaret Cousins, became an important proponent of women's rights in India.[9] A stream of politically engaged people visited their home, and Lakshmi was

further exposed to the ideas of those fighting for Indian political freedom
and gender equality. She liked Gandhi's activism but disagreed with him
on several points, particularly his 'unenlightened' view of women and his
campaign for young people to leave school to join the civil disobedience
movement.[10]

In Madras, Lakshmi was known as a social butterfly. A familiar sight
in her chocolate coloured Fiat racing through the streets and along the
beaches, she was stopped several times by the traffic police for speeding.[11]
While still enrolled at university, Lakshmi eloped with B.K. Naujindra Rao,
a pilot flying for Tata Air, a small private Indian airline, but after just six
months of marriage they had run out of topics for conversation and she left
her husband without obtaining a divorce.[12] She completed her education
as a medical doctor and having fallen in love with Matthew Abraham, a
Christian Indian and fellow medical student, she followed Abraham to
Singapore in June 1940 while still married to Rao.[13]

In 1941, many wealthy Indians fled Singapore in anticipation of the
Japanese attack, but Lakshmi chose to stay: 'I was actually quite keen to get
actively involved in a war. I felt it would be an exciting and adventurous
experience.'[14] As a doctor and a member of the Singapore Civil Defence
force, she was ordered by the colonial government to treat the victims
of Japanese attacks. Although she did not want Japan to win, she enjoyed
the spectacle of the British colonial overlords 'reeling under the blows of
a fellow Asiatic'.[15]

Captain Lakshmi joined the Indian Independence League and was
one of the committee to welcome Bose to Singapore in July 1943. She
was immediately impressed by him and readily accepted his invitation to
become the commander of the female regiment in the INA. The next day
she left her medical practice and Matthew Abraham, her lover and business
partner, to join the Azad Hind Fauj. The departure was made easier as
she had already met the man she would marry after the war, INA officer
Prem Kumar Sahgal.[16]

Bose's choice of Dr Lakshmi Swaminathan as commander of the
RJR and as minister for women's affairs was an inspired stroke. Captain
Lakshmi was the perfect model for the new Indian woman: independent,

intelligent, well educated and beautiful. She was compassionate, funny, charming and fluent in several Indian languages as well as English. Her family background included the state of Kerala, her mother's home, and Madras, where she grew up.[17] Well before joining the INA she had violated notable Indian taboos: she had married out of caste without her family's blessing and left her husband for a Christian man with whom she had an open extramarital relationship. She supported herself, set up her own business to assist people who could not afford good medical care, and advocated for smaller families, more education and equal rights for women. Captain Lakshmi was the kind of woman that Bose asserted he wanted all Indian women to emulate.

Immediately after announcing plans for the Rani of Jhansi Regiment, Bose threw himself into a wide-reaching recruitment effort. He travelled to make dozens of public appearances; he wrote articles, gave interviews and made radio broadcasts to reach potential Indian female recruits in Malaya, Singapore, Burma and Thailand. Bose assigned the early Rani volunteers, especially Captain Lakshmi, to give recruiting speeches and to invite friends to sign up. Energetic and enthusiastic Janaki Thevar recruited her half-sister Papathy and several friends. Sixty-five years later, in 2008, two of those recruits, Anjalai Ponnaswamy and Akilandam Vairavapillai, were still Janaki's closest friends and the three veterans met regularly at Janaki's home in Kuala Lumpur.[18] Bose also enlisted personal acquaintances, prevailing on his physician Dr S. Sen to urge his daughters, Reba and Amba, to enroll.[19] Pratima Sen, a teacher in Burma, at twenty-nine, older than most of the other women who joined, met Bose at a political event in Burma and he personally convinced her to enlist. Pratima claims to have recruited twenty-five or thirty young women.[20] If correct, she alone signed up more than half of the Ranis who were raised in Burma. One of those recruits was her niece Mommata Gupta.[21]

Having accepted the position as commander of the RJR, Captain Lakshmi also travelled to the major cities of Malaya to make recruitment speeches and to meet with prospective Ranis and their parents. Several young women who were inspired by Bose's speeches needed Captain Lakshmi's help to persuade their parents about the value of girls becoming soldiers in order to get the required signatures on the enrolment form.

Articles in *Young India, Journal for Indian Youths in East Asia* and local newspapers, which were all under Japanese control, featured stories about the large numbers who were signing up to be Ranis. The published totals were inflated, but women did join. All reports on Bose's public appearances, whether by men or women, raved about the impressive, energetic, youthful and handsome man whose call for patriotic action moved them deeply. The decision to follow his call to service would have immense consequences for the recruits. It meant that they would break with tradition, leave home, and, of course, risk injury, illness and death. These girls and young women signed up anyway.

Every Rani interviewed remembered exactly how and when she first learned about the Regiment and the circumstances under which she enlisted. Janaki Thevar of Kuala Lumpur was seventeen years old, the daughter of a wealthy Tamil dairy farmer. She had heard that the INA was going to raise a regiment of women, and was curious. Not daring to tell her parents where she was going, she rode her bicycle to join a large crowd gathered on the *padang*, an open field within the city, to hear Bose speak. Janaki recalls, 'He spoke in such a way that we all listened and were very attentive. He said that we must work for India's freedom, that a regiment was being formed for us. And as he spoke, the feeling grew in me that I must join.'[22]

When Bose asked the audience for contributions of money, jewellery, anything of value to help the cause of freedom, spontaneously Janaki removed her diamond earrings and put them in Bose's hand. Just as she did, a photographer took their picture, and the next day she was on the front page of the newspaper her father read. It was difficult but unavoidable to confess to her family, but Janaki explained her new passion and invited Captain Lakshmi for tea. Together the charming recruiter and Janaki managed to persuade the reluctant Mr Thevar to sign the permission form.[23] Janaki's elder half-sister Papathy also joined, and they were among the first RJR recruits.

The Navarednam sisters, Rasammah, age sixteen, and Ponnammah, eighteen, heard Bose speak at a large rally in Ipoh in the state of Perak in northern Malaya. Although their family had recently arrived in Malaya from Ceylon (Sri Lanka), the girls were so enthused with the struggle for Indian freedom that they implored their widowed mother for permission to enlist. These Christian girls, the youngest of six siblings, were conservatively brought up, attended convent school, and took music lessons and needlework instruction. Their mother Nancy Navarednam, a schoolteacher, was appalled at the idea of her little girls going to war. Captain Lakshmi was in Ipoh, recruiting, and the girls invited her home to meet their mother. Lakshmi charmed and impressed Mrs Navarednam, promising her that she would take care of the girls as if they were her own daughters, and obtained permission for the girls to become Ranis.[24]

In other cases, neighbours of families with young daughters acted as recruiters. A pharmacist Mr Ponniah and his wife of Teluk Anson in Perak, northern Malaya, were visiting Singapore and heard Bose speak about forming the Rani of Jhansi Regiment. They were so impressed by Bose's idea that on returning home, they gave their whole pharmacy to the movement. Mrs Ponniah joined the Ranis and urged their good friend, Mr M. Suppiah, to consider sending his three daughters to enter the fight for Indian freedom.[25] Mr Suppiah's mother was born in India and entertained her grandchildren with great stories from the homeland. So when they heard about the Ranis, the Suppiah girls pleaded with their father for permission to become Ranis. Anjali was just sixteen and in the interview she laughingly confessed that she joined to see a bit of the world, perhaps even India, and that at the time she was entirely too young to be informed about politics. The sisters had not been exposed to the outside world, and that they were very young worried their father, but slowly Mr Suppiah was won over. Thinking that the best experience for the girls would be to enter the nurses' section of the RJR, Mr Suppiah accompanied his daughters to Singapore to talk with Captain Lakshmi. She assured him that besides the physical training, they would also learn medical care and would work as nurses in the INA hospital.[26] After two days as members of the Regiment, the sisters knew that they did not like to sponge bathe the sick soldiers and they asked for a transfer to the fighting unit. Captain Lakshmi demurred because she had promised their

father that his daughters would receive training as nurses. But since the
Suppiah girls insisted, they were allowed to stop nursing and became
fighters instead. Mr Suppiah only learned of this change of plans when
his daughters came home after the war.[27]

Simultaneous with the establishment of the main RJR camp in
Singapore, Indian Independence League activists also recruited Indian
women in Burma. In Rangoon, Colonel S. C. Alagappan of the INA came
to the house of the four young Ganguli sisters after they had attended a
meeting at the Indian Women's Organization, a nationalist organization
under the IIL. The Gangulis were a large and successful middle-class Bengali
Hindu family with five boys and four girls still living with their parents.
The day the colonel came recruiting, Mr Ganguli, a Public Works engineer,
was not home. But when the colonel explained Bose's plans for the RJR to
Mrs Ganguli, she promised to send at least one daughter to the Regiment.[28]
Mr Ganguli was a nationalist at heart, and in principle did not mind that his
daughters were interested in politics. However, he thought it unsuitable,
indeed disgraceful, that girls from a respectable family would go to live
in barracks.[29] When Aruna insisted that she wanted to sign up, he finally
gave his permission, and told his beautiful sixteen-year-old daughter to
be aware of bad men in sheep's clothing. Aruna did not understand her
father's warning until years later.[30] Altogether three Ganguli daughters,
Karuna, Aruna and Maya as well as one son, Krishna Prasad, joined the INA.

Women who lived in Malaya and Singapore were recruited and enlisted
in Kuala Lumpur, Ipoh and Singapore, and they received their first training
in the central camp in Singapore. In Burma, Indian women joined at a
succession of camps around Rangoon. One British Intelligence document,
'Chronology of Indian Activities in Thailand During the War' shows that
on 20 December 1943, '...nine Indian women residents of Thailand were
chosen as the first volunteer group from Thailand to train as members of
Indian National Women's Corps, and left for Singapore.'[31] This Women's
Corps is probably the RJR, but I found no other information about other
Ranis joining from Thailand.

In her memoirs, Captain Lakshmi asserts that immediately after the
announcement of the creation of the RJR, many applications were received

from girls from the mainland of India, but that she was unable to call them up until a proper camp was established.[32] However, no information emerged from my interviews regarding women who had grown up in India and joined the RJR directly from the subcontinent. A story from Burma illustrates that knowledge of the Rani of Jhansi Regiment was not widely available in India. In June 1944, an Indian fighting on the Allied side was wounded and surrendered to some INA soldiers who brought him to their hospital in Maymyo for treatment. Astonished at the sight of the uniformed Ranis parading carrying weapons, he said, 'In India not a soul knows about what is happening here.'[33] When talking with British Intelligence officers after her surrender at the end of the war, Captain Lakshmi said that she was the only Rani raised in India.[34] After the war, three INA officers were tried in Delhi for waging war against His Majesty the King Emperor of Great Britain. The trials of these freedom fighters stirred mass protests across India because new information about Bose's activities and the INA was presented to the public during the court proceedings. It became clear that the British effort to suppress news of the war in Burma had been almost completely successful and it seems unlikely that in fact many applications to join the RJR from girls on the mainland had been sent or received.[35]

It is important to emphasize that the Ranis interviewed for this research are not a statistically representative sample of the women who served in the RJR. The mere fact that these women were still alive in 2008 and were either known by other Ranis or were listed in telephone directories (meaning that they could be located) introduces a broad range of statistical uncertainties. No official INA list gives names, addresses or other formal information about the Ranis, and INA veteran S. S. Yadava's roster of the Ranis, compiled many years after the war, provides only marginally reliable information. According to Captain Lakshmi, British Intelligence and other Ranis, approximately 60 per cent of the Rani recruits were illiterate South Indian Tamils from the rubber plantations in Malaya.[36] In contrast to those RJR members, Captain Lakshmi reported that the Burma recruits 'numbered quite a high proportion of college girls'.[37]

Mehervan Singh, a civilian Sikh living in Singapore, enlisted in the INA in September 1942. Attentive to the number of Sikhs in the force,

he proudly estimated that 30 per cent of the Ranis were Sikh.[38] Sikh first
names are not gender specific, but all Sikh women have the same last
name, Kaur. About 20 per cent of the surnames on Yadava's list of Ranis
are Kaur.[39]

Unfortunately, I found no Sikh Ranis to interview. The RJR members
contacted and their sisters who were also Ranis but had died prior to
the beginning of this study numbered thirty-two. Of these, two women
hailed from the rubber plantation labourers in Malaya; sixteen were of
South Indian background but were educated and did not come from the
plantations; and fourteen were from families that originally came from
Bengal, Gujarat and Punjab.[40]

Yadava's catalogue of Ranis does list many South Indian first names.[41]
As is customary, many of these women do not have family names, but some
are listed as 'Daughter of _____', specifying the father's first name. Rani
Muniammah, daughter of Eelavan, and Anjalai, daughter of Ponnaswamy,
are two representatives of this group in this study. It is significant also
that the memoirs of Captain Lakshmi, S.A. Ayer, A.C. Chatterji and
Shah Nawaz Khan mention no individual woman from the plantations,
while they praise several other Ranis by name. In the interviews, and in
the memoirs of the other Ranis, Tamil volunteers from the plantations
are referred to only as 'the estate girls' or 'the sepoys'; that is, they are
mentioned only as a group.

These former plantation workers' marginalized role in the narrative
of the RJR is worth noting. It is difficult to explain other than that
the 'educated' Ranis who survived to tell their stories to me and the
lowest-ranked sepoys were separated as groups by language, class, and
most importantly, education. These factors correlate with the fact that,
despite the youth of some of the recruits from the plantations at the
time of enlistment, only two of this most numerous ethnic group in
the RJR were still alive in 2008. The reduced longevity of the illiterate
Tamil Ranis may be because many of these recruits were in fragile health
when they arrived at the RJR training camp, and they might have been
raised on a less nutritious diet than the Ranis from middle income and
wealthy backgrounds. In addition, because they lacked the education

that would have allowed them to find jobs that would provide a decent living after the war, they may have suffered early deaths because of hard labour, poor health and lack of medical care.

Another reason that more South Indian Ranis were not located and interviewed for this study might be that they returned to the plantations in Malaya after 1945 and lost touch with other Ranis, or that during 2008–11 they did not have telephones listed with the Malaysia telephone company. However, Janaki Thevar, who kept in close touch with many Ranis in Malaysia, did not think this was the case.[42] She was certain that I had found all members of the RJR in Malaysia who were still alive.

The youngest Rani who participated in this study was seventy-seven-year-old Anjuli Bhowmick who was born in October 1931 and had just turned twelve when she left home to enlist. The oldest Rani I interviewed was Captain Lakshmi who was ninety-three at the time of our first meeting. Finally, of the Ranis interviewed and their nine sisters who were Ranis, two were born into a Jain family, three were Christian, and the rest were Hindu. Some Ranis changed religion to adopt the faith of their husbands at marriage. One Rani was born in Japan, four in India, eight Ranis were born in Burma, and fifteen were born in Malaya.

Bose urged all Indian women to join the Regiment, insisting that it was their duty as Indians to fight for the freedom of their homeland, but I found no records outlining the necessary qualifications for becoming a Rani. No speech or letter from Bose delimits the admission of future Ranis. The young women volunteers believed that being Indian and wanting to liberate India were the sole determinants. After the war and primarily in response to the questions of interviewers, Captain Lakshmi described some general criteria she claimed had been in force.

The first qualification was that the applicant be an ethnic Indian woman. For political reasons Bose thought it unwise to accept girls whose fathers were Indian but mothers Malayan.[43] As a second official requirement, applicants had to have passed their eighteenth birthday. Married women and mothers were accepted, but a woman who was still nursing a baby could not join. Several couples served at the same time such as Labanya Ganguli Chatterji and her husband. P.N. Chatterji worked in the Azad Hind

Dal, the bureaucratic section of the provisional government, and Labanya was a nurse in the RJR.[44]

In our interview in 2008, Captain Lakshmi casually stated, 'No woman was accepted if her husband or father objected.'[45] To prove that there were no such barriers, unmarried applicants needed the signature of their fathers and married women of their husbands on the application form. In 2008 I was surprised to hear that it seemed acceptable to Captain Lakshmi that the Indian National Army had required permission from male family members to allow adult women to join the Rani of Jhansi Regiment of the INA, an organization that was intended to be based on gender equality.

These rules were not strictly enforced. Akilandam, daughter of Vairavapillai, at age eighty-two when we first met, looked like a tall Chinese woman. She proudly stated that her mother was Chinese and her father Indian. She had been welcomed into the RJR as a seventeen-year-old widowed mother of an infant. She did have her father's persmission.[46] Of all the Ranis I interviewed and their sisters, only four had passed their eighteenth birthday when they were accepted into the Regiment. A few had barely reached puberty. Anjuli Bhowmick had just turned twelve, Muniammah, daughter of Eelavan, was fourteen, as was Maya Ganguli, when they became Ranis with the approval of their fathers.[47]

It is, of course, to be expected that those alive to be interviewed during 2008–11 included those who were the youngest when they enlisted, but many other Ranis who died before the beginning of this study were also younger than eighteen when they joined the RJR. Lakshmi Nair saw an advertisement in a Singapore newspaper that the INA wanted female freedom fighters. Her father had just died, and there was no money for food in the home of her stepmother. Her father had hated the English, so Lakshmi thought it proper that she would go to fight them while also earning a little money for the family. When she reported for service at the Singapore camp, she was at first told that at fourteen she was too young, but when she assured them that she was a good worker, she was inducted. Her stepmother, needing the income, gave her reluctant permission.[48]

The rules also specified that the recruits should be physically fit. All Ranis had a thorough physical exam before induction, and some were rejected because of poor health. Although many arrived severely emaciated, they were accepted. Women who wanted to become Ranis but because of old age or overweight were judged unable to handle the rigours of jungle combat were admitted as cooks, clerks and cleaners. Women of all religions, castes and educational levels were welcomed. A few months into the recruiting campaign when a surprising number of illiterate Tamil girls had signed up, the recruiting emissaries began to appeal to 'educated women' to join.[49]

It is difficult to analyse and impossible to generalize why women enlisted in the Rani of Jhansi Regiment. Some Ranis stated their reasons concisely and probably with reasonable accuracy. Others seem to have been swept up by complicated emotions, resorting subsequently to the explanation that was most often cited by other Ranis. The question, 'Why did you join the Ranis?' was almost always at first answered, 'To fight for India's freedom' and 'To free our Motherland'. Most of the Ranis told me that they had felt a deep desire to answer Bose's call and to make a positive contribution to justice for India. As a fifteen-year-old, Rasammah Navarednam read about the 1919 killing of unarmed civilians in the banned book, *Jallianwala Bagh – The Amritsar Massacre*. A year later that account influenced her decision to join the Ranis.[50]

It appears that at least some of the young women joined the RJR at least partly because of their attraction to the young, handsome, dignified and seemingly accessible political icon.[51] Joining his cause was a romantic and exhilarating adventure.

When she first heard Netaji speak in 1943, seventeen-year-old Karuna Ganguli, born in Shwebo in the north Burmese plains, and feeling entirely Burmese, knew nothing about India's fight for independence. But shortly thereafter, deeply inspired by Bose's rousing speech, Karuna joined the Ranis together with her younger sisters Aruna and Maya. More than six decades later when I met her in December 2008, she was a widow whose husband had passed away many years ago and whose son, her only child, had died two years earlier. She lived in a small, immaculate and sparsely furnished room on Mahatma Gandhi Road in Kolkata with her most cherished possession – a tiny portrait of Bose. With a sweet smile that lit up her beautiful face, Karuna remembered, 'Netaji made me fight for India. My hope was to fight like Lakshmibai – she was killed fighting.'[52]

A few reverently likened Bose to Jesus. Even those many years later several Ranis spoke about Bose with the sexually tinged adulation that subsequent generations of young women have expressed for pop stars.

One powerful motivation common to almost every Rani was undoubtedly that Bose incited them to fight for something larger than themselves, to join a quest of a long-treasured and noble goal. Bose appealed to the honour and prestige attached to self-abnegation and sacrifice, traditional values instilled in Indian females from early childhood. Rani Rama Mehta expressed the feelings that all Ranis shared: 'We worked together to do good.'[53] The combination of the call to sacrifice for freedom and the charisma of the messenger cast a spell they could not ignore.[54] That they had grown up believing that India was their Motherland may have played a part in giving the girls who joined the RJR incentive to fight for the freedom of India. For most Ranis, however, the connection with India was much more tenuous.

In addition, the decision to sign up to go to war also brought instantaneous attention from family, friends and neighbours, and in most cases approbation as well. Several Ranis described to me how neighbours came to drape them with flower garlands and to say goodbye. On the trip from northern Malaya, people would gather to cheer the new Ranis along their way to Singapore. Almost all of the women said that they were excited about the opportunity to see a bit of the world and to experience something new.

For most of the women in this study, the idea of joining the Regiment was their own, and several had to work hard to persuade their parents to sign the permission slip. Bose's stirring speeches combined with Dr Lakshmi's glamorous example of what a modern Indian woman might aspire to become persuaded many to join. Some of the women, however, were strongly encouraged, even pressured by their parents to enlist to become a Rani. Asha Sahay's mother was a cousin of Subhas Chandra Bose and her father, Anand Sahay, a member of Bose's cabinet. Anand Sahay chose to transport his sixteen-year-old daughter on a perilous journey aboard a

Japanese bomber from Nagasaki in Japan to Bangkok in May 1945 so that she could join the Regiment in Bangkok for a few months after the other Ranis had returned from Burma. Although her parents were prominent members of the Indian expatriate community in Japan, Asha had been educated exclusively in Japanese schools, not the international school that most other Indian children in Japan attended. Asha spoke no English or Hindi, only Japanese and Bengali; in almost all ways she was a typical Japanese girl writing haikus in beautiful calligraphy. She explained to me that she had always tried to fulfil the obligations imposed on her; joining the Ranis was probably another manifestation of her compliance.[55]

Ranis Anjuli and Shanti Bhowmick were born in Dacca – now known as Dhaka – in what is now Bangladesh, into a large and proud Bengali Kshatriya family that strongly supported Bose's nationalist ideology.[56] Their father, Dhirendra Chandra Bhowmick and his three brothers were freedom fighters and members of Forward Bloc, Bose's group of radicals within the Congress. When the girls were about eight and ten years old, the family moved to Seremban, Malaya, where their father worked as an assistant manager at a rubber plantation. In order that their seven daughters and one son continued to grow up feeling as true Indians, their mother brought all the children back to Bengal once a year. When his three brothers joined the INA, Dhirendra Chandra Bhowmick also wanted to sign up but lamented that with his run-down body he would no longer be of any use to the freedom struggle.[57] His two eldest daughters, Shanti, fourteen, and Anjuli, twelve, grasped the chance and volunteered to fill their father's position. Their mother brought them south to Singapore to register at the RJR camp at Waterloo Street. The Bhowmicks were greeted by Captain Lakshmi who promised that she would now be the mother of the two young girls.

Rama Mehta's family lived in Rangoon, where for generations they had been engaged in the freedom struggle. Rama's grandfather, Dr P. J. Mehta, originally from Gujarat, Gandhi's home state, was a generous contributor of funds to support Gandhi and the freedom movement in India.[58] When Rama's mother became a recruiting officer and interim commander of the first RJR camp in Rangoon, her first recruits were her two daughters, Rama and Neelam.[59] Rama joined because of her mother's insistence, but after a little while the community of young women working together for a common idealistic goal won her over, and Rama declared with much emotion that the two years in the RJR had been the best years of her life, 'You felt so much for your country. You wanted to achieve something. I am very proud of my country.'[60]

During our long talk at her church on a Sunday after the service, petit and gentle Eva Jenny Murty stated forthrightly that she joined the Ranis in order to become a nurse.[61] Eva Jenny's father was a medical assistant and had had to interrupt his medical studies after two years. She had always also wanted to attend medical school, but when her father retired with eight children in the family, there was no money for Eva Jenny to go. Giving up the dream of being a doctor, she had become a teacher, but her mother advised her not to waste her time. Instead she urged Eva Jenny to join the Ranis because she could then get her medical education as a nurse in the Rani Regiment. At age twenty-three Eva Jenny travelled by herself from Port Swettenham, north of Kuala Lumpur to Singapore, and reported to Camp Commandant Thevar. Eva Jenny became a surgical nurse, and was grateful for the excellent training she received from the Indian doctors at the Bidadari hospital in Singapore. As required of all Ranis, Eva Jenny also did military training, but 'I did not like soldiering. And those long marches were hard. I was very good at shooting, but I was not interested in that. The gun was heavy, not very heavy, but on those long marches they were heavy. It was worth it for the nursing.'[62] Eva Jenny lived in the Singapore camp and worked as a nurse at the INA hospital until the general disbandment of the Rani Regiment in August 1945.

Three Ranis, Gian Kaur, Gauri Bhattacharya and Labanya Ganguli, worked as nurses while serving in the Regiment; and after the war, they returned to India, went on to medical school and became medical doctors.[63] Gauri was already in medical school in Burma when the war broke out, but she finished her education in India.[64] Gian worked as head of the nursing group in Burma and agreed with Eva Jenny that it was a waste for the nurses to keep up their military training; their days could be much better used if the nurses cared for the wounded soldiers full-time.[65]

In 1943 the Japanese military in Malaya demanded that all vegetation be cleared alongside many roads up to a distance of 300 metres, near airports and around other strategic sites.[66] This rule effectively prevented the traditional production of rice and vegetables on public land, a practice on which poor Malayans depended, especially since the Japanese occupation in 1941 had disrupted the import of rice. Instead, farmers began to cultivate roots such as tapioca and sweet potatoes that had low nutritional value. The result was widespread hunger and even starvation, especially for the Chinese residents of Singapore City and for the Indian labourers on rubber plantations and in tin mines.

Rani Muniammah, daughter of Eelavan, as many others from the rubber estates in Malaya, joined the Ranis in order to survive. As Muniammah tells, after the Japanese invasion her father lost his job as a rubber tapper at an estate in Perak, Malaya, and the family was destitute. According to Muniammah, her father and uncles decided to volunteer for the INA in order to get food. When Eelavan learned that Bose was recruiting Indian women for the Indian freedom struggle, although she was just fourteen years old, he urged his eldest daughter to join the Rani Regiment to get regular meals.[67] When I asked many decades later if she thought of herself as being Indian when she joined the RJR, Muniammah answered that her grandfather probably came from India, but that an Indian identity was never something that she had considered before she joined the Ranis.

She thought that it was a frightening experience when the group of Ranis trekked through the jungle ahead of the Japanese soldiers. However, in our interview it curiously turned out that she was not quite sure who the enemy was, the Japanese or the British and was not able to give any details of what happened on the punishing trek she says she endured. Her granddaughter Teevia laughingly explained to her grandmother that the Japanese were friends of the INA. All that was of no importance to Muniammah; she just repeated the familiar slogan of the Ranis and insisted that she had joined the RJR to free the Motherland. The family agreed; her ten children and grandchildren were very proud of her service. A large portrait of Netaji dominated the wall in the common room in their downtown Kuala Lumpur high-rise apartment, where Muniammah lived with her son, his family and her unmarried daughter. On the same wall next to Netaji hung a large framed document that on 14 December 1995 recognized the service in the INA freedom fight during WWII rendered by Chinammah. When I asked if Chinammah was a sister of Muniammah, the granddaughter explained that Chinammah was the name her grandmother had as a girl, but that when she got a passport the officials made an error and wrote Muniammah as her first name, so she changed her name.[68] In my research I questioned many Ranis, but only one who claimed that she had spent two years as a member of the RJR but did not know for which side she was fighting; only one who knew no detail of the Ranis' experience; and only one whose name on her Rani certificate of service was different than the name by which she was known.

Middle-class families in northern Malaya were also affected by the food shortage. Rani Eva Jenny Murty explains in her memoirs that her father, who worked extremely hard as a medical aide to feed and educate his large family, one day felt so desperate with the complaints of his hungry boys that he screamed, 'I will line you all up and shoot you down!'[69] That night Eva Jenny made sure that the guns were empty before she went to bed, and as a devout Christian she trusted in God to do the rest.

The food shortage caused a substantial rise in mortality due to malnutrition. From 1941 to 1944 the overall mortality rate in Malaya more than doubled.[70] In Burma widespread starvation accompanied the Japanese occupation. Aruna Ganguli observed that like several other families in her middle-class Rangoon suburb, their neighbours gave their two eldest daughters away 'in marriage to anyone who can provide them with food, clothing and medicine'.[71]

In addition to Ranis Muniammah and Lakshmi Nair, many others also enlisted in the Regiment to get regular meals.[72] A friend of the Tamil Ranis, middle-class 'educated' officer Ponnammah said that most of those girls in her platoon were honest and admitted that they joined because the Ranis had food and they were hungry.[73] As a doctor and the person in charge of health checks prior to admittance, Captain Lakshmi realized that almost all of the Tamil volunteers from the plantations had more than likely enlisted for their own survival rather than out of a desire to sacrifice themselves for Indian freedom; still, all were welcomed into the ranks of the Regiment.[74]

Dr Nasira Kiani who conducted some of the medical examinations of recruits in August and September 1943 also observed that women arriving from the plantations were weak and emaciated. In Dr Kiani's opinion as she expressed it to her British interrogators after her arrest under suspicion for collaboration with the enemy, 'the recruits mostly joined simply to obtain food'.[75] Dr Kiani's husband, Mohammad Zaman Kiani, served as major general in the INA, which automatically made her a person of interest to British Intelligence.

Janaki Bai was born in 1922 in Sabak Bernam, Selangor, Malaya, and grew up on a large coconut estate in Malaya, where her father, El Fateh Singh, a Rajput, worked as assistant manager. As a young bachelor he had come to Malaya in search of adventure. He was a man with progressive ideas for 1920, and when he met a young Tamil widow with two children, he challenged societal disapproval of widow remarriage, and they wed. Janaki Bai had one brother who was about two years older, and then there were so many brothers and sisters that she was not sure how many siblings she had. All the children, boys and girls, went to boarding school and were well educated.

Janaki Bai had studied to become a certified teacher, but at age twenty-one she was living at home with her family on the coconut estate, because when the Japanese occupied the peninsula all the Europeans left and schools closed. 'For many months we did not see the Japanese and we were not much affected by the war. My father used to get newspapers from Singapore and I read about the Rani of Jhansi Regiment. ... You know mothers want their children to get married quickly and my mother was no different.' Janaki's mother had arranged that her daughter should wed a much older wealthy Chettiar man, a moneylender, who wanted Janaki as his bride and she urged Janaki to agree to the contract. Arranged marriage was anathema to the young intellectual, 'I think this Indian custom of marriage is silly. You must know the person first. The thought was odious to me. He assumed that just because he fancied me, he could simply buy me! My father saw that I was unhappy, and one day he said, "Why don't you join the Rani of Jhansi Regiment and that way avoid the marriage?" I said why not? Then a young man from the Indian Independence League in Selangor came by the estate canvassing for volunteers to join the Ranis. We were three people signing up from our area – I was one, a Hindu. Another was a girl called Grace, she was a Christian and a couple of years younger than I. The third was a shopkeeper's wife, but they sent her back because she had a growth and was not healthy. So the two of us went.'[76] After the war Janaki Bai married a man of her own choice.

Many of the women who joined the Regiment from the large rubber estates in Malaya lived and worked under conditions that approached slavery. Sexual abuse by the mainly white estate managers was a common occurrence. The Rani of Jhansi Regiment offered an environment where for the first time the young women found themselves respected and free of the social stigma of 'coolie' status. Now with their heads held high, they experienced a level of egalitarianism in the company of their Rani comrades that they had not known before. As Rasammah expressed it, 'They became soldiers for India's freedom and their own liberty.'[77]

When giving their reasons for enlisting in the Regiment, only a few, notably Captain Lakshmi and Rasammah, referred to the larger political issues of the conflict in Burma, or of World War II as a whole, or speculated as to what life in India might become after the war. Only Janaki Thevar mentioned feminism and gender equality as reasons for joining the Ranis. She claimed that most of her comrades had agreed with her that 'the women's question' was a motivating factor. Recounting their time in the RJR, almost all the veterans I interviewed focused on life in the camps, the community of the Ranis, and importantly their personal interactions with Bose. Several did mention their disappointment that the efforts of the RJR had not had any lasting impact on equality for Indian women.

TEN

SINGAPORE – THE RANIS PREPARE FOR WAR

IN THE FALL OF 1943, young women began to enlist in the Rani of Jhansi Regiment of the Indian National Army in Singapore and in Rangoon. The RJR needed a base camp in Singapore, a facility that would provide secure lodging for the female soldiers as well as sufficient space outdoors for military training. To the Japanese military authorities, female infantry was a preposterous waste of money and when they learned of Bose's idea, they protested.[1] Regarding the RJR, the Japanese officers found it completely incomprehensible that Bose would allocate precious ordnance and rations to women.

One way the Japanese sought to prevent the creation of the Regiment was their unwillingness to allocate real estate in Singapore for the training of women for combat. The Japanese administration refused every abandoned property that Captain Lakshmi found and proposed as possible housing for the RJR.[2] In the end, the Ranis did receive quarters, weapons, uniforms and training, but the cost of the RJR was borne entirely by donations from Indians living in Burma, Singapore and Malaya to the Azad Hind government, while the Japanese government financed only the male forces of the INA.

The chairman of the Singapore branch of the Indian Independence

League, Attavar Yellappa, a barrister, consequently took upon himself the task of finding a home for the Regiment. He persuaded some of his wealthy Nattukottai Chettiar banker clients to fund the refurbishment of a dilapidated building, formerly serving as a refugee camp and currently belonging to the IIL.[3] The property was enclosed with a high fence to shield the female soldiers from the curious eyes of Singapore citizens, and several new barracks were erected. The standing buildings were fitted with new plumbing, and bathing facilities were installed.[4] After three weeks of around-the-clock activity, the Singapore Central Camp, the Ranis' first training centre, was almost ready for the first contingent of volunteers to move in on the birth anniversary of Rani Lakshmibai of Jhansi.[5]

In his inaugural speech at the RJR training camp on Waterloo Street in Singapore on 22 October 1943, Bose welcomed 'the first one hundred and fifty women' who had moved in the evening before.[6]

> The opening of the Rani of Jhansi Regiment Training Camp is an important and significant function; it is a very important landmark in the progress of our movement in East Asia. To realize its importance, you should bear in mind that ours is not a merely political movement. We are, on the other hand, engaged in the great task of regenerating our Nation. We are, in fact, ushering in a New Life for the Indian Nation, and it is necessary that our New Life should be built on sound foundations. Remember that ours is not a propaganda stunt; we are in fact witnessing the re-birth of India. And it is only in the fitness of things that there should be a stir of New Life among our womenfolk.[7]

Bose went on:

> Since 1928, I have been taking interest in women's organizations in India and I found that, given the opportunity, our sisters could rise to any occasion. ... If one type of courage is necessary for passive resistance, another and more active courage is necessary for revolutionary efforts, and in this too, I found that our sisters were not wanting. ... Unfortunately, Jhansi Rani was defeated; it was not her defeat; it was the defeat of India.

She died but her spirit can never die. India can once again produce Jhansi Ranis and march on to victory.[8]

Outlining women's noble participation in the freedom struggle, Bose remembered the spectacular show at the Congress party meeting in 1928 where he had organized 'the volunteer corps of 500 women ...[who] with their parades and discipline gave us great hopes and confirmed my belief in the fact that, given the impetus and opportunity, Indian women could perform duties entrusted to them in a befitting manner'.[9] Bose closed the welcoming ceremony with the fervent hope that very soon the Singapore camp would have 'at least one thousand potential Ranis of Jhansi'.[10] Bose also met with the recruits and encouraged them in their new endeavour. In a long and sincere talk, he stressed the dangers awaiting them on the battlefront. Telling me about her introduction to the Regiment, Janaki Bai fondly remembered the 'brave son of India' whose ideas had brought her to Singapore and whom she met personally for the first time on this occasion.[11]

The exact number of women who had enrolled in the RJR at the inauguration date is not known. One photograph shows about thirty women in uniform presenting their weapons to Bose, but Captain Lakshmi thinks that there were just over one hundred recruits on that day. At the beginning, conditions at the Singapore camp were spartan, and they never became comfortable. As more women joined the Regiment, in addition to the renovated barracks some Ranis were housed in tents and Nissen huts, where privacy was non-existent.[12] On arrival, each volunteer was given a mat, a blanket and a pillow. It was then up to her to find a space to settle. The beds were narrow wooden platforms and the issued mat, blanket and pillow were the only permitted bedding.[13] Each Rani had a small area for her personal belongings: typically a change of clothes, a Gita or the Bible and a family photograph.[14] Meals were served in a mess tin, tea in a metal mug. There were too few tables to seat everyone, so the recruits ate sitting down on stairs or any clear, dry spot they could find.

In our conversations, only a few Ranis expressed dissatisfaction with the training camp facilities. Janaki Thevar, the daughter of a prosperous Tamil

dairy farmer, had a crisis after the first week.[15] Should she stay or go back
to be pampered in her affluent childhood home? She complained, 'The
wooden bed was most uncomfortable, ... the bath and toilets were terrible,
especially when we were made to clean them ourselves.'[16] Despite this
inauspicious introduction to military life, Janaki Thevar became a lifelong
devotee of the RJR. Several of the other Ranis also came from well-to-do
families, and the transition to camp life for them was also difficult.

Captain Lakshmi was appointed to serve as the first commandant of the
Singapore camp. Two-and-a-half months later, on 5 January 1944, when
Bose reassigned Captain Lakshmi to Rangoon, her second-in-command,
Manoranjitham Satiavati Naidu, assumed leadership of the training camp.
Naidu's background seemed perfect for the job. She was a mature woman,
in her early forties, who had served as headmistress of a girls' school and
therefore was assumed to have experience enforcing discipline.[17] However,
to the expressed strong dismay of Rani Janaki Thevar, the new commandant
incorrectly called her Mrs Thevar 'because she was the mistress, not even
second wife' of Janaki's uncle.[18]

In May and again in August 1944, 'in recognition of her good work' Bose
promoted Camp Commandant Thevar first to the rank of lieutenant and
next to captain.[19] In several letters over the summer of 1944, Bose, who
paid close attention to every aspect of Rani training, informed Thevar that
he had been observing camp conditions and had concluded that discipline
needed tightening. He had been apprised that the Ranis would dress in
their civilian clothes and go in a group to visit friends or to see a film on
Sundays. They only had to write in a log where they were heading and be
back by six o'clock.[20] Bose found such practices objectionable. His new
instructions were that the volunteers should not be allowed to leave the
facilities at will, and visitors' access to the camps was to be restricted.[21]
Endeavouring to ensure that the Ranis would sound and behave like real
soldiers, he also instructed Captain Thevar, 'Please tell all the girls of your
Regiment that while greeting anyone they should simply say [the official
INA greeting] *Jai Hind*', [Victory to India] and not *'Jai Hind Sahib'*.[22]

In our interviews, several Ranis expressed intense dislike of Camp
Commandant Thevar. They claimed that under Captain Lakshmi's

authority there had been a genuine feeling of fellowship and service to a greater goal, which deteriorated into pervasive antagonism between her replacement and many of the soldiers. Rasammah recounted how Captain Thevar unfairly disciplined and demoted her for an alleged breach of the rules. When Thevar stripped away one of the stripes from the corporal's insignia on Rasammah's shoulder, Rasammah defiantly ripped off the remaining one herself, to wear the uniform of a private although she continued to carry out her duties as a non-commissioned officer (NCO). Once Rasammah left Singapore as part of the Rani Burma contingent, she was out of Thevar's reach and her rank was quickly restored.[23] Apparently, Thevar may have regretted the incident because she wrote to Bose asking to promote Rasammah from sepoy to havildar, from private to sergeant. Bose's response to Thevar was harsh, 'This sort of thing cannot be done and I hope that you will not make such recommendation in future. ... I have promoted Rasamma[h] from Lance Naik to Naik. ... She must wait for her turn before she can be promoted Havildar.'[24] It is striking that this level of attention during wartime was lavished on one sixteen-year-old, seemingly temperamental and insubordinate soldier by her camp commandant, and even more remarkably by the Supreme Commander of the INA for whom no detail of the RJR was too trivial for his personal attention.

Several Ranis found that Captain Thevar was partial to Tamil-speaking members of the Regiment. The term 'Tamil-speaking' is probably a euphemism meaning 'uneducated Ranis' or soldiers who came from the rubber estates. Mild-mannered Eva Jenny, who arrived in Singapore after Captain Lakshmi had left for Burma, recalls her reception in camp with some rancour, 'Mrs Thevar did not like me. She had a prejudice against educated girls. When I just came she said we did not invite you to come.'[25] Captain Thevar chided Rasammah and Ponnammah that the freedom battle was not their battle. Since their family came from Ceylon, they were Ceylonese Burghers, not Indian and they were not wanted. 'But,' said Ponnammah, 'my father used to tell us that we were part of India and India was part of us. We were Indian.'[26] Rasammah asked her elder sister to complain about Captain Thevar's discrimination to Colonel Bhonsle, the INA senior officer in charge of the Ranis' training.[27] The issue of having

'Ceylon Burghers, both male and female' as members of the INA, had been discussed by the Azad Hind government, and the two Navarednam girls became valued members of the RJR.

Ponnammah's complaint and other reports reached Bose on a visit to Singapore, and he immediately reminded Thevar that she was 'the Officer-in-charge of a Training Camp and not the manager of a lodging-house' and that she had 'to be strictly impartial towards girls coming from different parts of India and speaking different languages'.[28] As almost all Ranis were born in Burma and Malaya, Bose did not mean to say that the girls had arrived directly from India; he meant that their families and therefore their customs and traditions came from different areas of India. The camp commander was ordered to be firm, but friendly to everyone. According to the Ranis, Thevar was indeed very firm, but no one thought of her as 'friendly'.

None of the women I interviewed mentioned Ranis being dismissed from the Regiment for misconduct. Asked whether she had been aware of any disciplinary problems, Ponnammah giggled with delight as she recounted an incident in which she and a couple of other Ranis broke in to the storage room where Camp Commandant Thevar kept the sugar under lock and key.[29] Ponnammah admitted that it had been her idea to steal the sugar, and she was a bit embarrassed that she had done so as an officer, while her partners in crime were just sepoys. An investigation failed to identify any of the culprits.

The security of the Ranis was of greatest importance to Bose and the young women did feel protected. As Rama warmly expressed it: 'He took great care of us. We had our own campus and no one was allowed to come in, except for the military instructors. Very strict.'[30] In Rangoon the Ranis lodged in wooden barracks with openings high on the walls instead of windows. One night a male INA soldier climbed the wall attempting to enter the women's quarters. He was caught in the act and promptly transferred out of the camp.[31] The camps in Singapore and Rangoon were completely barricaded and guarded day and night. In Singapore, after being trained in sentry duty, the Ranis took turns patrolling inside the camp at night and also outside during the day. A new password was issued every day, a practice that resulted in a memorable episode for one Rani.[32]

Mommata was on sentry duty one night in Rangoon when Bose appeared at the gate and requested access. She immediately recognized Bose, but because it was the duty of the guard not to admit anyone without the current password, she demanded it from him. Neither he nor his bodyguards knew the password, so the Rani denied them entry. Bose did not press the matter; his party left, but the next day he sent word praising the Rani for her proper conduct. When telling me the story, effervescent still at eighty-two, Mommata embraced herself for comfort; so many decades after the incident, the memory of 'sending Netaji away' was still unsettling. Several other Ranis were so impressed by Mommata's daring that they also remembered the event and recounted the story to me with perfect details.

In a speech at the Netaji Seminar in 1979, Captain Lakshmi poked fun at the Japanese general Fujiwara, who was in the audience. Even if the Japanese friends of the INA would not like to be reminded of it now, she said, during the war they had 'violently objected to the idea [of the RJR] because they thought that special arrangements would have to be made and another army would have to be created to protect the Rani of Jhansi Regiment!'[33] Although Captain Lakshmi ridiculed such trepidations, in point of fact male INA soldiers were assigned to protect the Ranis' camps both in Singapore and in Rangoon and travel with them everywhere they went. British Intelligence observed: 'When the Regiment moved into their Halpin Road Camp [outside Rangoon], the immediate vicinity of the camp was placed out of bounds to INA troops but remained inbounds to officers of the rank of major and above. ... The camp was guarded by an INA detachment under a Garhwali lieutenant, Second Lieutenant Sardara Singh (Sikh) 6/14 Punjab was liaison officer/Q.M. for the guard.'[34] Captain Lakshmi did not live together with the Ranis in the Burma camps; she served in the hospital closer to the fighting and may not have known the details of camp life, but male INA soldiers guarded the women against low-ranking INA and Japanese soldiers as well as Burmese guerrillas and civilians.

It was an INA rule that Hindus, Muslims and Christians were served the same food, prepared by the same cooks. Soldiers of all religions and castes ate together – an exceedingly novel concept for Indians, but reportedly a positive experience for all. Bose's principle was that since everyone volunteered to work for the same goal, identical meals would do for officers, for sepoys and for himself. Bose made efforts to assure that the Ranis' food supplies were satisfactory. His concern about the health of the Ranis was apparent: in a letter of May 1944 to Captain Thevar, head of the Singapore camp, he asked that she 'introduce a fortnightly weighment' to monitor the health of the volunteers.[35]

As is the case in every army, in the INA the food served was a matter for much gossip, discussion and complaint. The male soldiers were dissatisfied because they believed that the Ranis' were allotted better food than they. Captain Lakshmi remembered, 'We did not have anything special. We ate what was available. It was all vegetarian. We had a department of cooking. All the volunteers had to take turns cooking.'[36] Actually, Bose did not want the Rani fighters to spend their time doing household chores, and none of the Ranis I interviewed ever cooked while in the RJR. They all reported that their meals were prepared by Ranis who were too old or unfit to be nurses or fighters, and in Burma the cooks were male INA soldiers. As Mommata remembered, 'The Rani officers did not do the cleaning, that was [done by] those girls from the estates and from Burma, the mothers and the grandmothers. They were women who had had their children early and they cooked for us and cleaned.'[37]

Captain Lakshmi mentioned several times in our meetings, and also in her speeches and her memoirs, that the food was simple, delicious and nutritious, and that in fact the Rani cooks used the same ingredients that were provided to the male soldiers, including Bose. According to one story that Captain Lakshmi cited repeatedly: once, groups of male recruits from other camps were invited for Sunday dinner just to prove to the men that the women were not favoured with better supplies.[38] The men were asked to examine the ingredients used, and afterwards they had to admit that the skill of the female cooks made all the difference in the quality of the meal.[39]

Some Ranis told different stories. They said that because they were women they were given more meat, fish and eggs than the men. INA soldier Mehervan Singh, who was responsible for distributing funds to both Ranis and male soldiers, agreed with these Ranis and contradicted Captain Lakshmi's assertions of equal treatment:

> The [Ranis] had special treatment because Subhas Chandra Bose had in mind to use them for a purpose. Not necessarily to fight in the field, but to spiritually lift the people. So they were very well trained people, they were in good health, they were given better food than the other soldiers. I knew it because I was providing them with the funds and I used to have lunch with them whenever I went.[40]

Unlike the male soldiers, most of whom grew up in India where their families still lived, many Ranis both in Singapore and Rangoon were raised locally, and received care packages from friends and family.[41] Almost all Ranis agreed that the camp food was not especially tasty. The menu was most often simple dal and rice, or rice mixed with fish, but since they were hungry after their hard work and physical exercise, the simple fare was not a problem. The only Rani to complain seriously about the food was Janaki Thevar. She was not used to having her food dished 'into a cut open milk can'. For several weeks after joining the Regiment, she found it hard to eat 'the slop the Ranis were served, … Ragi Dosa, partly burnt and tea', but once she had decided not to go back home, the quality of the food apparently also ceased to trouble her.[42]

Long, heavy, glossy hair is an important mark of female beauty among Indians, and until recently, it was unusual for an Indian woman to cut her hair before marriage. For a soldier stationed in the tropical rainforest of Burma where vermin abounded and opportunities for bathing were few, those tresses could become a life-threatening impediment. RJR regulations therefore specified that hair should be shoulder-length or shorter. Describing the Regiment in our interview, Captain Lakshmi asserted that short hair was the rule. She claimed that she was particularly happy to finally have a valid reason to shear her knee-length locks, thereby circumventing her mother's long-standing insistence that she keep her hair long.[43]

Manwati Panday from Meikthila in central Burma had quite long hair when she joined the INA, but she and all Ranis in her troop cut their hair while travelling from Rangoon north to Maymyo, closer to the front. When I asked whether it had been difficult to give up her long hair, she answered with a peal of laughter, 'We were ready to give our heads, so who cared about the hair!'[44] General Chatterji's account concerning the Ranis' hair is consistent with what the Ranis reported in our interviews: many had short hair and others used nets.[45] As it is against the Sikh religion for either men or women to cut their hair, this regulation was waived for Sikh Ranis, and they wore their hair braided. Judging from available photographs of the Regiment, it appears that about nine out of ten Ranis had short hair.

Finding suitable guns for the Ranis was problematic. General Chatterji, who was in charge of supplies for the INA, writes that the Lee-Enfield 303 rifles used by the male soldiers were too long and heavy for small South Indian women. Instead, according to Chatterji, this problem was solved by issuing Canadian Ross or the 'Dutch' rifles to the RJR.[46] The Canadian Ross was, however, known to be notoriously inefficient. In addition, the 52-inch Ross rifle is eight inches longer than the Lee-Enfield 303. At a weight of almost nine pounds, it is also two ounces heavier than the Lee-Enfield and for those reasons Chatterji's explanation is thus unconvincing. The Lee-Enfield rifle had been the weapon of choice for the British Imperial Army since 1895, used by British soldiers everywhere. The INA men who were former British Indian Army soldiers were most probably familiar with it. Ammunition for the Lee-Enfield was also easier to procure than ammunition for the Ross. The Ross was known to jam in many situations; it was difficult to clean, and, critically, its bayonet tended to fall off when the rifle was fired.[47] To replace the bayonets lost from their Ross rifles, says Chatterji, the Ranis were instead issued short swords.[48] However, in photographs of the Ranis marching and training, the rifles appear to be Rosses fitted with bayonets. The Ranis did not shoot during regular practice so their bayonets may have remained attached. Two Ranis,

Aruna and Rasammah referred to their rifles as '303', but because the Lee-Enfields were in limited supply, it may be that some Ranis had Lee-Enfields and others had Rosses.[49] Chatterji probably also calculated that it was reasonable to issue the better weapons to the men.

In our interviews, the Ranis spoke with pride about their weapons, but the firearm mentioned most often and most enthusiastically was the Sten gun, a 30-inch sub-machine gun weighing just seven pounds. Its excellent firepower, despite its compact size, made it a suitable weapon for the women. Akilandam Vairavapillai and several others mentioned that they had also used the Bren gun, a light machine gun.[50] It weighed twenty-three pounds, more than a quarter of the weight of the average Rani and therefore cannot have been a weapon of choice for the Rani infantry soldiers. Physically fit Aruna did not mind the burden, 'As far as I remember my rifle was eleven pounds and the brengun weighed twenty-three pounds. But over the time past, it all became just like parts of our body.'[51] In addition to a rifle, each Rani was issued a handgun and a knife. The women were also trained in handling grenades, but they were not taught to drive any kind of a vehicle, and they received almost no artillery training.

Girls like Asha Sahay, the Mehta sisters Rama and Neelam and others who came from wealthy families brought uniforms sewn by their regular tailors. Camp tailors with treadle sewing machines equipped everybody else. Each Rani was measured on arrival and by evening was issued her new uniform made of heavy beige cotton khaki. Rasammah loved the jodhpurs and thought her new uniform quite smart and comfortable. As one of the Ranis pointed out, it might have been more logical to issue them green camouflage uniforms like the ones worn by the Allied armies, given that the RJR was to be deployed in the jungles of Burma.[52] Instead, the cut of the uniform was copied from the men's, except that the trousers had a buttoned opening on the hip rather than in front. The first recruits were issued three sets of uniforms; later arrivals received just two sets. In the beginning the Ranis wore jodhpurs for parades, but those proved impractical, said Captain Lakshmi, so they switched to plain slacks and a bush shirt with pockets. For everyday training they wore khaki shorts and a short-sleeved shirt. Each soldier brought her own underwear.

The RJR volunteers wore military shoes like those of their male counterparts. Many Gurkha men were commissioned into the British Indian Army, and, as Captain Lakshmi happily reported, since Gurkhas typically have small feet, the relative small shoes they left behind were reissued to the Ranis. [53] Socks were in particularly short supply, but fortunately, the British had abandoned significant quantities of socks when they surrendered in Singapore in February 1942, and some of these were promptly redistributed to the Ranis. Jewellery, so important for women of all Indian cultures, was not allowed. Married women were permitted to keep around their necks the mangalsutra, 'the sacred thread', given by their bridegrooms at their weddings.

Most of the Ranis had never worn pants other than the traditional salwar-kameez, or pajama pants. However, not one of the Ranis I interviewed expressed any discomfort or hesitation at having to change her style of dress. They all found the new attire comfortable and they wore their uniforms with pride.

ELEVEN

DAILY RANI ROUTINES IN CAMP

MANMOHAN KAUR, A HISTORIAN of Indian women, quotes the pledge
of loyalty that the Ranis swore every morning:

> I shall fulfill our objective in the face of all difficulties. I shall sacrifice
> myself, my body, soul and properties, all for the fulfillment of my pledge.
> I promise I shall not do any such thing which may besmear the name of
> Hindustan and Netaji. I shall obey all the orders of superiors with heart
> and soul. I shall keep in good condition all the weapons Netaji has given.[1]

When I asked the Ranis whether they took this oath, no one had any
memory of it. Several gave detailed accounts of the morning flag-hoisting
ceremony, and an oath involving Bose would most likely have made an
impression. The Ranis liked to recount their rituals and several women
sang parts of their marching songs and their favourite freedom song '*Bande/
Vande Mataram*'.[2] In its wording Kaur's reported oath sounds very much
like something Bose might have composed to promote troop loyalty, but
perhaps it was never implemented.

Reports from the Ranis about their daily routine in the training camps
differ only in the exact timing of each activity, but they agree on the basic

components of the training schedule. The day began for every member of
the camp at 6 a.m. with the hoisting of the Azad Hind flag. It was the saffron,
white and green tricolour of the Indian National Congress flag, but instead
of the charkha, Gandhi's spinning wheel, it had a springing tiger. After the
flag raising and salute came forty-five minutes of PT (physical training).

Breakfast, a mug of tea and some bread, was served at 7.30 a.m.,
followed by two hours of parade ground drills. The next two hours
were reserved for bathing, washing and personal affairs. Each Rani was
responsible for her uniform, a demanding task for those girls who had
always had a dhobi assigned to do their washing at home. Janaki Thevar
remembered, 'Getting up very early in the morning, washing your clothes
and starching them, and later ironing them for the next day's use was
very tiring.'[3] Other Ranis did their laundry less frequently, and instead
of ironing they placed the damp uniform under the pillow or mattress
and slept on it. As Janaki Bai said in her minimalist manner, 'Some of us
managed to look quite tidy that way. It all depended on the individual.'[4]
Lunch was served at noon and consisted of standard Indian fare: chapatti,
rice, vegetable and lentils. Occasionally, each soldier would get an egg.
Then the Ranis had another hour of leisure time, followed by two hours
of classroom work.

Hindustani was the official language of the INA, and all military
commands and instructions were given in that language. Bose had
concluded that by teaching Hindustani, a mix of Hindi and Urdu written
in Roman letters, he could avoid making a choice between the scripts for
Hindi and Urdu.[5] Tamil speakers and illiterate volunteers had classes for
one hour each afternoon learning to read and write Hindustani.[6] Those
Ranis who were educated in both Hindi and English spent that time
studying map reading and other practical skills that military officers needed
to master. A second hour was devoted daily to lectures on Indian history,
especially the history of the independence movement.[7]

After class there were two more hours of physical training, and at
6.30 p.m. the Ranis took down the flag. The singing of 'Bande Mataram'
signalled the end of the workday. Dinner, served at 7 p.m., was the same
as lunch. Afterwards, the Ranis gathered to chat, sing or play music.

Volunteers with talent at some form of performance had a captive audience in their fellow soldiers until lights out at 9.30 p.m.[8] The Ranis wrote and performed several dramas about the freedom movement for audiences that often included Bose and the male INA soldiers.

The strain of the strict daily physical routines was initially hard, especially for the recruits who had arrived severely malnourished. Others had never exerted themselves physically, and none had ever exercised for several hours a day. Some older and married women signed up with the Regiment despite being told that they would not be sent to fight in Burma. Assigned to serve as cooks, secretaries and other general assistants in camp, they were required to participate in physical training, but did not go on the long marches. Most Ranis were young and resilient; the combination of a simple wholesome diet, hard work, and regular sleep quickly transformed them into strong, fit and energetic soldiers.[9]

Ranis could volunteer to be either soldiers or nurses, and Bose required that all Ranis be trained as soldiers, even those who eventually served as kitchen and maintenance staff. Bose wanted as many as possible to sign up for the military wing. Captain Lakshmi explained, 'The Fighting Group numbered about three hundred and was divided into three companies. Each company was divided into three platoons and each platoon into four sections.'[10] Rani Gian Kaur, who was a medical student at the beginning of the war and worked as a nurse in the RJR, told British Intelligence that Bose concentrated all his interest on the Fighting Group and that he did not like recruits to transfer to the Nursing Section.[11]

From Burma Bose continuously supervised the training of the women and maintained close contact with the superintendent of the Singapore camp. Bose wanted the Ranis to spend their days training and learning military craft. Consistent with his promise that the Ranis should be treated like the male soldiers, he wrote to Captain Thevar at the Singapore camp that he did not 'like the volunteers to waste their time unnecessarily in cooking and other domestic duties. These duties they have done enough at home.'[12]

Bose handpicked the male INA soldiers who would train the Ranis to fight in the jungle. The men selected as instructors for the Ranis were told not to use foul language, and to treat the young women with the respect they would show their mothers and sisters. According to Captain Lakshmi, Bose did not emphasize the importance of the instructors' teaching skills or knowledge of warfare as much as their fraternal demeanour.[13] Janaki Bai held the instructors in high regard: 'They were well-educated men from the INA, first trained by the British Army. They took pains to teach us. They spoke Hindustani.'[14] Besides the physical training and weapons handling, the Ranis also learned military history, map reading, geography and took long night marches.[15]

In April 1945, Captain Sayed Munawar Hussain of the INA, POW number M2734, was captured and interrogated about the RJR. The British were particularly interested to learn if Bose had intended for the RJR to be a genuine combat unit. In Hussain's assessment, 'The fighting group underwent complete military training including bayonet drill, route marches in full battle order, rifle and machine gun firing.'[16] Still not believing that Bose had meant for the women to serve as real soldiers, his conclusion was that the training was all purely for the propaganda effect inside India and to spur the INA men on to greater efforts. However, he added a story of an episode in which the Ranis applied their fighting skills when they found an opportunity. As he remembered, 'In October 1944, a detachment of the fighting group [of the RJR] was passing through Kamayut [neighbourhood of Rangoon] in a lorry when it saw a minor Indo-Burman street fight. The Amazons charged with fixed bayonets, cordoned off the two parties and restored order until Police arrived!'[17]

At the end of basic training, the Ranis were put to the test in marksmanship. Janaki Bai was surprised when her skills on the shooting range earned her a prize, a leather bag presented by Colonel J.K. Bhonsle, a high-ranking officer in the INA.[18] Similarly Rasammah, despite a long life with many achievements and honours, including the prestigious Malaysian title of Datuk, still bubbled with joy in recounting to me how she had scored second best after her friend Janaki Bai in target shooting.[19] General Shah Nawaz Khan observed the Ranis in Burma and was impressed by their skill level. In his opinion, '...within a very brief period of six months they had mastered all their training and were every bit as well trained and disciplined as any soldier of the *Azad Hind Fauj*.'[20] With this statement Shah Nawaz is probably showing his loyalty to Bose and his wish to support Bose's idea of female soldiers rather than describing the Ranis' genuine readiness for combat in snake-infested jungles. No matter how well trained in camp the Ranis were and how many parade performances on the Padang in Singapore they had given, it seems unlikely that teenage girls would have been able to haul 80 pounds of gear through knee-deep monsoon mud 25 miles a day, make safe drinking water, sleep in the open and live off the land as was demanded of the men.[21] They were never taught these skills.

At the outset Bose decided that only 'educated' girls would be considered for officers' training. To become an officer a Rani had to be literate in Hindi and English and had to have completed at least eight years of schooling. A consequence of the educational requirement was that none of the South Indian women from the plantations, who were almost all illiterate and spoke neither English nor Hindi, were eligible to become officers.

The training of Rani officers began as soon as suitable candidates signed up. Captain Lakshmi proudly reported that on 30 March 1944, after roughly five months' training, 'the first passing out parade of the officers of the Rani of Jhansi Regiment took place'.[22] Eight young women who had taken and passed the same tests as the men in the INA Officers' Training School became commissioned officers in the INA, Captain Lakshmi said. On that occasion Janaki Thevar was the only woman to achieve the commissioned rank of second lieutenant. Two members of the first Singapore cohort, Janaki Bai and Ponnammah Navarednam, said that they were among the Ranis who passed the tests on 30 March and became sub-officers.[23] Several other women became non-commissioned officers (NCOs); Rasammah Navarednam, became naik, or corporal.

In August 1944, a few months after the contingent of Ranis had left Singapore for Burma, Bose wrote to Mrs Thevar, who was in charge of training the next batch of Rani officers, that he wanted 'to see the Rani of Jhansi Regiment Officers as efficient as the men Officers of the INA, so that nobody can have any justification for thinking that promotions in the Rani of Jhansi Regiment are easy'.[24] British Intelligence observations confirm Bose's intentions for proper training of the RJR. The Regiment 'was without a doubt taken seriously by the INA as a unit which would be thrown into battle after entry had been affected into the more populated areas'.[25] Many of the male INA officers were promoted from illiterate British Indian Army sepoy to INA officer after just three weeks of officers' school, so comparatively more resources were spent on the RJR.[26]

When asked to describe their training, the Ranis generally first mentioned their marches through Singapore and Rangoon, looking smart, presenting their rifles and singing patriotic songs. The training regimen included 12-mile route marches at night with full gear, consisting of 'rifle with ammunition, a canvas backpack containing four days' ration and one complete uniform, socks, a first-aid kit and a water bottle'.[27] This rigorous regimen gave the recruits a sense of danger and elation. Their accounts of how happy they felt marching together, filled with a sense of purpose, and admired by onlookers, are reminiscent of Bose's notes two decades earlier on his time in the Indian Defence Force.[28]

When telling me their stories about military training, many Ranis volunteered that bayonet exercise was their favourite form of drill. Most of the sweet old women into whom the Ranis had aged by the time I interviewed them wanted to demonstrate that they still knew how to use the bayonet. If able to rise, they got out of their chairs; otherwise they remaining seated and pretended to wield their rifle and bayonet. With a grimace and a grunt these octogenarians thrust the rifle hard forward, and made a swift upward movement with the fancied bayonet. The training mantra still edged in their brains, '[Maaro,kheencho,dekho] – kill, pull out, look.' Then they usually smiled and said, 'That's how you kill the enemy.' General Shah Nawaz praised in particular the Ranis' skill and enthusiasm in bayonet fighting and commented that all of them were always ready and eager to use their bayonets against the British forces.[29]

Neither Lakshmi nor any of the Ranis mentioned to me any class or discussion that would prepare these young women psychologically for the effects of killing another human being, be it an Englishman or an Indian in the British Indian Army. Janaki Bai's uncle served that force and other Ranis mentioned cousins fighting on the other side. Many of the women were raised in deeply religious families, including Jains, Buddhists and

Christians. When I asked if they thought that they would have been able to kill an enemy, most Ranis rather lightly said that it would not have posed a problem. Rani Anjalai Ponnaswamy smiled shyly and admitted that she 'would not have killed anything'.[30] Sitting right next to her was her friend, Akilandam who agreed with several of the other Ranis and said that cutting open the belly of a British soldier would not have been a difficult task, 'because that is what we were trained for'.[31] The women explained that they had had many hours of training on cloth-covered hay bales that they had named Churchill and Roosevelt. Janaki Bai admitted that stabbing the dummies would not have carried over to bayonet a person: 'We went through the training, but to be honest I could not bring myself to actually do it – I am not bloodthirsty enough.'[32]

Altogether five of the Ranis who were contacted for this study had changed their minds about killing and admitted regrets about having joined the INA. They now considered killing a sin and were sure they would never have harmed anyone.[33] 'We were children and did not know what we were doing,' said Veesa Mudeliar.[34] Eva Jenny Murty, a Christian, did not regret her participation in the RJR. As a Rani she worked as a surgical nurse helping Indian soldiers, and was happy that she never had to make the decision whether to kill another human being.[35]

Until the end of the war, Ranis continued their training while living in camp and thus had quite a different experience from that of the male INA soldiers who were sent into the Burmese jungle poorly equipped with such weak supply lines that they had no choice but to live off the land. More INA men died of hunger and disease than from bullets and bayonets.[36]

The young women who volunteered to be Ranis were united in their wish to become soldiers and participate in the liberation of India. The other characteristics they shared were that they were female, of Indian background, and bold enough to leave home for a journey into the unknown. These few areas of similarity left room for significant differences among the women. In pre–World War II Indian society, demographic factors such as caste, religion, geographic origin, and mother tongue, constituted effective barriers against socializing and collaboration. Perhaps because the Rani volunteers were instructed that social fragmentation was incompatible with the freedom struggle, the customary social barriers did not have a significantly divisive impact within the microcosm of the RJR. As one Rani tersely remarked, 'we didn't do much praying', indicating that religion was of little importance in everyday life in the camp.[37] Sharing the same meals, the soldiers often became friends across those traditional barriers.

As it turned out, however, educational background posed a significant basis for segregation. 'Educated' Ranis were separated out from the day of induction to receive officer training and were assigned sleeping quarters in the more comfortable front part of the dormitory.[38] In addition, they were chosen to perform in dramatic productions, and they were asked to carry the flag on ceremonial occasions. Being 'educated', in the context of the RJR, meant more than simply being literate. As earlier indicated, to be considered educated in the Regiment, a girl had to have finished the equivalent of the eighth grade.

Several Ranis noted that differences in levels of education between the Tamil girls from the estates and the Ranis who came from families that sent their daughters to school resulted in some de facto segregation. Janaki Bai found, 'When educated and uneducated people have to interact it is difficult. You don't know what they are thinking about. We who are educated think in a different way than those who are housewives.'[39] Aruna pointed out the main reason that no Tamil girls from the plantations could become officers: 'They could not write!' But while in camp, Aruna learned some Tamil in order to speak with the sepoys in her platoon.[40]

Many of the Ranis were brought up completely bilingual, fluent in one Indian language, Tamil, Hindi, Punjabi or Bengali as well as English, often speaking the Indian language with other children, servants and one parent, while using English in school and with the other parent. Generally, the Ranis who worked as tappers and weeders on the rubber plantations in Malaya spoke only Tamil and had attended inadequate plantation school at most for five years. According to Captain Lakshmi, nearly all were functionally illiterate.[41] Of the RJR veterans interviewed for this study, all the native speakers of Hindi, Bengali, Urdu and English, as well as those girls educated in English schools, had finished eighth grade, and those who were old enough had completed additional schooling.

As noted above, Bose wanted all RJR members to learn Hindustani, the official INA language, and Captain Lakshmi claims that illiterate recruits, whether native speakers of Tamil, Malayalam or Hindi, all learned not only to speak but also to read and write Hindustani in Roman letters – within three months of enlistment![42] Captain Lakshmi's report appears exaggerated. Based on testimony from the Ranis, many of the women in fact lacked a common language and were therefore unable to speak directly with one another. Most monolingual Tamil speakers were able to communicate only in their language even after the Hindustani lessons, and native speakers of the other languages did not know Tamil.

With so many young women living together in primitive and stressful circumstances for almost two years, one would naturally expect annoyances, disagreements and squabbles; and indeed there is some evidence of occasional disharmony in the RJR. On 6 June 1945, Asha Sahay confessed to her diary that she could not 'understand why the girls fight and talk so loudly. If they spend energy quarreling with each other, how can they fight against the Britishers?'[43] It may be that Asha, who came from an upper-class Indian family, grew up in Kobe, Japan, and had a passion for composing haikus, failed to understand that the quarrels were more rambunctious than hostile.

Notwithstanding Asha's observation, the curious fact is that in our many interviews more than sixty years later, with a few exceptions the Ranis consistently maintained that there was rarely a rough word exchanged among them. Of those minor disagreements recounted by the interviewees, most were resolved quickly and quietly. For example, Ponnammah discovered that her Bible was missing from her locker. She saw that some Tamil girls were looking at it and asked for it. At first they were unwilling to give it back, but when she told them that to her, a Christian, this book was as treasured as their Gita was to them, they promptly returned it.[44]

It is remarkable that no Rani I interviewed mentioned communal differences as a problem. Second Lieutenant Janaki Bai explained that the Ranis in general were not very religious. Chuckling, she told one of several instances when religious differences caused havoc, but no ill feelings. She explained that the Hindu women especially had a habit of going into a trance which made others believe that they were possessed by demons. One day in the dining hall, while the Ranis lined up waiting for their dinners, one Hindu girl went into a trance saying odd things. Hearing this, 'all the Tamil girls from the estates took fright and made a stampede to get out'. Janaki Bai pressed herself against the wall during the rush out of the dining hall, but her friend Grace was caught in the pandemonium and had a curry shower when somebody threw a large pail of the day's lunch. Janaki laughed, 'I was lucky, for her hair was completely washed in sambhar with dal.'[45]

As second lieutenant in charge of a platoon, Janaki Bai was responsible for keeping discipline among her troops and a few rowdy characters required special attention. She recalls '…one big Punjabi girl, Kartar Kaur, a rough, tough-looking one. She was quarrelling with some Tamil girls, and I remember three or four Tamil girls sitting on her trying to keep her from being violent. There was not a lot of violence among the girls, this was an isolated incident, but she had to be sequestered because she was violent. … She was under quarter guard, the military called it, in a room partitioned off in the barracks, but when we looked up, she was sitting on the roof. She had climbed out.'[46] Ranis remembered 'no clashes', only insignificant misunderstandings between the Tamil girls from the estates and the so-called educated girls, little arguments arising from their different upbringings, experiences and expectations. More than likely, the Rani memories of those halcyon days of comradeship are somewhat selective, but almost to a woman they agreed that their service in the RJR was the best period of their lives. In any case it seems clear that Rani interactions with one another were remarkably harmonious.

How would young girls, a few not yet teenagers, handle being away from family and normal life? How much did they know about the war and the Indian freedom struggle, and how could they possibly be prepared to live in the jungle alongside men, to kill enemy soldiers who most likely looked like their neighbours and brothers? In 1980, Janaki Thevar, who at age eighteen became second-in-command of the Rani Regiment in Burma, answered on behalf of the Regiment, describing the Ranis' state of mind as they were leaving the Singapore training camp:

They were fully aware of the hardships that awaited them in the battlefield along the Indo-Burma border. They were prepared to face the trials and tribulations that lay ahead under all circumstances. The future was uncertain. Our girl and women soldiers fully knew that in the national struggle all that they could expect was suffering and sacrifice. What else could one expect at the battlefront [sic] other than hunger, thirst, fatigue, bombing, injury and death? They were all the time conscious of the honour and dignity of Indian womanhood, and were totally inspired in this life and death struggle for India's freedom.[47]

The Ranis, when they told their stories in the interviews, agreed that Janaki's statement was also true for them. As old women looking back on how young they were then and how inexperienced with life, they still believed that they were prepared to march into battle and tolerate the horrors of war. They knew that they might die, but they were eager to sacrifice themselves for their Motherland. Several Ranis, including Janaki Thevar, the keenest of all the soldiers, admitted that at the beginning they cried every night. But as time passed, homesickness gave way to camaraderie and the euphoria of higher purpose.

When young women, almost all unmarried, and men who were either single or who had been away from their wives for years, work and spend much time together in a war zone, and remain isolated from the rest of the world, sexual attractions are to be expected. When I asked if there had been fraternization between the Ranis and the INA soldiers, Captain Lakshmi was adamant: '...there were never any such problems, no untoward incidents at all. Can't imagine it, really.'[48] To my further question of whether any Ranis became pregnant, Captain Lakshmi's answer was another firm no. There had been only professional relationships.[49] She explained, the male soldiers and the Ranis met both as soldiers and at social events, but dating was not allowed. Bose had instructed the men to look at the Ranis as their mothers or sisters, and apparently expected that admonition to control the soldiers' sex drive.[50] After all, this was consistent with the teachings of Bose's favourite gurus, Ramakrishna and Swami Vivekananda on transcendence of sex-consciousness.[51] In his political

campaigns, Bose had differed with Gandhi on birth control. He argued
then that there was no evidence for the efficacy of proscribed celibacy.
Because of the soldiers' reverence for both Bose and the mission, that
approach was, according to Captain Lakshmi, entirely effective. Bose took
the additional precaution of keeping the Ranis heavily guarded at all times.

Like Captain Lakshmi, most of the other Ranis claimed that they had
no knowledge of any fraternization. One reason for that answer may have
been that they were uncomfortable talking about sexual matters. These
Indian women were brought up during a time when sexual relations were
not discussed, especially not with a foreign stranger. Or perhaps being
very young and inexperienced with life outside their homes, they may not
have been aware of any incidents of male and female soldiers becoming
involved. In any case, all the Ranis agreed that romantic relationships had
no place in an army camp.

Other Ranis, however, stated unequivocally that fraternization
had indeed occurred, but most declined to elaborate. Ponnammah
Navarednam, who had lived in the United States for several years and
seemed more comfortable discussing sexual matters than the other Ranis
whom I interviewed, laughed at the question. 'First, everyone knew about
Captain Lakshmi's romantic relationship with Prem Sahgal. They were in
love. We saw that. We knew that. She was in the office and he would come
to see her, we could see them from our barracks. We watched them.'[52]
Several other Ranis had also heard that the reason why Captain Lakshmi
had been sent up to Burma early was because Bose had concluded that
she was a poor example for the other young women in the RJR Singapore
camp because of her relationship with Prem Sahgal.[53]

Ponnammah was not nearly as tolerant of romantic feelings when it
concerned herself. She had an experience that still made her uncomfortable
when telling it to me. Sahir, a Muslim officer whom she met at a tea party
given by Bose, kept staring at her and at the end of the evening gave her
a book about India. When she got back to camp she found a letter inside
the book in which Sahir described his feelings of admiration and desire
for Ponnammah. Apparently, the infatuated officer needed to share his
feelings with others and prattled on about his passion for Ponnammah in

the officers' mess. When General Shah Nawaz Khan, a family friend of the Navarednams, got wind of this ungentlemanly talk, he put an effective stop to it, and informed Ponnammah that he had done so. 'All rubbish,' Ponnammah scoffed as she recounted the episode. 'I was too young.'[54]

Another Rani, whose pregnancy caused her to vomit frequently, created quite a disturbance, but she subsequently lost the baby, said a Rani, 'one way or another'.[55] Karuna was timid and careful when telling about her life, but to the question whether any soldiers fell in love during the war, she answered forthrightly, 'Nobody was supposed to fall in love. Ranis lived separately and the men lived separately. Two or three Indian girls, not Bengalis, had a baby and were sent home.'[56] Karuna is the only Rani to tell me that a Rani was discharged for reasons other than illness, injury or not being able to handle the hard physical demands.

Rama knew that her good friend Janaki Bai was very much in love with a major of the INA. The two arranged to meet outside camp whenever possible. Janaki Bai, however, did not volunteer information to me about having had any romantic alliance, and to the direct question if any of the women had fallen in love with any of the INA men, she firmly answered, 'Life was so full with training and instruction, there was no time for that.'[57] Manwati said that she was aware of one relationship between a Rani and a male soldier, but did not elaborate. She may have talked about herself, for according to a CSDIC(I) report: 'Manwati Panday divorced her husband and started to live with Lieutenant Sita Ram Goswami.'[58]

Janaki Thevar, commander of the Burma RJR camp, also enjoyed her share of male attention. Ponnammah asserted, 'Janaki Thevar had a boyfriend, a Sikh man,' and a little later in the interview she mentioned Janaki Thevar's dalliance with another man, 'Janaki had fun with Colonel Zai, she was in love with this fellow.'[59] Janaki herself happily bragged to me, 'When I rode my tall, grey horse past the male INA garrison every morning, the whole army used to turn up in full force happy to see me trotting along – lots of cat whistles. ... Some officers got really interested in me. Of course, I took no notice of them.'[60]

In her unpublished memoirs Janaki mentions a revealing episode. At the end of the retreat from Burma when the contingent of which

Janaki was in charge had reached home and the Ranis were dismissed, it took but one moment before a woman from Janaki's group stepped forward, slapped Janaki's face several times and said, 'You are no more our Commandant.' According to Janaki, the reason given for the assault was that it was retaliation for Janaki's not allowing the Rani to be friendly with the male soldiers.[61]

British Intelligence reports also include many references to Ranis who had affairs with INA soldiers. For example, 'Mrs. Dolly was discharged from the Regt. owing to illicit connection with Captain Saleem,' and 'Captain (Lieutenant Colonel) [A.I.S.] Dara and some others have girl friends [sic] in this [Rani of Jhansi] Regiment.'[62] According to a CSDIC(I) report [Rani] 'Gori Bhattacharji [Gauri Bhattacharya], daughter of Bhattacharji, Advocate, Insein, Had illicit connection with B1018 Captain Tehl Singh.'[63]

Captured INA soldiers gave lengthy lists of INA officers who they claimed had sexual relationships with Ranis. Captain Lakshmi's name appeared so often in connection with so many officers that it had to reflect at least to some degree idle gossip – or wishful thinking.[64] There is, of course, no way to evaluate such assertions with certainty.

Further evidence that not all INA men thought of the Ranis only as their mothers and sisters is found in this poem circulating among the soldiers composed by INA officer Ehsan Qadir:

I

Jhansi paltan ko banane ka khyal achchha tha –
Thik sardar bhi chun lete to kam achchha tha,
woh na samjhenge bura kya hai, ya achchha kya tha –
Jin ko maalum nahin kaun pati achchha tha
Khahi shen inki mita den, ya mita den paltan,
Warna yeh fouj ki khahish ka banega madfan.

I

The idea of such a regiment would have been all right if only (he – Bose) had chosen the right leader. One who does not know which husband she likes best, cannot tell between right and wrong.

Either kill her passions or abolish the regiment,
Because it will otherwise become the grave of
the passions of the whole INA.

II

Chikni chupri jo suna dete hain har dam jhuk ke,
Zati jhagron men hi par jate hain unke sukh ke,
Khah woh bekar hon ya kam karen ruk ruk ke,
Woh bhula dete hain qisse jo hain qaumi dukh ke.
Aise hathkandon se chhoton ne barai leli –
Baz ko tu ne zabardast barai de di.

II

Those who only say palatable things in courtly fashion,
entangle you in their personal intrigues. Whether they
are idle or whether only working by fits and starts, they
make you forget the troubles of the people.
With such underhand tactics some of the scum have risen high.
While on certain others you yourself have trusted greatness.

III

Dost ko milke unhen sara jahan bhul gaya – Jhansi ka
khyal, khuda jane kahan bhul gaya.
Ustaraf doston ko asalakaman bhul gaya – Fouj bhi bhul gai
Foujinishan bhul gaya.
Phir yeh ummeed hai, maidan men ja kar woh maren,
Jang kahee ko karen, kyun nah woh Lachhmi pe maren.

III

She forgot rest of the world when she met her lover.
God knows how she forgot her (own state of) Jhansi.
On the other hand, her lovers have forgotten the 'Supreme Command',
the army, and its colours.
But still some people believe that they (lovers) would die in battle,
Why should they when it is much simpler to die for Lakshmi.[65]

Several Ranis mentioned to me the unwanted male attention that they were able to deflect on their own. Asha Sahay's experience with Ram Singh as described in her diary was perhaps typical. 'How the man was restless to talk to me. How shameless he was. I tried to be aloof but he was always after me. Well, now he cannot come. Sometime I pity him and decide to be nice to him when he comes next time. But as soon as I see him all pity vanishes and cruelty creeps in.'[66] Asha was also very unhappy with the attention of Abid Hasan Safrani, *Kaka*, 'uncle' Hasan, Bose's aide-de-camp who kept touching her. When she complained to her father, Anand Sahay, he told her not to make a fuss. Hasan, who was a Muslim from a different part of the country, was not familiar with their ways, her father explained; Hasan was probably just missing his own family.[67] The truth is that Anand Sahay chose to ignore his friend's transgressions rather than protect his daughter. He knew that Abid Hasan had grown up in Hyderabad, in a well-educated, anti-colonialist family, that he was a poet and a man of letters. As an engineering student in Germany, he had met Bose and then become active in the freedom struggle.[68]

The young Ranis prudently tried to avoid advances without antagonizing their pursuers because as Indian women, they knew that calling attention to themselves with complaints of male attention would most likely make matters worse. What seems clear is that Bose and the Ranis tried hard to ensure that the soldiers of the RJR were never mistaken for 'comfort women' of the sort the Japanese army notoriously procured for their soldiers. Captain Lakshmi was a practising gynaecologist. During many hours of interviews, she spoke freely about sex in other contexts. Either she believed, as she claimed, that fraternization would have been out of the question given the strong cultural values of both male and female soldiers, as well as the Ranis' robust commitment to their training and camp regimen; or more likely Captain Lakshmi denied the occurrence of fraternization because she did not want to tarnish the reputation of the RJR. But clearly there was considerable sexual tension and activity in the Rani camps despite Captain Lakshmi's denials.

Desertions and voluntary capture were a serious problem in the INA as a whole. Bose had expected the Indian commissioned soldiers of the

British Indian Army to change allegiance and join the INA when the two armies met on the Indian frontier, but that event did not happen as Bose had hoped and envisioned. After the joint INA and Japanese army attempt to cross the Indo-Burma border had failed and the INA retreated from Kohima and Imphal in torrential rains and knee-deep mud, nearly every soldier suffered from malaria and dysentery.[69] Shah Nawaz Khan saw men eating horses that had been dead for four days. Hundreds of Japanese and Indian soldiers lay dead along the sides of the road. They had died from illness, starvation, exhaustion or suicide because they did not want to be taken prisoners. The British tried to subvert the morale of the defeated soldiers by dropping propaganda leaflets urging Indians to switch sides if they wanted to eat, get medical treatment and live to see their children again. Shah Nawaz claimed, improbably, that as tempting as the offer sounded, only one man deserted.[70] British Intelligence documents tell a different story: 1,500 of the 6,000 INA soldiers sent to capture Imphal and Kohima deserted.[71] An estimated 2,500 died.

Bose reacted to the reports of these large-scale desertions of INA men with fury and a feeling of personal betrayal. The INA soldiers' loss of fighting spirit and nationalist fervour, he concluded, might be the result of his own absence from their ranks on the front, and he decided not to let the Japanese again deny him access to the battlefield.[72] But not a single Rani deserted or surrendered. In Burma, Rama knew of only one girl who found the strenuous training too hard and asked for permission to go home.[73] The few Ranis that were interrogated by British Intelligence officers 'impressed us greatly with the sincerity and fire of their beliefs – a sincerity which but few of their men folk [sic] have found it in them to express'.[74] Manwati Panday was still working for Bose's cause in 2008 and claimed that the Ranis never wavered in their loyalty to Bose or in their certainty that Bose was leading them towards freedom for their country and equality for them as women.[75]

TWELVE

THE RJR IN RANGOON AND MAYMYO

IN OCTOBER 1943, WHEN the Rani of Jhansi Regiment began to enlist volunteers in Singapore, simultaneously the Indian Independence League in Rangoon was recruiting young Indian women for the Burma contingent of the RJR. Many years later, Aruna Ganguli expressed pride that she was the first Bengali girl to sign up to be a Rani.[1] Mrs Lilavati Chhaganlal Mehta of Pagoda Road, a prominent member of Rangoon society and a staunch freedom fighter, was a recruiter for the Ranis. To underscore her rhetoric of persuasion at recruitment meetings, this 'formidable lady', as Captain Lakshmi described her, brandished a sword borrowed from an INA officer.[2] Lilavati Mehta's two daughters, Rama, age sixteen, and Neelam, seventeen, had no choice but to join, and by enlisting on the opening day of the training camp the Mehta girls, whose family several generations back, originated in Gujarat, became the first Ranis born in Burma.

Together with Mrs Chandran, an early RJR organizer in Burma whom Captain Lakshmi described as 'a motherly sort of person who had been a teacher', Lilavati Mehta spearheaded the effort of setting up the Rani camp in the Rangoon suburb of Thingangyun.[3] The camp was officially inaugurated on 22 October 1943. Colonel Alagappan of the INA opened

Courtesy Ponnammah Esther Navarednam

Rani of Jhansi
Regiment led by
Lt. Janaki Thevar,
1943-44

*Courtesy Janaki Thevar
Athinahappan*

(L-R) Gen. A.C.
Chatterji, Gen.
Mohammad Zaman
Kiani, Col. Habibur
Rahman and (seated)
Subhas Chandra
Bose, Burma, 1945

*Courtesy Dr Lakshmi
Swaminathan Sahgal*

The Ranis with a
portrait of Rani
Lakshmibai of
Jhansi, Singapore,
late 1943

*Courtesy Netaji
Research Bureau*

Supreme Commander of the
INA, Subhas Chandra Bose,
Burma, 1944-45
Courtesy Karuna Ganguli Mukherjee

The Mehta women
volunteers – Lilavati
Chhaganlal Mehta
and daughters
Neelam (left) and
Rama, Rangoon,
Burma, 1943
*Courtesy Rama
Mehta Khandwala*

Ranis train with weapons built for northern European men,
Singapore, 1944 *Courtesy Janaki Thevar Athinahappan*

(L-R) Ranis T. Suppiah, Papathi Thevar, Lakshmi Naidu and
Dhanam Lakshmi Suppiah, Singapore, 1944

Courtesy Ponnammah Esther Navarednam

Commander of
the RJR, Capt. Lakshmi
(Dr Lakshmi Swaminathan),
Burma 1944-45

*Courtesy Dr Lakshmi
Swaminathan Sahgal*

Bose inspects the Rani
Regiment with Khin Kyi,
wife of Burmese War
Minister Gen. Aung San,
Rangoon, Burma,
June 1944

*Courtesy Janaki
Thevar Athinahappan*

Rani Rama Mehta
prepares for jungle
combat, Burma, 1945

*Courtesy
Ponnammah Esther Navarednam*

Weapons training, 1944

Courtesy Janaki Thevar Athinahappan

Janaki Thevar, first female commissioned lieutenant of the Indian National Army, March 1944

Courtesy Janaki Thevar Athinahappan

Ponnammah Navarednam on guard duty, Rangoon, Burma, 1945

Courtesy Ponnammah Esther Navarednam

Early morning, Dr Lakshmi Swaminathan Sahgal opens her clinic, Kanpur, India, January 2008

Photo taken by author

Rani nurse Eva Jenny Murty Jothi, Tanjung Malim, Perak, Malaysia, March 2008

Photo taken by author

Friends since their RJR days, veterans Janaki Thevar Athinahappan, Akilandam Vairapillai and Anjalai Ponnaswamy, Kuala Lumpur, Malaysia, March 2008

Photo taken by author

Datuk Rasammah
Navarednam Bhupalan,
Petaling Jaya, Selangor,
Malaysia, March 2008
Photo taken by author

Lt. Janaki Bai, Rasah Jaya,
Seremban, Malaysia, March 2008
Photo taken by author

Dhanam Lakshmi Suppiah
Ratnam (left) and sister
Anjali Suppiah,
Georgetown, Penang,
Malaysia, January 2009
Photo taken by author

Rani Aruna Ganguli
Chattopadhya, Kolkata,
India, 2007
Courtesy Aruna Chattopadhya

the facility, and Major Salim, who would serve as weapons instructor and physical fitness trainer, was also in attendance.

Bose visited the Burma Rani unit for the first time on 3 January 1944, the day before the transfer of the Azad Hind headquarters from Singapore to Rangoon, and a date that remained indelible in the mind of Rani Manwati Panday.[4] Bose's speech calling for 'Total Mobilisation', including involvement also of women, resonated with Manwati's previous efforts to activate Indian women. She immediately presented Bose with a list of suggestions on how to engage women who were still observing purdah. He was impressed with her energy and ideas and asked her to join his team. The following day she went to work as the secretary of the Women's Department of the Azad Hind. Because she did not participate in the weapons training, Manwati, strictly speaking, did not become a Rani, but she worked as a member of the Regiment. As she pointed out to me, being an only child, she broke with an important Indian tradition when she left home and her old parents had nobody else to look after them.[5]

Anticipating victory for the upcoming Japanese–INA advance on Imphal, Bose sent for Captain Lakshmi in Singapore to come to Rangoon and prepare for the arrival of the Singapore Ranis as soon as they had finished their training. In Rangoon, a few days later, Captain Lakshmi took over responsibility for running the Rani camp and relieved Mrs Mehta and Mrs Chandran.[6] She immediately realized that the trainers working with the Ranis to ready them for combat were not up to their task. As the experienced INA soldiers already in Burma were about to proceed to the front lines, Captain Lakshmi requested from Bose that skilled INA instructors immediately be sent from Singapore to prepare the Burma Ranis.[7] In February, Major Salim, POW B961, was released from his duties as trainer for the Ranis but still 'visited the Amazons' Camp daily', as he told his British interrogators when he was captured towards the end of the Burma Campaign.[8] At the same time Rani Dolly Khastagir was discharged from the Regiment 'owing to [her] illicit connection with Captain Saleem'.[9] Captain Lakshmi would not have tolerated an instructor who fraternized with the Ranis.

The dormitory for the Regiment, a two-storey bungalow located on a large compound in Thingangyun, provided temporary and primitive quarters for this small group of the young Indian women. Some of the Ranis slept on the floor, while others spent nights in bamboo huts that were also used as classrooms in the afternoons.[10] There were no tables, so the girls sat on the ground and used benches as tables when eating.[11] Rani Rama Mehta, who came from an extremely wealthy and prominent Gujarati family in Burma, said that she and her elder sister spent the first month in camp crying every night for the food and comforts from home. The Ranis who had grown up around the city left camp to visit their friends and families, and at the beginning they had their food brought by their servants. Demanding military discipline, Bose quickly put an end to that luxury. The Mehta girls did accustom themselves to live like soldiers – Rama hurried to assure me that she thought that life in the Regiment was the greatest of times for her, because she was working for a higher ideal.[12]

The first camp at Thingangyun quickly proved inadequate and too small to house and train the anticipated contingent of Ranis arriving from Singapore. Once again Captain Lakshmi went off to search for bigger quarters. The Regiment next moved to Kamayut, a residential area on the outskirts of Rangoon. The new location with facilities large enough to house the expected eighty or ninety Ranis arriving from Singapore was in a dense bamboo forest, where the camp would not be as visible to Allied bombers.

Conditions at the camp were not quite spartan by contemporary standards, but they were certainly austere. There was no electricity; the Ranis relied on candles and kerosene lamps. Also privacy was non-existent. Mommata, Aruna and Maya shared a room on the second storey next to quarters of their officer, Pratima Sen. Everyone slept on the floor with just one blanket and a small pillow, except for Mataji, a kindly Tamil woman, whose legs were chronically painful because of her weight problem; she was given a cot to sleep on.[13]

Karuna Ganguli joined her two younger sisters at the Kamayut camp. One night soon after her arrival, air raid sirens went off. Running for the trenches in the dark, Karuna fell down an unguarded stair well. Aruna, Manwati and Reba Sen carried the bleeding and unconscious Karuna back up the stairs and placed her on a bed. The doctor was summoned, but did not arrive until the next morning. He ordered Karuna moved to the hospital, where she stayed for the next five months with a skull fracture.[14] During a heavy Allied bombing raid in September 1944, the buildings in the Kamayut camp were seriously damaged and the Ranis had to find new quarters once again. The INA 1st Brigade had vacated a huge mansion on Halpin Road in Rangoon, and in September 1944, the Regiment took over these more comfortable and more secure lodgings. The Ranis had to decamp immediately, each carrying all her gear, and move on foot into their new lodgings. The Halpin Road camp was guarded by an INA detachment under Lieutenant Sardara Singh, and no outsider or INA soldier below the rank of major was allowed inside the compound.[15]

During the spring of 1944, the major joint Japanese–INA offensive was being fought on the Indo-Burma frontier. The Ranis were eager to join the fighting, where they could put their six months of 'intensive infantry training' to use.[16] Bose had tried for months to arrange for the Ranis to leave Singapore for Rangoon so that they could be ready to join the first Indian soldiers crossing into India, but to his extreme frustration, transportation for the women for the 1,200-mile journey through the jungle was again delayed in mid-May.[17]

Finally, on the last day of May 1944, the first contingent of Rani of Jhansi soldiers comprising about 100 officers, sepoys and nurses, left the confines of the Singapore camp for Burma in excited anticipation of joining the INA men on the battlefields of Imphal and Kohima.[18] To assure their safe arrival in Burma, the women were accompanied by a platoon of male INA soldiers, two officers and several members of the Hikari Kikan, the Japanese administration.[19]

The departing group did not include all the women who had just finished basic training. The Ranis I interviewed did not know if any formal selection criteria were in place, but everyone I spoke with was satisfied with their assignment. All but three of these Ranis had been stationed in Burma, either because they were born and therefore enlisted there or they were deployed to Rangoon from Singapore. Eva Jenny, a devout Christian, was pleased to remain in Singapore to nurse the ill and wounded soldiers at Bidadari Hospital and fulfil her wish to learn more medical science. The Suppiah sisters who had joined partly to see more of the world would have liked to go to Burma, but were left behind because Dhanam had developed what was thought to be appendicitis.[20] Due to a strictly enforced RJR rule that sisters would never be separated, the Suppiah sisters remained in Singapore. While hospitalized, Dhanam became 'a one-woman Rani of Jhansi ward' at the Bidadari hospital. She recovered without surgery, but by that time the Burma-bound contingent had left.

The beginning of the trip from Singapore up along the Malay Peninsula to Thailand, with RJR members cramped in cattle trucks, was comparatively easy.[21] The next stage of the journey, however, through Thailand from Bangkok and on to Burma via the 'Death Railway' was a harrowing experience. The Regiment moved only by night, packed together in camouflaged freight cars because of the danger of Allied air attacks. At first light the train stopped and the Ranis took cover in the jungle for the day; there at least they could stretch their legs and wash in a stream.

The Death Railway was built by the Japanese from June 1942 to October 1943, using thousands of prisoners of war and the forced labour of Indian workers from Malaya. Over 100,000 of this enslaved workforce died as a direct result. Before the journey, most Ranis who mentioned the Death Railway in interviews were under the misapprehension that it had got its moniker because of the hazards of travel on it, and they were certainly afraid to cross the River Kwai.[22] En route, some Ranis noticed white men clearly in poor health labouring on the tracks, and they realized then the reason the railway had earned its sinister name.[23] Anjuli, Shanti and Rasammah understood that the emaciated British POWs they saw during their daylight stopovers along the tracks would not survive much longer. Rasammah was also reminded of the Japanese propensity for cruelty she had witnessed and feared at home in Ipoh, Malaya. Although she wanted the British to leave India, she was disturbed by the plight of these men and the viciousness of the Japanese soldiers guarding them.[24]

Despite the rigours, the women survived the journey without major difficulties. They had no problems – or any interaction at all – with the Japanese soldiers. When washing in a stream the Ranis took turns standing to shield each other from male eyes. Food on the trip was mostly dry rations and there was no meat or fish, but on a few occasions the monotony was broken by a 'feast' of *dal-bhat-tarkari*, rice and lentils with a bit of vegetable curry.[25] When the Rani contingent reached the first Burmese town, they switched back to a regular passenger train that carried them the rest of the way through Moulmein to Rangoon. To Bose's relief, the long-awaited Ranis arrived safely and settled in their camp in Kamayut on 21 June 1944.[26]

In Rangoon the smartly uniformed and physically fit Ranis caused quite a stir. Female soldiers were unheard of.[27] Since the Japanese army routinely provided their soldiers with 'comfort women,' Bose wanted to avoid any misunderstanding about the duties of the Ranis. He arranged immediately to have the Regiment demonstrate its military training. President Ba Maw of Burma and General Aung San of the Burma National Army watched together with officers of the Japanese army as the Ranis marched and exhibited their proficiency at weapons handling and especially bayonet charging.[28] Rasammah told me that the Ranis considered this exercise a huge success and rejoiced that 'Netaji's faith in the bold and unique step he had taken to establish an all-women's fighting force was clearly vindicated'.[29] The women took pride in the rumour that General Aung San was so impressed with the display of female bellicosity that he asked Bose for help in training Burmese women so that they could join Burma's armed forces.[30] The Ranis were in high spirits as they resumed their martial activities.

In April 1944 Captain Lakshmi was transferred permanently to the base hospital in Maymyo, and eighteen-year-old Lieutenant Janaki Thevar became commander of the Burma contingent of the Ranis. Havildar (sergeant) Aruna Ganguli described her commanding officer as a terror.[31] Janaki, the strict disciplinarian, noticed every detail in the dress and behaviour of her subordinate officers and sepoys and never failed to object to a pair of dusty shoes, an imperfectly pressed uniform or a cap worn at the wrong angle. Several Ranis commented that Janaki's not-so-secret weapon was her extremely loud voice. Many years later, Rama proudly claimed to me that hers had been the second best voice in the Regiment, almost as good as Janaki's.[32] Privately the Ranis did admire Lieutenant Janaki to some degree, but they feared her scathing criticism. They also made fun of her and the joke among them was that she had been born with an extra set of eyes.[33]

Janaki confirmed to me that as camp commander she had tolerated no breach of the rules. One incident in particular demonstrated that she showed no favouritism. Aruna together with Janaki's four-year-elder half-sister Papathy had slipped out of camp in uniform to go to town on a borrowed bicycle, where they had a minor accident and were sent back to the compound. As punishment they were ordered to run laps around the parade ground equipped with full battle gear, heavy boots, rifle and full backpack, in the sultry Rangoon heat. As extra embarrassment Janaki had arranged for all the other Ranis and the male instructors to watch. When the two girls were staggering in exhaustion, Lieutenant Janaki finally yelled 'Stop', and they fell to the ground.[34]

Ponnammah noticed that Janaki relied on the intelligence and social skills of her sister Rasammah, especially with the Tamil girls, 'because Janaki only knew to make a noise'.[35] Ponnammah also found it difficult to take orders from Janaki Thevar. As she stressed in our interview, 'I am very sorry to say it, but now I am over eighty years old, I will admit it. We used to fight in the camp. I said to [Janaki] one day, "You are telling me I can't do this and I can't do that. Who are you to tell me that? I will throw you down the stairs."' It never came to fisticuffs, but Ponnammah, like some of the other Ranis, resented Janaki's loud piercing voice and what they thought was unnecessarily harsh discipline.[36]

At Halpin Road the officers had a separate mess and dining room, but Ponnammah, commander of the second platoon, unlike the other 'educated girls' and officers, found friends among the Ranis from the plantations. 'I used to move with the sepoys. I would eat with them. I talked with them in broken Tamil. I used to do well with the sepoys.'[37]

As the Ranis anticipated being sent to the front to fight for their country, their daily schedule followed the same training programme as in Singapore: dawn flag raising, PT, marches, weapons training and afternoon lectures. Lieutenant Karam Chand and five or six other INA soldiers trained the

RJR women in rifle, pistol, Tommy gun (Thompson sub-machinegun) and Bren gun (Bren light machine gun). Their visits to the firing range where they went for practice every two weeks paid off. According to Aruna, most of the Ranis hit the bulls-eye 'any number of times'.[38] Shanti mentioned that 'time-bombs planting, hand-bombs throwing, and long route-marches' were also part of the regimen.[39] INA soldiers, when interviewed by the British after capture, reported having seen the women 'parading with breeches, shirts, and short-pattern rifles' through the streets of Rangoon.[40] Once a week they went out on route matches, carrying rifles and pistols and wearing their Japanese-style peaked caps.[41] Demonstrating his strong commitment to the RJR, Bose made many visits to the Rani camp to make sure uniforms were in order and that training was progressing. He knew all the Ranis in Burma by name and had a kind word for each.[42]

The Ranis who had chosen to become nurses continued their training in Burma. After flag hoisting and PT, which they participated in alongside the other Ranis, the trainee nurses travelled by bus to the Mayagon hospital in Mingaladon, the northernmost part of Rangoon, for their medical education and work. Ponnammah originally thought that nursing would be the best way for her to contribute, but in Burma she realized that daily life in any hospital would always be the same and she asked to switch to the fighting group.[43] Several INA soldiers including R693 Chajju Ram noticed the Ranis as they went through town to the hospital for 'training in nursing duties'.[44] To the disappointment of the British interrogator who wanted to learn as much as possible about the Regiment of women, Chajju Ram 'did not ask where those women were to be employed after such training and what their total strength was'.[45] Another report from January 1945 states that a dozen or so of the women performed nursing duties at the base hospital at Mayagon.[46]

Sundays were different. In Singapore the Ranis would catch a matinee movie, go out for ice cream or relax on the beach. In Rangoon the local Ranis were allowed to go home after morning flag hoisting provided they returned on time for flag lowering.[47] Transport was provided so that each girl could travel safely.[48] When Bose visited the camp in Burma and discovered the leisurely life the Ranis enjoyed while in training, he expressed strong disapproval of these Sunday indulgences. He believed they led to slack discipline. However, he was either unable or unwilling to enforce stricter rules, and the Ranis continued to enjoy their weekly home-cooked Sunday dinners.[49]

While quartered at the Halpin Road camp, the Ranis were allowed to ride the fifteen or twenty horses stabled there for their trips into town, but having two 'pips' on her shoulders, 'Camp Commandant Lieutenant Janaki Thevar' was the only Rani allowed to leave camp whenever she liked.[50] Janaki was granted the use of a beautiful grey horse for her morning commute from Halpin Road to the hospital to visit with the wounded soldiers, have a cup of tea with the doctors and nurses. The Rani nurses who had been on night duty at the hospital returned to camp in army vehicles. For the young commandant the way back to Halpin Road was pure enjoyment: 'I was thrilled. Seated on horseback I used to feel as though I was the real Jhansi Ki Rani and was very proud of myself,' and she was in camp by 9 a.m. for company inspection. One day Bose was driving by and stopped to give her pointers. He showed her how to make the horse walk figure eights, a trick that did not speed her on her way but did enhance her prestige among the troops. Janaki was proud of the personal attention from her idol 'Netaji', and recounted the episode to me with tears in her eyes these many years later.[51]

Bose was fond of music and dramatics and encouraged the Ranis to put on variety shows for the whole INA camp, and occasionally also for the general public in Rangoon halls. Rani Maya Ganguli was particularly surprised and impressed when 'Netaji, the Supreme Commander of this Army' took charge of a show to be performed at the Rangoon City Hall.[52] The entire programme was Bose's idea and he was so intent on success that he came to the RJR camp as often as twice a day to see rehearsals. He directed every skit and sang along with the girls.[53] For Bose's favourite segment of the show, he picked two exceptionally beautiful girls, Aruna and Maya Ganguli, to lead the Ranis on to the stage in full uniform with rifles, singing 'Chalo Delhi, Chalo Delhi'. The two sisters were flattered at the attention and did their utmost to please Bose, but even at age fifteen Maya did find it surprising that with all his other responsibilities Bose devoted that much time, effort and concern to perfecting the performance.[54]

On the big night, he arrived at the hall long before the audience; the girls were inspired and the show was a great success. Bose was overjoyed and the next morning he sent baskets of sweets and presents to each of the performers.[55] Bose and the young Ranis enjoyed many evenings together with song, plays and group discussions, and after the entertainment he would offer them tea or dinner. Bose also often invited them to his bungalow to watch documentary movies together with the INA officers. When requested, he even sang German songs for them and explained the text. Aruna marvelled, '...he was just like a father.'[56]

On 18 March 1944, as Japanese troops and INA soldiers crossed the Indian frontier, Bose made elaborate plans for the infrastructure of independent India: he reshuffled his administration, added new ministers to set up a civil administration for India, created the National Bank of Azad Hind, issued Azad Hind postage stamps for use in the liberated areas and even printed sample currency notes.[57] On 7 April, with the launch of the campaign on Imphal and Kohima apparently off to a good start, Bose moved his headquarters from Rangoon to Maymyo, close to Japanese army headquarters in Burma, and the Ranis were told that as the INA was now marching on to Indian soil, the Burma RJR contingent needed to advance to Maymyo.[58]

Captain Lakshmi was in Singapore to supervise the passing out parade of the first RJR officers in March. In her absence, Manwati Panday led a group of about twenty Ranis on the 400-mile trip northward from Rangoon to Maymyo.[59] Aruna and Maya Ganguli wanted to be part of the first Rani group at the front lines, but their mother refused to let them go unless they were together with Captain Lakshmi who had promised to protect them as her own daughters.

As soon as Captain Lakshmi was back in Rangoon, she gathered a small group of Ranis and they also set off towards Maymyo 'so as to be as far forward as possible in the event of a successful invasion of India and to be in a position to call forward quickly the rest of her Regiment'.[60] In Captain Lakshmi's cohort were the two Ganguli sisters, Mommata Gupta, three other Ranis, a few INA officers including parade instructor

Hari Singh, drivers and other assistants. Maya remembered with pleasure travelling in comfort and style in a convoy of a station wagon, two sedans and a truck.[61]

The Ranis set off in the late afternoon because it was safer to travel at night, and so many years later Aruna still remembered 'the dead eyes' of her youngest sister Kamal, who watched her two elder sisters drive off to the front.[62] Along the way the little caravan was welcomed and celebrated by Indians who offered them lavish hospitality and praised their willingness to sacrifice themselves for the liberation of India.

One Muslim Indian family invited the group to stay at their house; after a night riding in the open truck, everyone appreciated a bath and a bed with clean sheets. The local girls had heard about the Regiment, but had not believed that girls would actually engage in combat and they flocked to meet the Ranis.[63] The group of Ranis went through Meiktila in Mandalay Division, and continued into the mountains arriving in Maymyo on 19 April 1944.[64] At an altitude of 3,500 feet, the Ranis needed warm vests which were provided, and they immediately settled in with their RJR comrades who had arrived a month earlier with Manwati Panday.

Maymyo was an abandoned city, with overgrown gardens and crumbling houses. As young children Maya and Aruna had come to visit their uncle and their cousins who had lived in Maymyo, but like most Indians they had fled. Only a few petty shopkeepers were still selling fruit, vegetables and trinkets.[65] The city was surrounded by tall mountains, which made it impossible to hear the attacking Allied fighter planes until they were immediately overhead. Even though they were 300 miles from ground combat at Imphal and Kohima, the Ranis realized that they had arrived in the war zone. Nightly air raids often forced them to flee their barracks and hide in trenches or air raid shelters.

On 30 April Bose organized a variety show in honour of INA troops leaving Maymyo for the front. These INA soldiers marched off to war clad just in their khaki shorts and bush shirts, with one thin cotton blanket to keep them warm at altitudes of over 6,000 feet, much higher than Maymyo.[66] This lack of essential equipment for a successful campaign had been the INA deficiency from the beginning. The Japanese did not supply even a minimum of needed ordnance, rations and medicine as was agreed in the contract between Bose and Tojo.[67] The evening immediately following the farewell dinner for the soldiers, Allied bombers hit the school building where the Ranis were temporarily lodged.[68] Rani Lily was knocked unconscious by a collapsing beam inside a trench. When the bombing stopped, Aruna helped to carry Lily out of the trench, and then she looked for her sister. Maya was not to be found. A trench next to the kitchen had also collapsed when the kitchen took a bomb, and Aruna feared that Maya might be lying injured beneath the buckled wall. With the help of INA jawans Aruna and other Ranis dug away the debris and Maya was located, unhurt. Eventually, every Rani emerged safely and no one was seriously injured, but all RJR possessions and equipment except the uniforms on their backs were lost.[69]

While the Ranis searched for what could be salvaged from the rubble, Bose arrived. The Ranis all saluted and stood at attention. Bose then ordered them to do a quick march down a paved path to see if they were hurt. Every Rani except for Lily double-marched to the end of the path, even the bruised Maya. That night they received new blankets, and the next morning Chatterji brought everything they required: blouses, lungis, underwear, slippers, hair ribbons, toiletries, mess tins, plates, bowls, cutlery and more.[70] Unfortunately, the replacement firearms issued after the bombing were not the popular 303s, but the less reliable Dutch rifles.

Because Maymyo was a ghost town with many uninhabited houses intact, it did not take long to relocate the Ranis to a different site, a wooded lot with a two-storey bungalow that would provide better cover from air attack. On the way to their new camp their truck was hit. The well-drilled Ranis dropped into a ditch and kept their heads down for several minutes until the two Allied fighter planes ended their assault and flew off. Once again, every Rani escaped unscathed. Bose, who had watched the strike from a distance, was anxiously waiting for them at the gate to the new camp. He was obviously relieved to see their 'happy bright faces'.[71]

After this incident, the rules were changed. The bungalow of the new RJR quarters was surrounded by a ditch 3 feet deep and 2 feet wide; for extra safety additional ditches were dug around each tree in the garden.

On the ground floor, a large room with a cement floor was blocked out
to accommodate a dining room, a sitting area, an office and a sickroom.
The bedrooms were upstairs, and wooden verandas surrounded the house.
Every Rani was instructed to keep her kitbag packed and ready so that
when the air raid siren sounded, she would grab her bag and rifle before
heading for shelter.[72]

Gian Kaur, a thirty-year-old Rani nurse, did not like being forced to
spend her afternoons undergoing exhausting military training with the
fighting group, including bayonet drills. She knew that Bose concentrated
his attention on the sixteen or seventeen Ranis who made up the fighting
group, objecting when any of them wanted a transfer to the nursing unit.
Kaur believed that as a result of Bose's strong focus on the Ranis as a fighting
force, the rest of the INA at Maymyo began to take them seriously. When
held as a POW, number L3968, she explained to the British Intelligence
officers that finally the Ranis had felt 'as a unit which would be thrown
into the battle after entry had been affected into the more populated areas
of India'.[73]

Twelve new recruits, one Indian nurse and several Gurkha girls,
joined the Regiment in Maymyo, and the training of the fighting group
intensified.[74] The Ranis were put through all-day tactical battle exercises,
and their trainer, Major Rahturi, led them out on night forays. Gian Kaur
observed, 'They all reveled in it.'[75] Rahmat Bibi from the IIL recruiting
office was in Mandalay when she saw the fighting group, 'dressed exactly
like other INA soldiers'. They had just marched from Maymyo to Mandalay,
about 40 miles, carrying full equipment, and, to the Burmese woman,
they 'seemed quite happy in spite of what especially to Indian girls must
have been an extraordinary novel existence'.[76] In fact, the Ranis, together
with Captain Lakshmi, actually did march from Maymyo to Mandalay, but
they covered the distance in two stages.[77]

Aruna tells the story of when Captain Lakshmi arranged a Sunday
outing for five Ranis from the fighting group. One Rani, Parul Bhattacharya,
was recruited in Maymyo, but her family had moved away to Chiun, a
sleepy hill village three miles away. The group had planned an afternoon
visit to the Bhattacharya family, but the day began dark and gloomy, and

after breakfast the rain came in so fierce that Captain Lakshmi hesitated to set out. Seeing the girls' disappointment, she decided to proceed despite the inclement weather. As the group was leaving camp at noon, a guard asked where they were going in that weather. 'Just out for a stroll. It won't be long,' Captain Lakshmi said. A little farther along they met Colonel Tehl Singh on a motorcycle; he also questioned Captain Lakshmi about their plans. Completely drenched, the group carried on. The sentry at Bose's gate called, 'Children! Where are you going like this? You will fall ill.' Captain Lakshmi waved to him, and the group continued up the hill into the forest. Two hours later they reached the hut where Parul's family lived. The wet Ranis quickly washed off the red mud and settled down for tea and omelettes; then it was nearly sunset and time to leave and return to camp.

The rain had stopped but the jungle was dark and they quickly lost their way. Stumbling over tree stumps, they walked and walked, realizing several times that they had just walked a big circle. As they were about to give up and wait for morning to come, they saw a faint light. It turned out to be a group of villagers at a humble small tea shop. The village headman Yakub Achchha introduced himself and offered to guide the way with his flashlight, warning that the hillside was treacherous in the rain. Just as he said that, he lost his footing in the mud and the girls had a hard time refraining from laughter. As they progressed, however, all the girls slipped again and again. Late in the night, Aruna put her ear to the ground and heard approaching footsteps.

It turned out that the RJR camp, the hospital, guard, and the sentries had mobilized several search parties to find them. The commander in charge of the search told them that the doctors at the hospital were worried that they would catch pneumonia and had six beds ready for them. Manwati sat waiting with candles and in no time had arranged hot baths for them all. They received fresh warm clothes and hot coffee. As it turned out, in her haste to make everybody comfortable, Manwati had put salt in the coffee instead of sugar. The Ranis laughed till they cried and fell asleep still chuckling. Their legs felt heavy and their leg muscles hurt for a few days, but otherwise there were no negative repercussions from their adventure in the jungle.[78] Aruna Ganguli, who told the amusing story, did not mention if the Ranis or their instructors concluded that more rigorous training of the RJR was necessary for combat readiness after their afternoon stroll required emergency rescue.

During the two years of spending every hour together in close quarters, the Ranis learned the details of each other's lives. Many Ranis told corroborating stories about the difficult lives of some of the other RJR members. Labanya Ganguli's life had never been easy. Her mother died when she was two and her father sent her from Calcutta to Singapore to be raised by her older sister. In 1942, when Labanya was thirteen, her sister passed away, leaving no one to take care of her. A year later when she heard Bose speak in Singapore, she immediately decided to join the INA and become a Rani nurse.[79] When I asked if she was also trained as a soldier, she answered indignantly, 'Of course, I was trained – I was a soldier.'[80]

In Singapore Labanya met P.N. Chatterji who served in the Azad Hind Dal, the administration of the Government of Free India. They married and both were deployed to Burma, where she worked at the INA hospital in Maymyo and Chatterji's team was sent out by Bose to set up a civil infrastructure for India to be ready for the bureaucratic demands of independence. In May 1944, six months after their wedding, Labanya's husband drowned when two INA troop transport boats collided on the monsoon-swollen Chindwin river. Hearing the news Labanya tried to commit suicide. Manwati discovered Labanya. Bose was concerned, called on her and attempted to console her, but Janaki Bai, Labanya's platoon commander, chose a different approach and addressed the crisis by scolding instead of coddling her. Captain Lakshmi watched her closely for a few days, and Maya arranged to work in a room next to Labanya so she was never left alone.[81] This RJR teamwork lasted until the young widow was again able to concentrate on her work as a nurse.[82]

After the war, Labanya went to medical school, became a doctor and never married again.[83] It was difficult to persuade Labanya to talk; she was a bit cantankerous and somewhat hard of hearing. She complained that she was on death's doors, but actually looked rather well. At the appointed hour for the interview, she was returning from a walk with her brother with whom she lived in a nice part of Kolkata. She did not mention the tragedy of her husband's death or her suicide attempt; rather like almost all the other Ranis, she repeated several times that those two years in the INA were the best years of her life. She was happy being taken care of by Bose and being in the company of her friends in the RJR.

In August 1944 Bose was finally becoming aware of the full extent of the disaster that his 1st Division had suffered with the failure of the Imphal campaign. He had been spared or had ignored the reports from Chatterji about promised deliveries of materiel that was not being delivered to the INA.[84] Many soldiers had died of disease and starvation, and survivors in terrible physical shape flooded the medical facilities at Mandalay, Meiktila, Toungou and the INA hospital in Maymyo where the Ranis were ready to help.[85] Of the 2,500 INA soldiers who returned from the failed Imphal campaign, 2,000 men urgently required medical care.[86] The Ranis worked round the clock as nurses at the base hospital at Maymyo, treating the soldiers straggling in from the Imphal campaign for 'septic gun shot [sic] wounds, dysentery and malaria'.[87]

Because extra help was urgently needed, all Ranis over the age of fourteen were required to take a three-week course in basic nursing.[88] Realizing the magnitude of the task of caring for the returning soldiers, several of the Ranis from the fighting group volunteered to serve as nurses until trained nurses arrived from Rangoon. Aruna was assigned duty in the operating theatre. Even with thirty-eight nurses, some of whom were locally recruited women with no training, the job was overwhelming. Aruna's description gives an impression of the horrors:

> Most of the time we were in trenches. Too many wounded soldiers were coming from the front line. Local wounded were also many. All doctors, nurses and social workers worked day and night. Some wounded were hurt in the chest some in the back. The splinters came out from the back tearing the back making big holes through the chest and some splinters came out from the chest entering through the back – these were mostly gone cases. Some were groaning loudly and some were senseless. Everywhere there was blood. All the wards and verandas were all full.[89]

In October 1944, Shah Nawaz Khan was visiting the Maymyo hospital
with Bose when he noticed Bela Dutt, a sixteen-year-old Rani, caring for
eighty-five men with acute dysentery. Bela attended to all their needs, and
the men praised their young nurse, telling Bose that even their mothers
or sisters could not have looked after them better.[90] The Ranis served in
twelve-hour shifts, day and night, as they saw the horrible effects of war.

After his trip to north Burma in September to personally assess the
situation, Bose returned to Mandalay and called a meeting of senior officers
and members of the cabinet for an update on the war. Captain Lakshmi was
surprised that as he laid forth in detail all the dismal news about Germany's
failed offensive in Russia and the Japanese losses, Bose still insisted that the
INA must press on. He wanted to spread 'the truth about the INA and the
Azad Hind' fight to reach India. He was determined to remove the stigma
of the INA being known only as Japan's puppet army. As Bose said, when
the truth of the INA's independence from the Japanese became known, he
was convinced that the INA would be welcomed in India as a revolutionary
army.[91] The soldiers were told not to commit suicide if captured, because
courts martial would offer more opportunities to tell the truth about the
INA. After the meeting, Bose asked Captain Lakshmi to stay back and then
informed her that he was sending the Rani fighting section back to Rangoon.
She and the nursing section, however, should remain in Maymyo.

To the Ranis the recall came as a shock. 'Netaji week', the celebration
of Bose's first year as Supreme Commander was carried out with 'much
pomp and grandeur, sports, plays, music, conferences, variety shows,
eateries' in mid-July.[92] That happy event was followed by an onslaught of
wounded soldiers and hard work for the RJR, and it therefore seemed
incomprehensible when suddenly Captain Lakshmi told the fighting group
to pack. First the Ranis had experienced joyful extravagances, then the
horrors of war and now abruptly they were being redeployed away from
the battle without an explanation. They wept all night, and in the morning
Captain Lakshmi, also in tears, embraced the girls and told them 'to be
friendly with the Singapore girls' who had arrived in the Kamayut camp
in their absence.[93]

This time on the reverse journey the Ranis, truck was not part of a large convoy. They left for Mandalay after dusk, accompanied by Colonel M.Z. Kiani and other high-ranking INA officers. In the moonlight the driver took many wrong turns and the girls were frightened, but eventually they reached Mandalay and camped for three days. Bose was also there and invited the girls over for dinner. During the meal, an Allied aircraft buzzed his house and when it sounded as if the plane crashed, the Ranis went to investigate. They found nothing, but Bose was proud that they had dared venture outside to look. Aruna thought, 'Netaji was just like our mother. Netaji knew when we needed anything and what. [At] the table Netaji and we had long talks on many different topics. We came and sat in the drawing room after we finished our tea.'[94] The Allied continually bombed traffic going to Rangoon, but the Ranis arrived safely at the Halpin Road camp.

Much had changed since the group left for Maymyo five months earlier. The Regiment had moved to a large building and the contingent from Singapore had arrived. As company commander, Janaki Thevar came out to receive the returning Ranis. In the Halpin Road camp, formal protocol did not allow free mingling of officers and sepoys, a distinctly different experience for the Ranis from Maymyo when all together they had waved goodbye to Bose.[95] Here the officers had their own individual bedrooms and an officers' dining room with a separate cook. Several Ranis thought that reversal of equality a negative, and Ponnammah continued to eat with her platoon.[96]

The RJR contingent in Rangoon was divided into three platoons, which again was split into three sections with ten soldiers in each section. The three platoon commanders were Aruna Ganguli, Ponnammah Navarednam and Janaki Bai, and fortunately, I was able to interview all platoon commanders for this study. The Maymyo girls not only became friendly with the Ranis from Singapore, as they had promised Captain Lakshmi; they began to learn to speak Tamil.

In anticipation of his forty-eighth birthday in January 1945, Bose appealed to Indian civilians in Burma for a special birthday present. He wanted volunteers to sign up for a suicide squad, the Janbaz, modelled on the Japanese Kamikaze Special Attack Corps.[97] As described to British Intelligence by an INA soldier, the work of this squad 'would be to infiltrate into British positions in disguise and to attack senior Allied officers at opportune moments; to carry mines on the body, and to jump in front of oncoming tanks'.[98] POW B1021 Captain Asiruddin D. Jehangir, called 'Prince Jehangir', when interrogated, revealed to British Military Intelligence that he had collected names of seventy-one volunteers signing up for suicide missions. Another INA informant, identified as POW B985, asserted that there were forty names on the list.[99] According to these two surrendered INA soldiers, among the volunteers 'most of them Tamil recruits, [nineteen] girls from the Rani of Jhansi Regiment signed a pledge with their blood offered to sacrifice their lives in the cause of India's freedom'.[100]

As discussed previously, several Ranis reported to me that they did indeed sign their names in blood, but that was a petition asking Bose to allow them to go to the front to fight, not for any other suicide mission. Rasammah's experience was different and is not easily explained. Her application to volunteer for the Janbaz was rejected. Deeply disappointed, she asked Bose why having asked for their blood, he would deprive her of the honour of sacrificing her life for India's freedom. He answered, 'What would I say to your mother, if you never came home?'[101]

Dhanam Suppiah was certain that if there had been a suicide unit in Singapore, she would have known about it, but she had never heard a word.[102] On the other hand, Meenachi Perumal, a woman about whom much more will follow, alleged to Joyce Lebra in 2008 that she was proud to be 'one of five Ranis' who were asked by Bose to join 'the Janbaz "suicide unit"'.[103] Prominent at Rani gatherings and appearing on YouTube as a Rani spokesperson, Meenachi Perumal is controversial within the society of Rani veterans.[104] All efforts over a long time to locate her for this study were unsuccessful. Asked for help in locating Meenachi, Janaki Thevar and other Ranis were dismissive: 'Meenachi was not a Rani. She just says she was a Rani to get the freedom fighter pension.'[105]

On 23 January 1945, Bose's forty-eighth birthday was celebrated in high style. In Rangoon his weight was matched in gold contributed by supporters of the revolution; a short play to celebrate his life was performed; the Ranis exhibited his favourite marching routines, and 'a blood sealing' ceremony for the Janbaz, the suicide volunteers, was held by the INA. Each Rani was given Rs 48, an entire month's wages for a havildar. Janaki Bai spent her bonus on a small cake of soap.[106] Captain Asiruddin Jehangir gave Bose a list with the names of the Janbaz volunteers, and they walked by him. An officer standing next to Bose pricked the right thumb of each INA soldier and took a thumbprint on paper, the signature for membership of the suicide squad. Despite all these theatrics, the Ranis agreed that no one was ever asked to perform a suicide mission.[107] Jehangir told his interrogators the same.

The Ranis kept insisting that Bose let them go to the front. The young women were bored with their training routines and clamoured for permission to fight. They sent many appeals to Bose begging to be permitted to do what they had been trained to do, win freedom for India. The only extant document that mentions, however, any consideration to deploy the Ranis to fight is found in an unpublished summary in Japanese of General Kawabe Masakazu's handwritten diary, *Boeicho Senshishitsu*.[108] On 22 June 1944, Bose heard directly from General Kawabe Masakazu, newly returned from the battlefront, that the situation looked desperate. According to Kawabe's diary, Bose responded by 'ask[ing] that the Rani of Jhansi Regiment be sent to the front immediately'.[109]

Bose's alleged urgent call for the Ranis' deployment is mentioned only in Kawabe's diary, and without any other information it is impossible to know what was on Bose's mind with regard to the Ranis at this time of crisis. The main contingent of Ranis had just arrived in Rangoon from Singapore, and experience had shown that it would take weeks to reach Maymyo from Rangoon, which was still hundreds of miles and many days of strenuous trekking across 6,000-ft-tall mountains away from the border. It is also not likely that Bose would have considered the Rani fighting unit that was stationed in Maymyo suitable for deployment to the front. It was just twenty women strong, not nearly enough for the impact Bose wanted the Regiment to make. In any case, the women of the Rani of Jhansi Regiment never made it to the front lines, never went into battle as an infantry unit, never fired a weapon against the enemy and never fulfilled their dream of fighting for their country.

THIRTEEN

RJR RETREATS FROM RANGOON

WHILE THE RANIS IMPATIENTLY anticipated their deployment to the front lines, Allied forces emerged victorious in the protracted Battle of Imphal, which began in March 1944 in the region around Imphal, capital of the Indian state of Manipur. During their long retreat south, the exhausted INA troops endured serial military disasters, and a year later, in March 1945, Bose had no other option than to seek to evacuate the wounded soldiers remaining in the path of the British sweep.

Bose's other chief concern was the safety of the 150 Ranis camped in Rangoon. He felt morally responsible to their parents for their safe return.[1] INA captive B956 testified that '[Bose] used to say that he would be very happy if those girls died fighting in the cause of the country, but he would have no face to show if anything else happened to them.'[2] In Bose's value system, sending the Ranis into a battle that might result in their deaths and make them martyrs for Indian freedom was a worthy moral choice and the Ranis shared that point of view. Bose was concerned that it would be difficult to persuade these committed women to leave Burma while other INA soldiers remained on the front lines. He was right. Forcefully, the Ranis voiced their plea to stay to the end; they did not want to be sent home. They had come to free India or die fighting for that goal.[3] They had trained hard for two years and that would all have been a waste.[4] Bose insisted that they obey military orders.

Rasammah was deeply moved by an anguished and angry speech that Bose gave on 13 March 1945, when nothing was going well for the Azad Hind Fauj. In 'his most impassioned speech' to his army, Bose denounced INA officers who had deserted and become informants to the British.[5] He ordered a purge of cowardly and treacherous elements in the army and commanded soldiers of all ranks to shoot any other soldier 'if he acts in a treacherous manner'.[6]

After a series of heavy Japanese losses at Pyawbwe near Mandalay in mid-April 1945, General Kiani conveyed to Bose that Japan had given up the defence of Burma.[7] General Slim, head of the Allied forces, described what followed as a race with elements of comedy as the Japanese army and the INA men, deprived of supplies and without communication to know the location of the enemy, attempted to outrun the Allied soldiers through the jungle in an effort to reach Rangoon before the onset of the monsoon.[8]

When the withdrawal orders were issued by the Japanese to withdraw from Burma despite Bose's 'overriding ambition to get the army into India at all cost', the decision was welcomed by General Mohammad Zaman Kiani of the INA.[9] He had been caught in heavy British shelling of the divisional headquarters that immediately followed the defection of Major B.J.S. Garewal, the second-in-command of the Guerrilla Regiment. Garewal was the officer in possession of INA and Japanese battle plans that included maps and the positions of various INA and Japanese headquarters.[10]

When the five staff officers, four of them majors, failed to return to the 2nd INA Division at Popaywa, their commanding officer, Colonel Prem Sahgal, wrote in his diary, 'I am certain they have gone over to the enemy – the treacherous swine.'[11] Once on the other side, these defectors signed with their own names a new series of pamphlets that Allied pilots dropped on their former INA comrades who upon Bose's orders still defended their posts in Burma. Until then the INA men had expected to be shot by the British if they tried to defect. Now they saw proof that was not the case, and hundreds more surrendered to save their lives.[12]

The magnitude and effects of this continuing treason was emotionally unbearable to Bose, who threatened suicide should it happen again and remained in his room for four days.[13] In this condition, he was unable to face the first Japanese ambassador to the provisional government who came to present his credential to the head of state. When it turned out that Ambassador Hachiya Teruo had not brought his formal credentials, Bose used that as a less embarrassing pretext to send away the Emperor's envoy.[14]

After Bose had regained his equilibrium, he re-emerged and was increasingly determined not to risk the Ranis' capture by the rapidly advancing British troops. At first, half of the contingent, fifty-one Ranis, whose homes were not in Burma, was dispatched onwards to Bangkok.[15] INA soldier, Lieutenant Khushal Singh Rawat had been posted in Rangoon as chief weapons instructor to the RJR, and as he reported to the British interrogators after he was captured, in his last assignment Bose ordered him to accompany 'the Amazons out of Burma to Thailand'.[16]

Rasammah, one of these 'Amazon' women, penned a detailed account of the trip.[17] The Ranis were ordered to pack their gear and board a freight train leaving Rangoon for Bangkok on 29 March 1945.[18] Platoon officers Ponnammah and Janaki Bai led the sad and disappointed group of bewildered young women. Just nine months earlier they had travelled the same route via the Death Railway, filled with enthusiasm for the opportunity to fight for India's liberation. Rasammah expressed the feelings of the entire regiment: 'All of us felt deeply that we had been denied the opportunity to prove our mettle on the front line.'[19] The song and laughter that had characterized the outward journey was missing, but the women still hoped that they would be given another chance to engage the enemy.

Because of the danger of air attack, all travel was done during the night. At dawn the train would stop and the Ranis would try to find shelter in the villages and huts abandoned by Burmese peasants. The villagers had devised a system by which they alerted each other by drums of the approach of Japanese or INA soldiers. At the alarm the locals gathered their few supplies and hid in the jungle until the soldiers had moved on. The Ranis' first night on the run was spent in comfortable huts at Sittang, and they were looking forward to remaining there for another night. However, the women were not to enjoy that shelter, because at nine in the evening,

Lieutenant Rawat, their escort, suddenly ordered the group to clear out of the village because of a possible Burmese guerrilla attack.[20]

Burma's declaration of war on Japan on 27 March 1945, and Burmese General Aung San's negotiations to change alliances and instead support the British and American forces made it very dangerous to travel south through Burma on Japanese trucks in the company of Japanese soldiers. Burma National Army (BNA) guerrillas dressed like the locals and attacked all non-Burmese travellers.

The Ranis sought refuge in a temple, each woman clutching her rifle all night. The RJR soldiers realized that they were on a treacherous journey when with gunfire rattling nearby, they were next transferred to a bungalow held by the Japanese. Here they stayed for several days and the Ranis' nerves were frayed. During the day Allied aircraft dropped bombs, and at night they feared attack by the Burmese guerrillas and the Burma National Army who had turned against both the INA and the Japanese.

At nightfall on 4 April, after resting at the Sittang river, the group was ordered into one railway carriage for the onward escape towards Bangkok.[21] It was dark and the train was moving slowly through a paddy field with the Ranis sitting on the carriage floor on their packs when the carriage was fired upon. Janaki Bai stressed to me, 'Suddenly, the bullets were whizzing, whizzing, whizzing past. I could feel the shooting flying over my head, I could not sit up.'[22]

'It was the first time we were under enemy fire,' said Rasammah, 'but we had been trained, we knew to throw ourselves on the floor and stay down although we could hear that someone had got hit.'[23] Ponnammah felt overwhelmed by the smell of blood and by a voice moaning nearby in the dark, but they did not turn on their torches and could do nothing to help the wounded. All Ranis stayed quiet as the train accelerated in order to get out of the range of fire.

Janaki Bai and Ponnammah sitting together, ducked low. Years later Janaki Bai recounted to me, 'Because "Pono" [Ponnammah], when she was nervous, she would both laugh and cry, I remember putting my hand over her mouth and putting her head down in the dust while they were shooting overhead.'[24] As soon as the firing had stopped, the women turned on their torches. Sitting right next to Janaki Bai and Ponnammah were two friends, Josephine and Stella. Janaki Bai still remembered the gruesome scene in detail: 'Josephine's brains had been blown out, but she died very quietly. It was a horrible sight. Next to her lay Stella Thomas, a Christian Rani and a large girl; she had been shot in the chest or the arm and was bleeding profusely.'[25] Fortunately, nobody else was hit. Several of the Ranis were trained nurses, but they had no means to help Stella and stop the massive loss of blood. Ponnammah remembered, 'She would not die. She was in great pain, but would not die. She was not married. All we could do was pray.'[26]

At dawn on 5 April the train stopped at Chambpoori. The Ranis carefully carried Stella into an abandoned hut. Josephine was also brought into another hut where the Ranis cleaned her up and changed her clothes. In the morning light, a group of Ranis was detailed to bury Josephine in the jungle. The women also saw that the train carriage was blood-spattered, and cleaned it thoroughly. Stella was still alive and cried, unable to endure the pain. A Japanese doctor from the army camp at Chambpoori was called for, but as the group of Ranis was returning to the hut after burying Josephine, someone came running to say that Stella had also died. The two fallen Ranis were buried in the jungle, side by side. Stella and Josephine were both Christian, and Lieutenant Janaki Bai was relieved that they could be given a dignified burial according to their religion without endangering the location of the whole group as might have happened by rising smoke from a Hindu funeral pyre.[27] Male cooks travelling with the Ranis dug the two graves, and the women gathered wild flowers to decorate the simple burials.

It was a traumatic RJR episode which was mentioned by almost every Rani I interviewed, even by those who had remained in Singapore. The girls were devastated at having to bury two of their comrades in the jungle in the middle of nowhere. Janaki Bai said, 'I remember how we were standing at the graveside crying and crying – my thin handkerchief was soaked through. We were not related but we felt so close, it was very sad.'[28] Shanti Bhowmick asserted, perhaps wrongly, that when she retreated from Rangoon to Bangkok with the second RJR contingent three weeks later, she was walking along a river and saw a big tree with the names of the two Ranis 'scribbled in somebody's hand' on the trunk. She said that her group paid homage to their dead comrades with military salutes.[29]

Rasammah was particularly sad at the way her two sisters-in-arms had died. 'All of us would have gladly given our lives in the battlefield and been proud of that. The desolate feeling which engulfed us at that moment was that these two Rani of Jhansi soldiers had died while we were forced to retreat.'[30] The Ranis conjectured that the train had perhaps been attacked by Burmese snipers.

Kuala Lumpur resident Meenachi Perumal has contributed a lively account of this attack on the retreating Ranis, which Joyce Lebra in her book highlights as 'a definitive eye-witness [sic] account'.[31] Perumal's version differs, however, on several fundamental points from those of all the other Rani witnesses. First, Perumal claims incorrectly that Janaki Thevar was the commanding officer of the group that was attacked. As the leader of the second contingent of retreating Ranis who left Rangoon a month later, Janaki was not present during this incident. Second, Perumal is the only person to claim that Stella Thomas had brought an adopted child along on the retreat. From all reports, neither commander Janaki Thevar nor the other officers in the Regiment in Burma would have tolerated a child in camp or on the retreat and no one else mentioned one. Third, the train was not bombed. There are many other details that combine to suggest that Perumal was not a member of this first retreating RJR force; that she was not present when the two Ranis were shot; and that as other Ranis have asserted, she was never a member of the Regiment.

The remaining forty-nine Ranis crouched behind their packs on the floor of the carriage as they continued their dangerous journey. After crossing the Salween river by sampan, they arrived in Moulmein on 6 April and stayed there for several days. According to Rasammah, their INA guard Lieutenant Rawat, who was also a fitness instructor, made sure the Ranis continued their PT to keep them combat-ready.[32] Departing Moulmein by rail, the Ranis were granted the use of three freight cars and experienced more comfortable transport, although the monsoon rains had begun and the women sometimes had to spend an entire day inside the wagons. The group passed safely through Wang Poh, Nombrodok and reached Narkon Fathom just six miles outside of Bangkok on 23 April. They spent the night there at an abandoned school building and then moved to a camp set up by the IIL in Bangkok. When I pressed her, Janaki Bai reluctantly remembered some inconveniences of the journey: 'When we got to Rangoon people stepped back because we smelled so badly not having had a bath for many days. When we came by a stream we wanted to take a bath. Once we came by a stream and wanted to take a bath but then we saw several Japanese men stark naked standing there. We were shocked and ran the other way. We were horrified. We had never seen a naked man before standing like that. A bad habit being naked for the whole world to see!'[33]

Back in Rangoon, Bose refused the Japanese offer of a special plane for his own use because he knew that if left in Rangoon, the second contingent of the Ranis would be captured. He finally agreed to retreat to Bangkok, but only on the condition that the second group of the Rani of Jhansi Regiment be evacuated by train.[34] The Japanese officers, who lacked transportation for their own wounded soldiers, promised to arrange a train for the Ranis from Rangoon to Waw on the evening of 23 April.[35]

On 21 April 1945, without offering explanation, Janaki Thevar told the remaining Ranis that Bose had invited them to come for an interview with him. Aruna accepted the offer and told me that when she and Bose were by themselves in a room, he asked her first if she was well and then whether she had any complaints about the two years of training and living a soldier's life. Aruna answered that she was well and had no complaints, but she did have a question: Why had she not been promoted? She was sure that she 'was the best cadet in the whole Regiment'. Bose smiled and said that she was too young; she was then dismissed.[36] Aruna was then seventeen years old. In their interviews, several Ranis stated that they had asked Bose why they had not been sent to the front, but had received no answer.

Immediately after breakfast the day following the individual meetings with Bose, Janaki Thevar ordered all the girls who had joined from Burma to come to the parade ground with their packs. Three tongas, light horse-drawn carriages, stood waiting at the gate. The group from Kamayut, consisting of the three Ganguli sisters, plus Mommata, Ranu, and Neera stood together. The girls from Mandalay formed another group. Rama and her sister Neelam were also there. They were all wondering what was going on. Janaki gave the crisp command, 'Just now you are provided with transports to go home. Tongas will [take] you home, Jai Hind.'[37] The British Intelligence (BI) account of the event was phrased equally tersely: 'The disbanding of the Regiment began with sending the fifty or so local recruited Ranis back to their homes.'[38] INA soldier B985 reported to BI, '…the Burma-born girls of the RJR discarded their uniforms, were paid six months' salary, and were sent home.'[39]

The Burma Ranis felt stricken when they realized that they had been disbanded.

Mrs Mehta was notified and brought the family car to the camp to pick up Rama and Neelam. When the tonga stopped at the home of the Ganguli family who had sent four children to join the INA, Mrs Ganguli 'was very much surprised to see [her three daughters] coming back like that, disbanded. It was so sudden.'[40]

The following day Aruna heard that Bose would give a goodbye speech at a local high school and she ran all the way to be on time to hear him, but as was his habit Bose was hours late. The Supreme Commander of the INA explained to the gathered Indians, 'We failed this time. We were late. We will come attacking again and again. Like waves of the ocean.'[41] Aruna never saw her idol again. In their interviews with me, Manwati, Karuna, Mommata and Aruna each spontaneously agreed that the day they were disbanded to give up their fight and had to bid farewell to their friends from Malaya was the saddest day in their lives.

On 23 April, two days after the Burma contingent of the RJR was sent home, and while the remaining fifty Ranis from Malaya were still billeted in the Halpin Road camp, Bose received the news that the British spearhead had broken through at Pyinmana in central Burma.[42] Since British troops could easily reach Rangoon within a matter of hours, in a last burst of noblesse oblige, Bose promoted all INA officers in Burma one step in rank, paid all soldiers six months' advance pay, and added two hundred rupees as a gift from their commander.[43] Six thousand INA soldiers were assigned to remain in Rangoon under Major General A.D.

Loganadan (1888–1949) in order to prevent mayhem.[44] Rangoon fell on
3 May and the 6,000 INA soldiers requested they be treated as prisoners
of war captured from a foreign army rather than as Indian Army soldiers
who had defected to the enemy.[45]

Japanese officers of the Hikari Kikan continued to be worried that
Bose might be taken prisoner and insisted that he leave forthwith. Bose's
friend and member of the Azad Hind cabinet, Subbier Appadurai Ayer,
claimed that Bose was offered the use of an airplane that would take him
to Bangkok in less than two hours, which he declined.[46] The Japanese also
made available an evacuation convoy of trucks to escort him and his advisers
out of Rangoon. Bose agreed on the condition that the Ranis leave earlier
by train. Trusting the Japanese promise to provide a train carriage for the
rest of the RJR, Bose sent a confidential letter ordering INA Captain Ehsan
Qadir 'to depart that evening by train for an unknown destination, and to
look after the Rani of Jhansi Regiment'.[47]

When the Ranis with their packed haversacks had waited for hours
on the train platform only to see the Japanese claim the train for their
wounded soldiers, Qadir, who wanted to stay to fight the British in
Rangoon, sought Bose's permission to do so. Bose was adamant; he ordered
Qadir to obey orders. According to B978 Qadir's interrogation testimony
to British Intelligence, Bose appeared 'to be very agitated and expressed
annoyance with the Hikari Kikan for not permitting the evacuation of the
Rani of Jhansi women'.[48] Other reports also state that Bose was furious
and refused to leave Rangoon unless transport was provided both to the
Ranis and to his own party.[49] He was promised that trucks would be ready
for departure the next evening.[50]

Clearly it was of the utmost importance for Bose to secure a safe
return of the Ranis to their families in Singapore and Malaya, therefore his
choice of Captain Qadir as the guide to lead the Ranis through the jungle
is puzzling. Qadir was considered by some INA officers to be 'anti-Bose',
and had advised a fellow INA officer B978 Captain Abdul Rashid on the
best way to arrange his desertion.[51] Also Captain Lakshmi expressed the
strongest abhorrence for Ehsan Qadir's character and activities, considering
him a schemer and a sadist.[52] Bose may have been unaware of Qadir's

poor reputation, and fortunately no Rani mentioned Qadir's presence during the trek.

The dramatic story of the twenty-one-day retreat by the second RJR contingent through the jungle, largely on foot, and of Bose's efforts to bring these fifty Ranis safely home was recounted to me by several of the participants on the trek and confirmed by Hugh Toye, using British Intelligence information. The major accounts are by two Ranis, Janaki Thevar and Shanti Bhowmick and by two members of the Azad Hind cabinet, Subbier Appadurai Ayer and A. C. Chatterji. Janaki made available to me her typed unpublished memoir for this book, and sections from her diary are included in the memoirs of Shah Nawaz Khan.[53] The details of Janaki's accounts of her time in the RJR and of this perilous journey are characterized by her great exuberance, and they are often quite different from other Ranis' reports of the same events. Janaki Thevar has told the story of the retreat several times, and she asserts that on this trek from Rangoon to Bangkok she commanded 500 soldiers of the RJR, not fifty Ranis as told to me by all other women on the trip and stated in British Intelligence reports.

The escape route was to go via Pegu, Waw, cross the Sittang river, continue south to Moulmein and then through the Three Pagodas Pass into neutral Thailand and on to Bangkok. In late April 1945, the monsoon had further eroded the poor roads, and bridges across rivers were destroyed by bombing. In addition to the danger of Allied air attacks and Burmese guerrilla raids, both road and rail travel was dangerous and difficult.

Before leaving Rangoon, Bose issued a special message: 'Brothers and Sisters! I am leaving Burma with a very heavy heart. We have lost the first round of our fight for Independence, but we have lost only the first round. There are many more rounds to fight.'[54]

On the afternoon of 24 April, Havildar Shanti Bhowmick had just returned to the barracks in the Halpin Road camp after the day's parade and training classes. She expected to have a rest, eat dinner and end the day's work with night attack practice, when at 5.30 p.m. camp routine was broken; the bell rang calling the Ranis to the parade ground. Lieutenant

JanakiThevar, their commander, gave them an hour to eat dinner, pack their possessions and equipment to clear camp for an unknown destination.[55]

At 9 p.m. on that bright moonlit night, a convoy of trucks with fifty Rani of Jhansi soldiers left Rangoon for Bangkok together with Bose. They were accompanied by most of the members of the Azad Hind cabinet, a party of about forty bodyguards plus some domestic servants.[56] General Chatterji, who was also a medical doctor, and Bose's publicity manager Ayer were tasked to look after the 'girls on the trek'. The convoy consisted of twelve trucks, three of which were reserved for the Ranis, and four cars, all heavily camouflaged with branches cut from the trees along the Rangoon–Pegu road that they would be travelling.[57]

The convoy had barely got on its way when Allied planes buzzed overhead. The entire party jumped out of the trucks and took cover along the sides of the road. According to Ayer, that routine continued about once an hour throughout the night. Several hours into the journey the rumble of artillery, believed to be from British troops, caused the convoy to stop and send a patrol ahead to find out how close the enemy was. The scouts returned with information that it was the Japanese who had set fire to ammunition dumps around the city of Pegu and in several villages. Avoiding these locations further slowed the convoy's progress. Shanti, like Ayer, observed the burnt fields and villages on the way to Pegu. She, however, believed that the destruction was the result of 'the enemy's, the Allied's Scorched Earth Policy', and not caused by the Japanese.[58]

After a long night's travel, the group reached a small hamlet near the city of Waw, about 75 miles from Rangoon.[59] Chatterji, Ayer and British Intelligence accounts agree about most of the first day's events.[60] Shah Nawaz Khan was not a member of the convoy and in his memoirs he focuses on Bose's legendary good luck. The group had a late start and, despite Burmese guerrilla attacks, they made it to a place beyond Pegu on the first night. One day later the British occupied Pegu.[61]

JanakiThevar, the commander of this second Rani retreat contingent, gave a dramatically different rendition of the events. She asserted that in Rangoon the Ranis were about to board the train when 'a barrage of bombs and machine gun bullets from American Bombers' caused everyone to lie down flat on the ground, but still 'some of our members' were killed.[62] As soon as the bombers had flown off, Janaki saw that Japanese soldiers tried to whisk Bose away in a car. But refusing the offer of safe transport, Bose instead began the trek to Bangkok determined to bring his Ranis safely home. That night, said Janaki, the group walked until they reached River Sittang.[63] Arriving at the Sittang River would mean that the convoy members had walked a distance of more than 100 miles in one night. It must therefore be assumed that Janaki compressed the story somewhat.

Shanti proudly recalled that when their trucks were hit by incendiary bombs on the road, all the Ranis got out 'in the twinkling of an eye'. As trained soldiers, they made sure to bring their arms and ammunition. No Rani was hurt, but all the trucks 'were reduced to ashes in no time with all [the Ranis'] other belongings on them'.[64] The women immediately continued on foot, their bayonets tied to a belt around their waists. In order to stay on track in the dark each Rani held on to the rifle of the soldier in front of her.[65]

Shanti remembered that at the end of the first long night's march, they arrived at a large rain-filled gully in which Bose's car was almost submerged. Even with help from Colonel Habibur Rahman and another INA officer, Bose was unable to lift out the car. Seeing the problem the Ranis rushed over to help them. Bose smiled and said, 'Ranis have now come here. We have no more any worry.'[66] The car, however, was left in the ditch.

All travel was carried out in the darkness of night, and days were spent under cover to avoid Allied bombings. In his report on the first morning near Waw, Ayer elaborated on Shah Nawaz's theme which all the reports share, Bose was unwilling to take the most basic precautions for his own safety despite the pleading of his companions. His preternaturally good luck carried him through. Out on a walk away from the group, Ayer saw a fighter plane strafing the precise location where Bose was resting, but he later learned that Bose was safe and concluded that a miracle had saved Bose from the machine-gun bullets.[67]

Janaki described the same morning: She was resting while Bose shaved under a tree when a fighter plane circled straight above them. Everyone else took cover, but Bose continued to shave. A little later they were crossing a paddy field where no cover was possible when the planes returned and Bose sat down, lit a cigarette and smoked. Janaki asked, 'The planes missed us, why is it that he is always having miraculous escapes? I think he is charmed against danger. Nothing can happen to our Netaji until India is free.'[68]

There are many examples in which people regularly attributed such magical powers to Bose, including 'second sight', or clairvoyance. He often said that the British bullet that would kill him had not been cast, that no enemy could touch him. Perhaps he did believe that he had been granted immortality until he had secured liberty for all Indians. Several Ranis told me of instances when Bose changed plans and thereby saved the lives of others. Janaki described how on 25 April, that first morning away from Rangoon, Bose sent a motorcyclist out to tell the Janbaz unit, the male INA suicide fighters, to leave the road and proceed instead along the railway line. A few minutes after the Janbaz unit had left the road, 'enemy tanks came charging down it. Our men had just been saved.'[69] Episodes like these continued to accumulate until the group reached Bangkok. To put perspective on Bose's supposed invulnerability, despite constant Allied bombardment and patrols by Burmese guerrillas in the jungle, only one member of that convoy accompanying the second RJR contingent was wounded and died on the entire trek.

From Rangoon the road to Waw leads due north but is the only way to ford the river after which it then heads south towards Moulmein. The last segment of the road had turned into mud in the monsoon, as a result, stranded Japanese trucks blocked all progress. Just before dawn on 26 April, hundreds of trucks cluttered the banks of the Waw river, all attempting to cross before first light when Allied planes would arrive looking for targets. The one ferry at the Waw river crossing was not nearly adequate for the task, and Bose therefore decided that it would not be safe for the Ranis to wait for passage on it. He ordered them all to cross the river on foot. Ayer brimmed with praise: 'The girls were simply wonderful. They waded through waist and neck-deep water and somehow managed to get across.'[70] Several Ranis remembered the event with pride and wonder that they all survived, because they could not swim.

Janaki's account differed. Japanese general Saburo Isoda suggested to Bose that he should cross to safety on the other side first, followed by the rest of his group. Janaki quoted Bose: 'Go to Hell, I will not cross over till all the girls have gone across first.'[71] According to Janaki, soon the shallowest ford was located, 6-ft deep, and she ordered all the girls to march to that place and swim across which they did carrying their rifles. It was at that time unusual for an Indian girl to be able to swim. Furthermore, most of the Ranis measured 5'1" or 5'2" in height, so even if the water was not exactly 6-ft deep, crossing the river was a feat. Shanti reported that when the Ranis came to a swift river, 'Taking the name of Netaji, we raised our weapons upward and crossed the river through neck-deep water very carefully.'[72] Janaki and Shanti both mentioned that one Rani lost her balance and was almost swept away, but Colonel S.A. Malik, a tall INA soldier, caught her and rescued her.[73]

At daybreak the whole group had barely crossed the Waw with Bose bringing up the rear. The contingent arrived at a dilapidated shelter close to the riverbank just as the first Allied aircraft were heard overhead. Bose ordered the Ranis to take cover but dismissed their pleas that he do so himself. With an impatient gesture, he stretched out and allegedly went to sleep on the platform in front of the old building and slept while a fighter squadron swooped over them firing their machine guns.[74]

The next night the escape route crossed monsoon-flooded paddy fields and predictably their new trucks provided by the Japanese got stuck in 4-feet-deep mud. The vehicles were abandoned and the Ranis slogged their way through soggy paddy fields all night, reaching a deserted village the next morning.[75] They cooked a meal of rice and curry, diving for cover every time a fighter plane droned overhead. After a day's rest, at midnight the Ranis set out with Ayer to cross the Sittang river. The bridge had been blown up several months earlier and had not been repaired; so the only way to cross was by ferry. Daybreak came with no chance for crossing, so the group returned to the deserted village. They risked setting out for the Sittang the next afternoon in broad daylight, but reaching the bank by dusk they encountered thousands of Japanese soldiers waiting for space on the ferry. The Japanese moved aside for the Indian group and after a leap into the overcrowded ferry, the Ranis reached the eastern bank of the Sittang in ten minutes and hurried on through burning villages to a hamlet a few miles away for a brief rest.[76]

Janaki's report of the crossing of the Sittang was death-defying but inconsistent with all other sources. Rather than embarking on a ferry, she remembered that the Ranis waded 'through water – infested with dangerous crocodiles', each Rani secured with a long rope tied to her waist and the other end of the rope tied to trees across the river.[77] It took a long time, but every one crossed wet but safe before morning light. In any case, the only vehicle conveyed on the ferry that night was Bose's car; all other cars and trucks remained on the west bank, so the Ranis would have to walk, and Bose would do the same.[78]

As the entire   contingent would have   to walk from Sittang to Moulmein, a distance of a little over 100 miles, Bose placed General Kiani in charge of the convoy in order to assure the most orderly daily progress. All participants, including Bose, were to follow Kiani's orders regarding when to march and when to take cover. In military fashion, the group marched with five-minute rest stops every hour. Ayer admitted that he quickly developed painful blisters, but Bose, according to Janaki, in his heavy knee-high leather boots and carrying his own pack pressed on, doing 3–4 miles an hour.[79] Janaki was also proud of '[her] girls'. She was happy to see that their excellent night march training enabled them to carry 35-pound packs containing all their personal belongings, rations, cooking tins, their rifles with ammunition plus some hand grenades without complaint.[80] The convoy covered 10 miles the first night across the Sittang river and 15 the second, but the Ranis were hungry, plagued by sore and bleeding feet, and approaching exhaustion. Bose also had difficulty hiding how painful it was to walk in his fancy boots.[81]

Rani Shanti was hungry and found it hard to continue enduring 'the endless strain of the continuous march' without food, but, she added, the Ranis 'did not lose [their] morale'.[82] Ayer confirmed the Rani of Jhansi girls proved wonderful. They were not in the least dejected. They continued in high spirits and helped with cooking and serving.[83] Janaki, concerned as always with Bose's comfort, persuaded him to take off his heavy boots so she could wash his socks. She was shocked at the mass of blisters on his feet.[84] Bose's replacement car was following the convoy with no passengers. His Japanese escorts constantly tried to get him to ride in the car because they did not enjoy the hike, but Bose staunchly refused to be driven until there was transportation for everyone.[85]

Leading the group, the next night Bose walked another 15 miles on blistered feet. Just as Ayer who also suffered with bleeding feet was planning to ask to be left behind, because it was too painful for him to continue, three or four trucks procured by the Japanese met up with the group. Ayer and some of the Ranis found space in the first truck and they drove off. Apparently, Bose had other plans that had not been communicated to the whole convoy. He became extremely upset and called the INA senior officers fools when the first two trucks did not halt at the intended meeting point. A car was sent after them demanding that they return. The trucks had arrived at the Bilin river crossing but came back as ordered. Half an hour later they were again told by Bose to proceed to the river crossing. Spirits flagged and one of the most senior INA officers was not pleased with the behaviour of the Supreme Commander, especially when he heard that he had been called a fool. For days he complained at having to suffer such an insult at his age.[86]

For once the group had a moment of good luck with the trucks. They did not skid off the loose planks lined up to board the tiny ferry that plied across the Bilin river. All crossed safely, but it did not take long before one of the two trucks transporting the Ranis broke down. A wild ride followed when the Ranis' truck was tied to the truck ahead and the driver apparently thought that with a truck in tow he had to drive faster. At 40 miles an hour in the dark the driver of the broken down truck on tow stepped hard on the brakes. That did not slow them down, but the brakes caught fire. Someone managed to alert the speeding driver who finally slowed down, and after a short while the group reached a village for the day's rest. The Ranis cooked what Ayer called a sumptuous meal using local ingredients bought in the village at exorbitant prices, and the mood would have been upbeat except that Bose, who was walking, had not yet crossed the Bilin river.

Late that night, the Ranis were approaching the town of Martaban on the west bank of the Salween river with Moulmein on the east side. The Burma–Siam railhead was just six miles away and the group was relieved when a truck rushed by, on its way to pick up Bose. One more river crossing and the group reached Moulmein and hoped that the worst of the trip was behind them.

On 1 May 1945, looking somewhat bedraggled, Bose arrived by truck at Martaban on the west bank of the Salween River at a time when intense Allied air activity was concentrating on the delta of the Salween between Martaban and Moulmein. Bose, again trusting his good luck, successfully crossed the estuary in broad daylight.[87] He joined the RJR members, and indomitable, having slept no more than a few hours a night for a week, 'Netaji work[ed] like one inspired.' He made sure that after a week with only one serving of a little rice and dal per day, everyone was now served delicious and abundant meals.[88] He arranged accommodations for all in the group and then persuaded the Japanese that his entire convoy should have priority on any available space on the Burma–Siam trains to Bangkok.

On 5 or 6 May, late at night, the Ranis were the first of Bose's group to leave Moulmein. They were again in freight cars, once more 'packed like sardines', and this time General Chatterji and Colonel Malik accompanied them.[89] They had been forewarned not to expect a continuous ride because Allied air forces were concentrating on the Burma–Siam Railway and had caused heavy damage to both bridges and rolling stock.[90] After several hours but only a short distance, the train ride ended. The track had been blown up by US bombers which Janaki considered a 'terrible nuisance', and she predicted that with the sheer weight of metal the Americans would win the war.[91] Once more the Ranis had to walk, 16 miles to the next railway station. Even at two in the morning, the resourceful Malik managed to find three bullock carts to transport the Ranis' packs, relieving their shoulders of the weight and the pain where the leather straps cut. The group reached the station at daybreak as the British and American planes began their search to destroy the remaining locomotives camouflaged under bamboo shelters.[92]

The trip continued for four more days, alternating between train rides and, when the track was damaged or bridges blown up, walking. Again the Ranis hid during the day in whatever shelter was available near little towns along the track, and limped towards Bangkok in all-night marches. Bose, who had been given another car by the Japanese, was in touch with the RJR members at several points along the way. Arriving in Bangkok on 14 May, one day before the Ranis, he contrived a hero's welcome for them. After twenty-one days on the run, crossing four rivers, slogging through muddy patty fields and dense jungle, with innumerable dives into ditches to avoid strafing bullets from low-flying aircraft, the Ranis straggled into camp. They were met with a nest of wartime luxuries: fresh clothes, fruit and milk.[93]

The two groups of Ranis reunited at the RJR camp about seven miles outside Bangkok to discuss and exchange details about their ordeals in the jungle.[94] Time to stretch out and rest, baths, fresh clothes and a full meal were mentioned by the Ranis as the most important rewards from the difficult journey, rather than safety in Thailand. One Rani in the second contingent, Goorjal Kaur, had become seriously ill on the trek and died shortly after arrival in Bangkok. Goorjal was married and had two adult 'adopted sons with beards', a fact curiously mentioned by all the Ranis I interviewed who were present in Bangkok. Ponnammah remembered sitting by Goorjal's bed when she died. Some of Goorjal's friends believed that she had succumbed to the stress and physical exertion of the trek; others thought that she had contracted either cholera or dysentery. The Ranis performed Sikh funeral rites for Goorjal with full military honours.[95]

After a few days rest, Bose ordered the Ranis to be sent back to their homes in Malaya and Singapore, but they begged to stay in Bangkok. They argued that the male INA soldiers were carrying on the fight and they wanted to do the same, promising to share cheerfully all hardships and sufferings. Still the Regiment was formally demobilized in Bangkok and General Chatterji found it a painful task because the Ranis again insisted that they had left their homes to win the struggle for India's freedom and did not want to quit until the mission was completed. In particular, Janaki Thevar's plea made an impression on Chatterji, but once more Bose

managed to persuade all the Ranis to go back to their homes.[96] Amidst
heavy Allied bombardment in Bangkok, the Ranis were again crowded
into train freight cars for the last stage of their return home to Malaya.

Janaki claimed that on the way from Bangkok to Malaya one Rani died
of typhoid and another from machine-gun wounds. She asserted that many
of the INA soldiers who went along as escorts 'lost their lives in trying
to protect us.'[97] Other Ranis remembered the constant bombing until
the train reached the Malayan border, but told of no casualties. In Kedah
and Penang, two states in northern Malaya, some Ranis said goodbye,
and in Ipoh, Perak, several more disembarked for home. The families of
the Ranis had been informed of the time and place they could welcome
their returning daughters. Janaki accompanied the last Ranis all the way
to Singapore, where she met with Bose for the last time. He told her that
they would meet again in Free India and that she should not worry about
him. 'The British will not take me dead or alive.' In her memoir, Janaki
mused that it was not long before Bose's prophecy was proven true.[98]

While trekking through the jungle, two Ranis, Rasammah Navarednam
and Loganayagy Suppiah, had fallen ill with malaria and were unfit to
complete the trip home when the rest of the Regiment boarded the train
in Bangkok heading home to Malaya and Singapore. Ponnammah wanted
to stay with her younger sister.[99] Three Ranis, Emily Xavier, who was born
in Burma, Janaki Devi and Chameli had come south on the trek with the
Malaya-bound girls but they had subsequently changed their minds and
now wanted to return to Rangoon.[100]

Despite the danger to his own safety and notwithstanding the many
other issues requiring his attention, Bose took time to arrange for
Rasammah, Ponnammah and Loganayagy to be transferred the next day,
17 August, to the French Convent in Bangkok, where for six months they
would stay as 'first class boarders' and continue their academic studies.[101]
Bose made sure that the IIL would also cover expenses for the three
Malayan Ranis' travel home to Ipoh and for the three Burma resident Ranis
to return to Rangoon. Rasammah treasured the memory of Bose placing
his hand on her head, assuring the girls that they would be safe even after
the Anglo-American forces arrived.[102] In response to a farewell request

from Ponnammah, Bose wrote in her little notebook: 'Live for others – if you want to live.'[103]

When the Navarednam sisters finally returned home, they flew from Bangkok to Penang and then went by newspaper delivery truck to Ipoh. Their mother was very happy to see them, but she told her daughters not to mention that they had served as Ranis.[104] The war was over and India was still a British colony. Several other Ranis also commented that they had wanted to share their experiences, to tell their stories when they came home, but they found no audience. Not even their families were interested. Most of the Ranis I interviewed stopped believing that others thought that having been a member of the RJR was something special. Rasammah, however, was not easily cowed, 'I was proud of my service and I still am proud. I never got any pension.'[105] Some Ranis did not want it known that they had been in the RJR because they were afraid that it would hinder their efforts to find good jobs. Ponnammah did not even talk to her husband about her experiences in Burma because to him 'it would be nothing'.[106]

In August 1945, when most of the Ranis had returned to their families in Singapore and Malaya, Asha Sahay, who had enlisted in the RJR in Bangkok on 15 May 1945, moved in with the family of Raghunath Sharma, the president of Thailand's Indian Independence League. As late as 23 October 1945, British Intelligence still refused to grant permission for the return of 'Miss Bharati Sahaya (alias Asha)' to her ancestral home in Bhagalpur, Bihar, India.[107] Born in Japan, Asha had never been to Bihar, but Bhagalpur was the village where her father's family lived, and that would be her future home. Only a few Ranis were retained by British Intelligence, but because of her father's position as minister in the Azad Hind government, apparently Asha warranted different treatment. Her interrogators eventually determined that Asha's experience in and knowledge of the RJR were limited, and in March 1946, Asha and her father were allowed to resettle in India.[108]

On 15 August 1945, the day following a grand performance of *Rani of Zanshi, A Play in Three Acts* by P.N. Oak about the life of Rani Lakshmibai, the Singapore Ranis received the dispiriting news that the RJR was to be disbanded, they would be sent home and the camp closed. As in Burma, the end came without ceremony. The Ranis were simply ordered to pack their gear and prepare for departure.[109]

Rani Dhanam was given a list with the names and hometowns of the twenty–thirty Rani of Jhansi women who were not Singaporeans, and was put in charge of their transfer to their homes in Malaya.[110] Dhanam reported that at the time of the disbandment in August 1945, they were about fifty or sixty Ranis billeted in the Singapore camp. A truck big enough to hold the girls from Malaya along with guards was hired. As officer in charge, Dhanam sat in the front seat next to the driver and thus the last of the Rani of Jhansi Regiment rolled out of camp.

They first went to Johor in southern Malaya, just across the strait from Singapore. They then proceeded to Kuala Lumpur where the Indian Independence League gave the group a nice dinner and put them up for the night. The following day the remaining Ranis continued northwards.[111] The IIL offices in towns along the route alerted the families of the return of the women so that they would come to meet them at the IIL offices. In many cases, it was the husband who came to pick up his wife, Dhanam noted, as she checked off each name on the list and officially closed the era of the Rani of Jhansi Regiment in the struggle for Indian independence.[112]

FOURTEEN

VARYING ACCOUNTS OF THE RJR

AS A RESULT OF Bose's order to destroy all records of the INA, extant documentary evidence of the Rani of Jhansi Regiment is scant. With the war concluded and Bose declared dead, Captain Lakshmi assumed custody of the Regiment and its representation to posterity. Her influence on the reputation of the RJR has been pervasive. An analysis of academic works in which the RJR is mentioned confirms that almost every detail, factual or not, can be traced back to Captain Lakshmi.

The use of female soldiers and their combat capabilities are controversial topics that tend to elicit emotional responses rather than critical analysis. Depending on a priori sentiments as to whether women should serve in the military or not, the Ranis' importance and achievements have been both exaggerated and deprecated over the past seven decades. Two questions have particularly intrigued partisans on both sides, despite the lack of reliable evidence: Did the Ranis engage in combat in the jungles of Burma, and how many soldiers were actually on the rolls of the RJR?

At the very end of the war, Captain Lakshmi wrote a romantic novel, *Jai Hind: The Diary of a Rebel Daughter,* a fictional account of a valiant Rani who is wounded in battle. [1] The manuscript was secretly brought out of Rangoon by an Indian journalist who published it anonymously for her in

India in 1945.[2] Captain Lakshmi claims that that was the way 'we were able to smuggle out the true story of the INA'.[3] However, Captain Lakshmi's heroic tale of Ranis in combat on the Burmese front is pure fantasy. In it the female protagonist imagines a scenario in which 'I suppose we all forgot our sex', where the Ranis attack the British Army, firing and firing again and follow up by charging the enemy with fixed bayonets.[4] In time, this fictional account of RJR courage under fire on the front has often become accepted as historical fact.

In a 1979 article, Captain Lakshmi mused, 'When a person has lived through a historical epoch and more so when one has been an active participant in a revolutionary movement, one is apt either to give a highly exaggerated account of events or to error [sic] on the side of understatement.'[5] Next she asserted, 'I realize that I have been guilty of understatement with regards to the part played by the Rani of Jhansi Regiment.'[6] In this article as in all her publications and speeches following World War II, Captain Lakshmi aimed to burnish the Ranis' aura of 'true heroism and sacrifice', a reputation she believed they deserve but had not yet been accorded.

In writing her 1979 article, Captain Lakshmi began with the first RJR deployment, recalling that when the Ranis 'left Rangoon to go to Maymyo and then to the front', they looked like schoolgirls.[7] In fact, the Ranis in the small fighting group heading for Maymyo were schoolgirls in 1944, but they were never deployed for front-line combat.[8] Instead, they were billeted for a few months in a camp near Maymyo, several hundred miles from the actual combat. At the end of the article, Captain Lakshmi repeated a tale of the Ranis' 'proudest hour', a fictional incident that she claimed occurred in the jungle during the retreat from Rangoon to Bangkok in April and May of 1945. She had already described this incident in a 1947 article, but there are important differences between the two accounts.[9] In the later enhanced version, Allied guerrilla forces fired at Bose; the Ranis 'took up positions and beat back the attacks', successfully protecting their Netaji. 'Two members of the Regiment lost their lives.'[10] None of this happened. In January 2008, Captain Lakshmi stated that during their service in Burma, five Ranis died in active battle and three or four others by bombings.[11] This information is also not corroborated by any other source, and although the grapevine connecting the Ranis was strong throughout their time in the INA and afterwards, no Rani I interviewed had heard of those events.

Shortly after its publication, the fictional accounts of Rani heroism in *The Diary* were republished elsewhere as fact. In her little book, *The Story of I.N.A* (1946), Indian journalist Kusum Nair asserted that the Ranis battled bravely on the Indo-Burma frontier, and that later, while withdrawing from Burma, they 'fought valiant rearguard action near Moulmein'.[12] More recently, in a two-volume collection on Bose and the INA that purports to present objective historical fact, Roma Banerjee quoted directly from *The Diary* as if it were a reliable historical source.[13] Banerjee reiterated the fantastic accounts of multiple Rani casualties, of Rani success in crossing the border to stand on Indian soil, and of courageous rearguard battles waged by Ranis in full retreat.[14]

Several independent accounts, including those by many Ranis who accompanied Bose on the retreat from Burma, described the trip through the jungle, but not one person mentioned anything like a deadly encounter with enemy guerrilla forces, other than the attack by unknown fighters on the retreating Ranis on the train leaving Rangoon. Moreover, no other report from the campaign in Burma alleges that Bose was personally attacked, or that it was necessary for the women to protect him. Indeed, at the time of this purported RJR skirmish in the course of retreat to Bangkok, Captain Lakshmi was far away trekking through jungles of the Karen Hills with the dying Attavar Yellappa of the IIL.

Based on archival information and extensive interviews with the Ranis, it is now clear that these incidents recounted in *The Diary* and persistently repeated elsewhere did not take place: they are entirely fictional. The Regiment was never deployed to the Indo-Burmese border, never entered India, never engaged the enemy, never beat back attacks between Rangoon and Bangkok, or anywhere else. In any case, as indicated earlier, the women of the Rani of Jhansi Regiment never made it to the front lines, never went into battle as an infantry unit, never fired a weapon against the enemy, never could fulfil their dream of fighting for their country.

In none of the memoirs, articles or speeches written by INA soldiers or members of the Azad Hind government about their experience in the Burma campaign is there any claim that the Ranis fought in combat or even approached the battlefront. The women begged to go, but Bose refused to send them. Although the bravery of all RJR members during the harrowing retreat from Rangoon to Bangkok has been widely admired, the INA soldiers interrogated by British Intelligence never mentioned any combat or other battlefront action involving the Ranis. The service rendered by the nursing section, however, is praised by many. Rahmat Bibi Ma Khin U, the IIL recruiter who was interrogated by the British, gave her concluding appraisal of the RJR, 'The Nursing Group put in some really good and useful work.'[15]

Without exception, the Ranis interviewed reported unambiguously that they did not fight. Many of them expressed great disappointment; they wished that they had been allowed to put their training to use and prove their courage. They wanted to charge the enemy with weapons and plant the tricolour flag on Indian soil. They wanted to sacrifice their lives for the freedom of their Motherland. They protested strongly but had to accept that they would not serve in combat, as they had been promised by Bose, fighting shoulder to shoulder with the men. No Rani claimed to have fired her gun except in the course of target practice, and none claimed to have seen, much less confronted, an enemy soldier.

In fact, a contingent of about twenty Ranis did set out from Rangoon for Maymyo (now Pyin Oo Lwin) in April 1944 believing that they were going to join the INA soldiers in combat. But that lovely highland resort town lies 300 miles away as the crow flies from the battlefront at Imphal and Kohima, across 10,000-ft-tall mountains and mighty rivers. The women camped in Maymyo until October 1944, when they returned to Rangoon, and no Rani got any closer to the front than Maymyo.

Although they never engaged in front-line battle, the service rendered by the Ranis in Maymyo should be considered heroic. Constant Allied air raids forced them to spend many nights in trenches, but they nevertheless managed to carry on tending to the wounded who were coming back from the front. The men had sometimes travelled for weeks to get medical care. Aruna describes some of the horrors of war: 'The wounded soldiers coming from the war front had newspapers as their bandages. They were all skeleton thin, hollowed eyed, their beard and hair grown in knots. Whole body swarming with lice. Opening the paper bandages, we stepped back. There it was all full of maggots.'[16]

In October 1943 at the opening of the first Rani of Jhansi Regiment training camp, Bose declared the scope of his grand vision: 'India has to produce and shall produce thousands of Ranis of Jhansi.'[17] Clearly, Bose intended his success to be measured at least partly in terms of how many women would take up arms to serve their country. Bose himself was not alone in expecting great things of this project. Captain Lakshmi reported that when Bose asked her on 12 July 1943, if she thought she would be able to persuade 100 women from Malaya to sign up, she assured him that at least 5,000 women would join the Regiment.[18] When it comes to tipping points in the history of gender relations, numbers alone do not tell the whole story, but to judge the impact of the RJR it is necessary to have some sense of how many women actually enlisted and how many Ranis were deployed to Burma.

RJR volunteers enlisted and were trained on an ongoing basis in camps in Singapore, Rangoon and Bangkok. Without enlistment records, there is no straightforward and definitive way to determine precisely how many Ranis in total joined the RJR. We do know roughly how many of those were sent to Burma. Some indication of the Regiment's strength might have been inferred from requests for small bayonets or lightweight Sten sub-machine guns issued to the RJR. Whereas such nominal rolls and supply information for the male INA members are contained among the extant INA Papers in the National Archives of India, no such information has surfaced for the Ranis. Despite these obstacles, nearly every historical account of the Regiment includes estimates of how many female soldiers participated. In addition, these assessments state or imply that all members of the RJR were deployed to Burma as members of the combat force.

Very few informants other than Bose and his few closest aides were in a position to have comprehensive information about numbers at the

RJR Singapore camp and in the Burma contingent; it is not clear whether Captain Lakshmi had access to this data. After her surrender in Mawchi, northern Burma, on 1 June 1945, Captain Lakshmi, as noted above, was debriefed by Captain Rashid Yusuf Ali, a British Intelligence officer, who was unsure of the accuracy of Captain Lakshmi's information because she had been out of touch with Bose and the RJR for a long time.[19] Indeed in May 1944, even Bose did not know how many women had joined the RJR and enquired in a letter to the Singapore camp commander Lieutenant M. Satiavati Thevar, 'I should like particularly to know the present strength of the [Rani of Jhansi] Regiment.'[20]

The commonly cited source regarding the number of Ranis in the RJR is Captain Lakshmi. Over the years, Captain Lakshmi's assessment of the strength of the Regiment fluctuated significantly. Captain Ali's report on Captain Lakshmi's debriefing, dated 4 August 1945, noted that she explained that structurally the RJR was divided into two groups: a nursing section and a fighting section.[21] By Captain Lakshmi's account at that point, 100 trained nurses were stationed at four camps: Singapore, Rangoon, Maymyo and Zeyawaddy. She specified that the 300 Ranis of the fighting group were divided into three companies, with two companies billeted at Singapore and one at Rangoon. That would mean that approximately 200 soldiers and twenty-five nurses were camped in Singapore. Captain Lakshmi also reported that the Burma contingent included an additional 100 locally recruited women, so that there would have been in total 200 Ranis in the Rangoon combat unit, plus about seventy-five nurses. It is conceivable, but seems unlikely, that Captain Lakshmi gave inaccurate information in order to mislead the British, and those numbers correspond to the Ranis' recollections and estimates.

The British military repatriated Captain Lakshmi to India in 1946 and her earliest non-fictional account of her war experience was published a year later. In a 1947 speech titled 'The Rani of Jhansi Regiment', her recollection of the strength of the RJR had more than doubled. Captain Lakshmi states, 'At the end there were over a thousand trained women soldiers. ... In addition to the actual combatants, there was a fine Nursing Corps.'[22] In a speech in Calcutta in 1979, her estimate took another leap forward as she described Bose's surprise that 'thousands of women volunteered for the Rani of Jhansi Regiment'.[23]

In most of her speeches, articles and interviews, Captain Lakshmi asserted that the RJR numbered 1,000 soldiers plus 200 nurses.[24] By 2003 the Regiment in Captain Lakshmi's reports had swollen to 1,500 Ranis, and in our January 2008 conversation, Captain Lakshmi specified that of the 1,500 Ranis, 500 remained in Singapore to complete their training and the rest went to the battlefront in Burma.[25] Thus, over the sixty-three years from 1945 to 2008, the RJR strength assessments grew from 500 as she reported to Captain Rashid Yusuf Ali in 1945 to three times that many in 2008, with at least one intimation that the total exceeded two thousand.

INA Captain Yadava's lists, compiled many years after the war's end, give the names of 200 Ranis, but there are many inaccuracies.[26] The spelling of many names differs from the way the Ranis themselves spelled them, resulting in redundancies. One example: Captain Lakshmi is listed twice, both as Colonel Lakshmi Sahgal and Dr Laxmi Sahgal.[27] Several Ranis are identified only by their first names, again with different spellings. At the same time, there are apparent omissions. British Intelligence documents provide several names of Ranis not on Yadava's lists, and the Ranis I interviewed for this study mentioned still other individuals. After elimination of obvious duplicates and addition of those known omissions, the count comes to 199 names, but that certainly does not include every woman who served in the RJR.

A few INA officers and others who worked with the Azad Hind have written about encountering Ranis in the field and their estimates of RJR numbers vary greatly. Colonel Prem Sahgal, who served as Bose's military secretary ('his right-hand man on the organizational and administrative side of the INA'), was stationed in Rangoon until January 1945 and may have been in a position to know the size of the total RJR enrolment.[28] In 1985 Prem Sahgal set the number of the RJR at 1,200. He asserted that when the Ranis reached camp in Rangoon, the strength of the unit had increased to 1,000, including local recruits.[29] That would mean that 200 Ranis were billeted in Singapore. Sahgal's estimate so many years after the war may also reflect Captain Lakshmi's influence, as the strength assessments by his INA colleagues are significantly lower.

Assigned by Bose to accompany the second contingent of Ranis from Rangoon to Bangkok, Azad Hind chief of propaganda, S.A. Ayer commented on the onerous responsibility of 'having to look after some one hundred girls on the three hundred-mile jungle trek'.[30] As mentioned earlier, there were only fifty Ranis with Ayer on that retreat so that by doubling the number of his charges, he also added a bit of extra drama when retelling the story five years later.

In his 1946 memoirs of the war, General Shah Nawaz Khan of the INA states that 600 volunteers, 'mostly from very high and respectable families', joined the Regiment in Singapore.[31] Shah Nawaz's effort to gild the lily was conspicuous in this statement: only Shah Nawaz characterized the families of those illiterate Tamil plantation girls who comprised 60 per cent of Singapore enlistees as 'mostly from very high and respectable families'. General Shah Nawaz began the march from Singapore towards Kohima and Imphal intending to enter India with the Subhas Brigade in February 1944. His journey ended when he surrendered his brigade near the village of Pegu, 40 miles north of Rangoon in May 1945.[32] It is therefore not likely that he would have known the number of Ranis in the INA.

General A.C. Chatterji, who trekked in April 1945 with the second group of retreating Ranis out of Rangoon to Bangkok, in his position as Azad Hind minister of finance my have had facts on which to base his assessment of RJR numbers. In a book published only two years after the conclusion of the war, Chatterji notes, 'The maximum strength of the Regiment in Singapore was about five hundred.'[33]

The British Intelligence reports allow a wider and more detailed view of Bose's operations in Burma than the accounts of individual partisans. Unlike Captain Lakshmi, Bose and the Ranis, the male sepoys who were interrogated had no vested interest in the triumph of the Rani concept and probably answered truthfully to the best of their ability. The information in these reports was, however, harvested from captives under duress. The soldiers may have believed that their responses, even about topics on which they had no factual information, would determine their future. They hoped for leniency and freedom after the war but feared a death sentence for treason, having suborned their oath to the British Indian Army. This may be one reason that reports on the same subject often disagreed in the details of events, dates and numbers. Another reason that the reports do not agree may be because the interrogations were carried out over a three-year period, beginning with the first deserters and captives in 1942 and continuing throughout 1945 when the last man laid down his arms. Even so, these interrogations add significantly to our knowledge of INA and RJR activities.

Five INA staff officers surrendered on 1 March 1945, and gave interrogators the following description of Captain Lakshmi and the Regiment:

> The Strength of this unit is about six hundred, of which two hundred are in Rangoon, under 'Maj.' Lakshmi. It is composed mostly of Tamils. Its main objective is to increase morale of the I.N.A.[34]

After the 'capitulation,' as the reporting officer called it, of Captain Lakshmi in early May, British Intelligence set the strength of the RJR in Singapore at 300.[35] In his final report on the RJR to the South East Asia Command (SEAC), dated 2 October 1945, Captain Ali concluded that precision was impossible, but agreed with the earlier Interrogation Report; he estimated 'the total strength of the Rani of Jhansi Regt. at 600'.[36] On the basis of all available information, including his own interrogation of Captain Lakshmi, Ali calculated that of these 600 Ranis, 170, including forty nurses, had been stationed in Burma.[37] It is notable that Ali believed that the Regiment had just 130 Rani infantry in Burma, too few for a combat force, but consistent with Bose's fantasy that a token presence of the women on Indian soil would exert sufficient psychological pressure to subvert the loyalty of the Allied Indian soldiers.

Because British IRs were unavailable to earlier historians and commentators, no previous histories of the RJR could have taken them into account. Due to Captain Lakshmi's prominence as the most knowledgeable source on the RJR, the inflated numbers that she gave were frequently accepted and repeated in serious scholarship. Several historians, including Professor Sugata Bose of Harvard University, assert without documentation that there were 1,000 Ranis.[38] He adds that of those 1,000, 'Lakshmi Swaminathan had come to Burma with several hundred soldiers of her women's regiment.'[39] In fact, Captain Lakshmi had left Singapore for Burma months before any of the Ranis began their journey northward from the Singapore camp. Leonard Gordon also states without reference to sources that the Regiment eventually grew to 1,000, all of whom were deployed to Burma.[40] Geraldine Forbes reports, again without citing evidence, that there were about 1,000 Rani recruits distributed among three camps located in Singapore, Rangoon and Bangkok.[41] Journalist Carol Hills and psychiatrist Daniel Silverman firmly allege that 1,500 women arrayed in breaches and boots fought for Indian freedom in the Burma jungle, but they cite no basis for that assertion.[42]

Indian historians have had a more diverse view. K.K. Ghosh, a respected Bose scholar, states that the Regiment eventually had an enrolment of 500. His source for this information, however, is a *Young India* news article written the day after the opening of the Singapore camp. This report from the Azad Hind's house organ cannot be considered a reliable source, especially considering that Ranis had only just begun to enlist.[43] H.N. Pandit arrived at a total of 800 Ranis, comprised of 500 from Singapore and 300 from the rest of Malaya.[44] This estimate seems skewed; it is highly unlikely that there were 500 Ranis from Singapore alone. As we know from other sources, female labourers from the rubber plantations in Malaya constituted the largest proportion of the troops, perhaps as much as 60 per cent of the entire Regiment.[45]

In short, most Western academic authorities recycle Captain Lakshmi's incorrect claim that the RJR numbered between 1,000 and 1,500 women, all of whom were sent to Burma, and in some cases that the Ranis fought bravely on the Indo-Burma border.

Finally, the assessments of RJR troop strength from the Ranis themselves are found in my interviews and their diaries. The response of almost every Rani to my question of how many women were in the RJR was usually consistent with the figure that had become generally accepted by the Indian public because Captain Lakshmi in her many speeches and publications had repeated it again and again over the years.[46]

In her July 1980 reminiscences, Rani Shanti Bhowmick wrote that Netaji's dream of 1,000 Ranis came true within one year.[47] Rani Janaki Bai, a thoughtful and serious woman, however, deliberated for a moment before she answered, 'I am not sure. Several hundred, I suppose, but not in the thousands. This kind of thing you should not invent.'[48] Most Ranis placed the total between 1,000 and 1,500, which for them, as for the scholars noted above, had become the canonical range. They did not specify their own cohort, or distinguish between the residents of the Singapore camp and the Burma combat group. Given that it would have been almost impossible for any individual Rani to have gathered information independently as to how many Ranis were stationed in a contingent to which she did not belong, the responses seem to confirm that, by and large, the interviewed Ranis had simply accepted Captain Lakshmi's numbers.

When pressed in later interviews with questions on the size of the Singapore barracks, the configuration of the dormitories, whether everyone ate at the same time, whether they knew the names of everyone in the troop, and so on, the Ranis' answers belied their previous estimates. According to their responses in our interviews, the purported 500 or 600 Ranis would simply not have fit in the Singapore barracks, transport trucks, or lunch queues.

This conclusion is substantiated by a male INA soldier captured by the Allies and identified as B1156 Corporal Badr-ud-din in British Interrogation Reports. He served as a drill instructor for the RJR in Singapore and stated that only twenty-five female recruits were being trained in November 1943.[49] It is unlikely that, in less than two years, the corporal had forgotten how many girls and young women he was asked to forge into combat soldiers. As there is no apparent reason for such a soldier to misrepresent the facts, the default conclusion would be that there were approximately twenty-five Ranis in the Singapore camp at the end of 1943, far fewer than the 150 that Bose said he welcomed when the camp opened on 22 October 1943.

Eva Jenny Murty, who remained in Singapore until August 1945, provided figures only for her own camp. After the departure of the Burma contingent, she said '300 Ranis, not all nurses' remained in the camp until they were sent back home.[50] The Suppiah sisters also remained in Singapore till the Regiment was disbanded. Dhanam and Anjali Suppiah thought that there were about fifty or sixty Ranis.[51] Anjali was quartermaster and responsible for distributing the daily rations to the cooks, so one might assume that she was quite aware of whether the Singapore camp was feeding fifty women or several hundred.[52] When they were disbanded, Dhanam was given the task of accompanying the women who were domiciled in Malaya to their homes. The sisters independently stated that after the local Singapore Ranis had gone home, some twenty or thirty women remained, all of whom fitted into one army truck for the journey north.[53] How can three sensible, earnest women have such divergent recollections, ranging from sixty to 300, when they were in the same place at the same time? This is an impossible question to answer.

Rani Lakshmi Nair was a member of a special RJR propaganda unit who remained in Singapore after the war. In 1985 she was interviewed for the Singapore Oral History Project and volunteered two pieces of erroneous information about the number of women soldiers. First, she stated that in her group 'there were many thousands [sic] of women, a whole battalion'. Second, she reported, 'Once at an estate in Kuala Lumpur ... I recruited 300 women over night [sic] at one big meeting. 300 women joined the Indian National Army.'[54]

When recounting about the journey to Burma on the Death Railway, without being asked about the number of Ranis being deployed to Burma, Ponnammah Navarednam volunteered, 'They said there were 100, but we were just about eighty or ninety.'[55] Ponnammah remembers that about twenty Ranis were already there when the contingent from Singapore arrived at the Burma camp.[56]

An independent account about the number of Ranis in the Burma camp was given by Major Salim of the INA, POW number B961 during his interrogation by British captors. As noted above, Salim served as a weapons instructor in charge of the Burma Ranis' physical training (PT) at the Thingangyun camp. He told interrogators that he had witnessed the camp inauguration in the fall of 1943, when forty young women had been rushed through basic training.[57] Subsequently only twelve of those soldiers wanted to remain Ranis, he said, but the group grew slowly and by December 1943 he was coaching twenty-three Ranis. Aruna remembered sixteen names of the first recruits in Burma: Aruna, Karuna and Maya Ganguli, Rama and Neelam Mehta, Amba and Reba Sen, Lakshmi Sen, Pratima Sen, Latika Roy, Suchitra Chatterjee, Abha Sanyal, Mommata Gupta, Neera Chatterjee, Nomita Chowdhury and Sabufa Khatun. Five of the these women were interviewed for this study. Mommata, who was sixteen when she joined in December 1943, remembers that many Sikh girls signed up at the same time as she did. Aruna thought that perhaps when the Ranis in all camps were included there would be one thousand Ranis, but she was 'very sure that there were only forty or at the most fifty Burma girls in Burma, plus of course the Singapore girls'.[58]

After Captain Lakshmi was assigned service at the hospital in Maymyo, Janaki Thevar became commander of the Burma Rani contingent; she claims that her force was 500 women strong. In a passionate speech in 1979 at the Netaji Seminar in Calcutta, Janaki depicted the Regiment as an iconic entity: 'Women in their thousands, young and old, poor and rich, educated and uneducated, skilled and unskilled, mothers and daughters and sisters of varying walks of life thronged the Indian Independence League Office for enlistment.'[59]

Considering all other evidence, Janaki's ebullient estimate appears substantially exaggerated, and not just in terms of the numbers. In her lecture, she went on to describe the unit in her command: 'Six months of almost non-stop and intensive training in Singapore fully prepared the Jhansis for the onward march to the Indo-Burma border battlefront. Accordingly, the first contingent consisting of five hundred women and girl soldiers of Rani of Jhansi Regiment left Singapore in late 1943, reaching Burma by early January 1944.'[60]

In addition to the number of RJR soldiers, Janaki's account is inaccurate
in several other ways. Given that the first women did not take up quarters
and begin training in the Singapore camp until October 1943, they could
not have been training for six months by late 1943. Furthermore, the
first male INA soldiers did not deploy in Burma until February 1944.[61]
Long anticipated, the arrival date of the Singapore Ranis in Rangoon was
21 June 1944 as confirmed by a letter from Bose to the Singapore camp
commander, 'You will be glad to know that the Jhansi contingent arrived
safely today after an uneventful journey.'[62]

Although in general the Ranis did not change their answers about
how many they were, it is safe to conclude that their initial responses
substantially overstate the true strength of the Regiment. In sum, all these
reports and interviews suggest that the total combined strength of the RJR
in Singapore and Burma was about 450, that the Regiment contingent in
Burma was at most 150, and that the fighting unit in Maymyo was about
twenty Ranis strong. Several Ranis who served in Burma told me that
they all knew each other by name, which would hardly be possible with
a force of 500.

Because Captain Lakshmi's fantasy of 'the rebel daughter' was more
dramatic and glamorous than the actual adventures of the RJR, her effort
to secure a place for the Ranis as Indian heroines may instead have served
to diminish the extraordinary nature of their actual experiences in the
public mind. Although they did not engage in combat against the enemy
and their numbers were smaller than commonly believed, the Ranis
were undoubtedly courageous individuals who broke ancient traditions
by leaving home, training with the intention of entering into battle and
dying for a country they had never seen. This sterling record needs no
exaggeration.

FIFTEEN

THE END OF THE QUEST

SOMETIME IN THE EARLY summer of 1944, a change occurred in the relationship between Bose and Captain Lakshmi. She no longer accompanied him on his diplomatic visits, but remained nominally the officer in command of the RJR and minister of women's affairs in the provisional government without devoting any time to either position.[1] Captain Lakshmi stayed in Maymyo as a physician to the INA. In our meeting, she explained her new focus: In view of the fact that the likelihood of the Regiment taking part in combat had become remote and also that the rate of casualties coming in from Imphal and Kohima was so great, she 'obtained Netaji's permission to work at the INA hospital which had been set up in Maymyo'.[2]

In apparent agreement, the British observers believed that Captain Lakshmi changed from being politically engaged to only wanting to serve as a medical doctor 'as the result of a change of heart inspired by the arrival of the 1 Div[ision] casualties'.[3] Earlier British Military Intelligence had surmised that Captain Lakshmi's change of heart had occurred 'after censure by Bose'.[4] Yet another report attributed it to 'ideological differences' between Bose and Captain Lakshmi.[5] Several Ranis had heard that Bose did not approve of the love affair between Captain Lakshmi and

Prem Sahgal; he felt that she did not set a good example for the Ranis. The exact reasons for the reported breach may never be known, but when the fighting group of the Ranis returned to Rangoon in late September and early October 1944, Captain Lakshmi stayed with the medical unit. For the next half-year, Captain Lakshmi worked far from Bose and the RJR at INA hospitals at Maymyo, Ziawadi and finally at Kalaw, a hill town in Shan State, halfway between Maymyo and Rangoon. She remained in Kalaw until forced to flee before advancing Allied forces in March 1945.[6]

The circumstances of Captain Lakshmi's surrender were dramatic.[7] After obtaining Bose's permission to concentrate on working as a doctor at the INA hospital in Maymyo until the end of the war, Captain Lakshmi treated both soldiers and civilians at medical facilities in northern Burma. During this time the area was under constant and heavy air bombardment and there were many INA casualties, both from ordnance and from disease. In March 1945 Captain Lakshmi was working at a small hospital in Kalaw when the town was bombed. Attavar Yellappa, who at this time was the minister of transportation of the Azad Hind government, had been sent north by Bose to organize the evacuation of INA patients as British forces were advancing quickly. During the attack, the building where Yellappa was staying took a hit and his leg was seriously hurt by shrapnel. Antibiotics were in limited use in WWII, none was available to administer to Yellappa, and he developed septicemia.[8]

The Burma National Army had declared war on Japan, their former allies, just a few weeks earlier. Consequently, when Captain Lakshmi, Yellappa and their Indian cohort were fleeing south towards Rangoon in April 1945, few places along the way offered refuge. Strapped to a stretcher, the feverish Yellappa was carried through the monsoon downpour towards Rangoon just ahead of the British troops. Captain Lakshmi realized that Yellappa would inevitably die from his massive systemic infection, and she did her best to keep him comfortable despite his high fever and the rigours of the retreat.

In her memoirs, *A Revolutionary Life: Memoirs of a Political Activist,* Captain Lakshmi told the story of the difficult and dramatic journey, and recounted the terrible episode in which she was forced to leave the dying Yellappa in a hut in the jungle with one assistant.[9]

On June 1, while we were in the jungle building a small hut for ourselves, a party of guerrillas – three Karens and one Gurkha – arrived, armed with sten guns. They spoke Hindustani and informed us that we were now their prisoners. They relieved me of my pistol and the two other rifles we had.[10]

A two-day trek together with her captors through the jungle brought her to British Post Force 136, commanded by a Colonel Edgar Peacock. Captain Lakshmi requested that Peacock send a team to recover Yellappa, but he refused claiming that he did not have the manpower.[11] It was learned later that Yellappa and his assistant were burned to death in their hut by a group of Karen guerrillas a few days after Captain Lakshmi left.[12]

Major Y.S. Bawa, the commanding officer of the INA hospital in Maymyo, was a member of the cohort fleeing with Yellappa, but he had left the group a month earlier to arrange for an official surrender to the British troops for everyone in his unit. He arrived at the British post and formally surrendered under terms of the Geneva Conventions. It is not clear if he requested that a British unit be sent for Yellappa and Captain Lakshmi. Therefore on 3 June 1945, when she reached the British post, claiming ignorance of Major Bawa's agreement with the British, Captain Lakshmi, as she called it, 'surrendered due to circumstances'![13]

The British Intelligence account of Captain Lakshmi's surrender differed somewhat from the version told by her elsewhere, and strongly suggested that she had a personal agenda that cannot be conclusively reconstructed but may have had something to do with her relationship with Sahgal. First, her surrender occurred a few weeks earlier than she claimed in her memoirs. The British Army Intelligence news-sheet, 'British Intelligence Weekly Letter' for the period 9 May to 15 May [1945] stated that Dr Lakshmi had 'capitulated'.[14] The account continued that Captain Lakshmi responded to a message from British troops to surrender, left Yellappa and an orderly with enough food in a friendly village, and contacted British patrols in order to give herself up, 'come in' as it was phrased. She surrendered to forward levies in Mawchi Area, Kayah State on 1 June 1945.[15]

The unusually enthusiastic intelligence report described the event in the liveliest of prose: 'The RANI herself who so fired the imagination (and hearts) of the INA came in unexpectedly at the end of the period under review after a month's involuntary attachment to one of our clandestine organisations in the Shan States. There can be no doubt at all about her personality or sincerity and she impressed us by her reasonableness in contrast to the rather shattering feminine fanaticism of her adherents. She has enabled us to obtain a much more balanced picture of the Rani of Jhansi Regt. ...[POW ID] L3719 [Captain Lakshmi] will at any rate be of extreme interest to CSDIC for her penetrating summing up of other INA officers.'[16] It is clear that the intelligence officers anticipated much valuable new information about the Rani regiments and the senior INA officers.

Captain Lakshmi noted in her memoirs that the British were friendly, did not imprison her and shared their provisions equitably with her.[17] After three weeks the British post was running out of supplies to sustain the POWs, and Colonel Peacock was forced to relocate the settlement. Along with other INA POWs and a mixed group of Karen and Gurkha refugees, Captain Lakshmi was escorted south to the encampment of a British Army unit in Toungoo, 100 miles away. By this time the head of the Ranis had, by her own account, 'become very friendly' with her captors.[18] The other INA soldiers from the relocated group were taken away as ordinary prisoners of war, but Captain Lakshmi received special treatment. She explained her preferential arrangements, 'I was different because I was a civilian and did not come under jurisdiction of the army.'[19] It was a curious point to argue because as the commandant of the RJR, she wore her uniform with the insignia as the rank of major in the INA, and she was still a minister in the Azad Hind government. She was hardly 'a civilian'.

British officers had already heard about Captain Lakshmi from other INA captives and defectors. Most notably they knew about her from her fiancé Prem Sahgal. Sahgal's diary, replete with confessions of love for the captain, had been impounded by the British to be used against him in his forthcoming trial at the Red Fort. The Fortnightly Report from the British Intelligence Unit of 9 August 1945, enthused, 'As regards individuals the star turn of the fortnight has of course been LAKSHMI, the gamin darling and later enfant terrible of the INA.'[20] Captain Lakshmi's charm, intelligence and beauty demonstrably served her well in her relationships with her captors. Every comment about her by British Intelligence officers was respectful and full of admiration for her energy, courage and honesty. By 4 August 1945, when the composite Interrogation Report was written up, Captain Lakshmi was expressing complete disillusionment with the Japanese and admitted that their intentions were purely imperialistic.[21] On a more personal level she stressed that she deeply resented the Japanese disapproval of the Ranis and of her as commanding officer of the Regiment.

The officers who handled her case emphasized that it was important to remember 'that for the last year she has been doing nothing but medical work'. It was decided that she not be confined to jail, and the official reason given was that 'as it is possible that her presence there might have an adverse effect on her followers in the ranks of the INA'.[22] Clearly, Captain Lakshmi used her brain and negotiating skills brilliantly and worked out with the British intelligence officers a good deal for herself.

In Rangoon she was kept in house arrest but was allowed to live in the homes of Burmese friends, where she quickly established a social circle of visiting journalists and resident Indians. The British officer who came to see her immediately after her arrival in Rangoon exceeded normal levels of helpful friendliness. She reports in her memoirs about British Major Harold Bow who was on his way to Delhi and offered to carry 'a personal message to Colonel P.K. Sahgal.'[23] Prem Sahgal was one of the three INA officers that the Raj had chosen to put on trial at the Red Fort in Delhi, accusing them of waging war against the King Emperor. Prem Kumar Sahgal was a Hindu and the two other officers brought to trial were Shah Nawaz Khan, a Muslim, and Gurbaksh Singh Dhillon, a Sikh.

In 2008, when Captain Lakshmi and I spent several days together at her lovely home in Kanpur, she added further details to the story about her surrender that she had told in *A Revolutionary Life*, the story of her service in the INA. Smiling impishly, she recounted that 'the British officer placed the note in his shoe, carried it from Rangoon to Delhi and managed to deliver it to Sahgal inside the prison'.[24] The clandestine message, she said, advised Sahgal to hire Bhulabhai Desai, a famous lawyer, to take over his defence as she was afraid that Sahgal would be hanged if found guilty.[25]

Sahgal hired Desai, but was found guilty and was sentenced to deportation for life. The trial of the three INA officers was followed by all of India and the publicity suddenly portrayed the INA soldiers as patriotic Indians. In the face of public outrage that Indian heroes of the war for freedom would be punished, their sentences were commuted and the prisoners released.

While telling the story to me, Captain Lakshmi further elaborated her account. Whenever Major Hugh Toye was in Rangoon, he came by her house for social visits. At this point in our conversation, it became clear to me that her fraternization with the British was a matter of considerable importance to her, because she provided an unusual amount of detail without being prompted.[26] Captain Lakshmi was still gleefully proud of having obtained useful assistance from her captors to help her future husband.

Captain Lakshmi's dismissal of her rights under the Geneva Conventions, described in her memoirs, needs to be understood in a larger context. As a major in the INA and a well-informed, educated woman, she would know the substance of the Conventions, and she would be aware that the terms of her surrender were important to her personally and as well to the Azad Hind and the INA. Even if she had not been familiar with the Conventions, Major Bawa of the INA could have explained to her in a few words that under the Geneva Conventions prisoners of war must give their names and rank, but were not obliged to give any other information. Also, the British would presumably have clarified the issue for her if she had inquired, but Captain Lakshmi instead chose not to surrender under the protective terms of the Geneva Conventions.

Peter Ward Fay, a friend of the Sahgals, sought in his book, *The Forgotten Army*, to exculpate Captain Lakshmi's 'coming in' to the British military and her social meetings with Major Hugh Toye, head of British Intelligence Unit in Singapore and others.[27] In their meetings with Captain Lakshmi, Fay charged the British intelligence officers of 'fraternization with the enemy – to be precise, fraternization with a turncoat', as Fay phrased it.[28] After acknowledging that Captain Lakshmi was a 'turncoat', i.e., that she revealed information about the INA and the Japanese Army because she had changed her allegiance, Fay's accusation that her interrogators, Captain Ali,

Major Toye and 'a dozen others' fraternized with Captain Lakshmi seems misplaced. At the time Fay wrote about Captain Lakshmi's surrender, the report of her testimony to the British Intelligence interrogators still lay undiscovered in the Indian National Archives, and Fay assumed that the information had not survived. Now these pertinent documents are available in full detail, it will be interesting to see what conclusions further analysis will bring.

At the end of the war there was much discussion among the members of the Government of India, the British government in London and the military regarding how to punish members of the INA without thereby causing a nationalist uproar in India. The IRs were an important basis for such British deliberations. One Forward Interrogation Unit document concludes with a tidy taxonomy of prisoners according to their threat to the Empire and a summary of the results of interrogations of 23,266 INA and IIL members in addition to a few civilians.[29] With Indian independence a looming prospect, those individuals deemed subversives and traitors by the Forward Interrogation Unit were increasingly hailed as heroes and martyrs by nationalists in India.

Because the INA soldiers were Indians and not foreigners, part of the purpose of British interrogations was to discover the extent of each subject's engagement in the Indian rebellion against the imperial Raj. All persons questioned were rated on a scale of white, grey and black, depending on the stringency of their political commitment to the movement against British colonial rule:

White: Genuine escapers or refugees whom it was safe to return to their Indian Army units or to release to their homes.

Grey: Men who had been affected by enemy propaganda but who were thought fit for return to service or release after rehabilitation and leave.

Black: Actual or potential enemy agents who would be a security risk if released.[30]

Like every surrendering INA soldier, Captain Lakshmi was assigned

an interrogation identification number; hers is L3719.[31] The debriefing of
Commander Dr Lakshmi Swaminathan of the Rani of Jhansi Regiment was
undertaken first during her house detention in Rangoon, and continued
while she was held in Kalaw, Burma, until she was repatriated to India in
March 1946.[32]

The overall British impression was that as a person with distaste for the
betrayal of friends, she maintained her personal loyalty to Bose, but made it
clear that she had lost hope that his movement would succeed. At the time
of her interrogation, she did not know where Bose was, but argued against
the likelihood of Bose having fled to Russia. Captain Lakshmi was drilled
on the personalities of senior members of the INA and, while providing
some useful information, she still remained 'loyal enough to her friends
and generous enough to her enemies to avoid getting them wittingly into
trouble'. Captain Ali, her interrogator and clearly her admirer, respectfully
accepted her limits.

The CSDIC(I) had since its creation sought information about the
RJR, but their earlier informants had not been sufficiently knowledgeable.
Captain Lakshmi asserted that Bose did not arrive in Singapore firmly
resolved to create the RJR as his companion on the U-boat, Abid Hasan
Safrani, claimed. A true politician, Bose had begun by sounding out Indian
expatriate opinion on the prospects of starting a women's military unit.
Only Yellappa had liked the idea, but he fought so effectively for the project
that despite the consensus among all other members of the IIL that only
five or six women would join, Bose decided to form the Regiment.

From the outset, the RJR was expected to play a dual role, fighting and
nursing. Captain Lakshmi stressed that the training for battle was carried
out in all seriousness, with machine gun courses, range practice, tactical
exercises and bayonet training. The Regiment never received orders to
move to the front because it was intended to operate only inside India
once the INA was marching through Bengal and Assam.

Captain Lakshmi insisted emphatically that the Ranis would have gone
to the front line, and that they had trained well enough to work together
as a coherent fighting unit. She tried to convince Captain Ali, her Indian
interrogating officer working for British Intelligence, that if the two of

them had met on the field in Bengal or Assam, she would first have tried to persuade him to join her cause. If he refused she would have taken him prisoner, and had he resisted, she contended that she would have shot or bayonetted him. Even after Captain Lakshmi's best attempts to prove to her Indian fellow countryman that the Ranis were professionally trained and skilled soldiers, he clearly found that proposition preposterous. With perhaps condescending humour he noted 'the Indian Army may well be thankful that it has been saved such an embarrassing situation'.[33]

In his evaluation of Captain Lakshmi, Ali recognized her achievement with the RJR: 'By her talents and inspiration she created the one unit in the INA which has almost without exception remained loyal to its leader and its beliefs.' Also, he pointed out, her excellent and unselfish work as a medical doctor in Maymyo and Mawchi hospitals 'can call for nothing but unqualified admiration'. Captain Ali thought that Captain Lakshmi was the type of woman India needed, but he was not sure what path she would follow after the war and therefore rated her 'Grey'.

Ali's commanding officer, Major W.P.G. MacLachlan reviewed the Interrogation Report and agreed that Captain Lakshmi's personality and drive had achieved 'the impossible with the RJR', and at the same time he doubted that her efforts had helped the INA cause. 'The 500 members of the Rani of Jhansi Regt have had no effect on the course of events in Burma, except for the blinding by propaganda of a few young and undeveloped girlish minds.' He continued, 'Never once have we heard that the example of the Rani of Jhansi Regt had inspired a soldier at the front to deeds of daring. Though trained to fight – after a fashion – they never, providentially, were near the fighting line, and whatever their nursing achieved is to be applauded.' MacLachlan considered Captain Lakshmi's work with the Ranis not only wasted energy, but that it also contributed to 'the corruption of the young'. He was not sure what rating to give her, but in the end raised her rating to 'Black'.[34] Captain Lakshmi was pleased to get a black rating, as it was a distinction conferred only on those who exhibited by word, deed or rank a fundamental disloyalty to the Raj.[35]

In her memoirs, Captain Lakshmi describes how she spent her captivity in Rangoon following the end of the war living in the home of Indian friends,

Dina Nath and Sardar Zahra Singh. Her good friend Rani Gian Kaur, the head nurse from the Maymyo hospital, also served her house arrest at the Singh house and the two women had a stream of Indian officers from the British army visiting. Lakshmi was now able to catch up on news of the INA and especially of Bose's last days in Rangoon. Two days after her arrival came word of Bose's death in an airplane crash. Knowing Bose, she dismissed the report and expected him to return at an opportune moment. Time in captivity passed slowly, until Dr Lakshmi's repeated requests finally resulted in permission from the British to work at a small medical clinic. She would both serve the many people who needed inexpensive medical care and also earn a bit of money so she could contribute to her living expenses.

According to a British Intelligence interrogation report, for one month during her captivity, Lakshmi – 'the RANI herself' – as the BI called her, was attached to one of their 'clandestine organisations' and 'enabled [them] to obtain a much more balanced picture of the Rani of Jhansi Regt' and several of her fellow officers in the INA.[36]

Captain Lakshmi has never given any details of her interrogation, but says that in early November 1945, when British Intelligence thought that she had become too politically active, she was transferred 400 miles north to the small hill town of Kalaw in the Shan state of Burma. Instructed that she would remain under house arrest until the trials of the INA at the Red Fort in Delhi were concluded, finally on 4 March 1946, she was escorted back to Calcutta by a British army officer in an air force plane.[37]

After Prem Sahgal's release from the Red Fort and Captain Lakshmi's divorce from B.K. Naujindra Rao, they were married and lived in Kanpur. Captain Lakshmi told me somewhat wistfully that Kanpur was not her first choice to settle and raise a family, but that was the only place her husband was able to find a job.[38] His service in the INA blocked his getting a position as a military officer after Independence.[39] Captain Lakshmi established a medical clinic for the poor in Kanpur and worked there every day of her long life. At age ninety-three she invited me to accompany her on the medical rounds she did early every morning. After finishing her examination of an obviously pregnant woman, she grumbled to me, 'It is still the same. This woman said that she did not have any children, but on examination I saw that she had definitely given birth before. I asked what had happened to the child, and she answered, "But that was a girl!'"

In their assessment of Captain Lakshmi's potential as a politically dangerous person for imperial rule in India, the British Intelligence officers mention several times that Captain Lakshmi was not interested in politics.[40] She proved them wrong. At the age of eighty-eight and after many years of active membership in the Communist Party of India, Captain Lakshmi ran for president of India as the candidate sponsored by several left-leaning parties. She acknowledged that she did not have a chance of winning but found it scandalous that no one else would represent the party. She lost to A.P.J. Abdul Kalam who was sponsored by both the Congress party and the Bharatiya Janata Party (BJP), the two major political parties in India.

The representatives of the Combined Section General Headquarters, India, decided to interrogate only five Ranis in addition to Captain Lakshmi, those they considered leaders of the RJR.[41] No sepoys were interviewed. The reason for not questioning more Ranis was a fear that rounding them all up would 'violently antagonise Indian public opinion' and serve no useful purpose.[42] From a British point of view that was the right decision for the Ranis would have welcomed the publicity and the opportunity to demonstrate their devotion to Bose and the Azad Hind.

The RJR was the only segment of the INA that was entirely recruited from the civilian population. Therefore, although the Ranis had sought to overthrow the Raj, they, unlike the former British Indian Army soldiers, could not be said to have suborned an oath to serve the King Emperor. The Government of India estimated that if all members of the Regiment were interrogated, half of the Ranis would be classified 'White' and the rest, except for Captain Lakshmi, 'Grey'.[43] In addition to Captain Lakshmi, the Ranis chosen for intense interrogation were L3239 Bela Mukherjee, a schoolteacher from Rangoon; L3267 Manwati Panday, a successful recruiter and person in charge of the camp in Burma; L3242 Gori Bhattacharji (Gauri Bhattacharya), a nurse; L3968 Gian Kaur, the nurse in charge of the RJR nursing group in Burma; and Janaki Thevar, the commanding officer of the Rani fighting group in Burma.[44] Each individual who was formally detained and interrogated was given an identification number, but no numbers or names were found for any Ranis apart from these five. Toye notes that interrogations were usually not hostile as 'most subjects were only too anxious to tell their stories, but that, even when true, the stories were often hard to believe'.[45]

Janaki Thevar reported that shortly after Bose's presumed death, her sister Papathy and she were taken to British Army headquarters in Kuala Lumpur for questioning. This continued every day for over two months, until the girls' father protested and the interrogations stopped.[46] Unfortunately, the IR for Janaki Thevar was not found. Shanti and Anjuli Bhowmick were interviewed several times at their home in Seremban, Malaya, but as Shanti wrote, 'due to want of sufficient proof they could not haul us up for any trial or punishment'.[47] British police did, however, arrest her two uncles, Haripada and Motilal Bhowmick under 'the Arms Act', and Motilal was sentenced to a six-month jail term.[48]

Several members of the Regiment, whom I interviewed for this study, stated that British Intelligence officials in Rangoon, Kuala Lumpur, Bangkok and Singapore had also questioned them and ordered them to stay at their homes; among those were Rama, Asha and Mommata. Apparently, the British did not categorize their conversations with these Ranis as interrogations. Rama's experience was typical. She was directed to stay at her parent's house in Rangoon for six months after leaving camp, but was allowed to continue her studies. A few polite police officers came to the Mehta residence to ask her why she had joined the RJR. She answered that she had enlisted in order to fight for Indian independence. Since she had no answers other than obvious ones, the interviews were terminated and the police officers left her alone.[49]

In interrogating the Ranis, the intelligence officers were surprised at the lasting impact of Bose's words on the volunteers. Two Ranis in particular gave the British officers 'much cause for thought. ... L3242 (Second Lieutenant Gauri Bhattacharya) and L3239 (Lieutenant Bela Mukherjee) impressed the British interrogators greatly with the sincerity and fire of their beliefs – 'a sincerity which but few of their men folk had found it in them to express'.[50] The Ranis, Gauri and Bela, tried to convince their interrogators that Bose was right, that they were still going to fight and win freedom for India. They were firm in their trust that as agreed between Bose and Tojo, the Japanese would leave liberated India and return home expecting to be reimbursed in cash for their services to help secure India's independence. The British interrogator clearly appreciated the intelligence and integrity of especially these two young women. However, he worried that given their complete ignorance of history and the world situation, the Ranis' blind faith in their Netaji, which he thought paralleled that of 'the Hitler Madchen', would make it difficult for them to fit into post-war Indian society.[51] The British Intelligence officer refers to German girls, Mädchen, who enrolled in the *Bund Deutscher Mädel in der Hitler-Jugend,* a society of young women who were fiercely devoted to the Nazi movement without understanding its depraved philosophy. This officer expressed the hope that all the Ranis would direct their nationalist energy into more conventional channels and find constructive ways of helping their country, like Gauri Bhattacharya, who went to medical school when the war ended.[52] Notwithstanding the pessimism of their interrogators, many of the Ranis interviewed for this study did serve their countries with honour after the war. Rasammah and Janaki, the two most outstanding public servants of the group, did not move to India but stayed in independent Malaysia where both received high awards from their country for their service. Several other Ranis became teachers in Malaysia, while others were trained as medical doctors in India and remained there.

The battle for access to India through Burma was lost. Bose arrived in Bangkok on 14 May 1945. After taking a cup of tea he went back to plan the next venue for continuation of the fight.[53] In public Bose dismissed the idea of defeat and called the evacuation from Burma a temporary setback.

In a speech delivered in Bangkok on 21 May 1945, Bose admitted, 'No doubt we have lost one round in India's War of Liberation ... [but] those of us who have left Burma have not withdrawn from the fight. ... The roads to Delhi are many.'[54] Despite the demoralizing defections of hundreds or perhaps even thousands of his troops, Bose still clung to his dream. He claimed to have learned from many battlefield encounters between INA soldiers and sepoys of the British Indian Army that his dream could still come true: 'If they [i.e., Azad Hind Fauj] succeed in advancing further, members of the British Indian Army would then come and join them.'[55] In preparation for that next battle, he summoned the Azad Hind ministers to lay plans and draw up maps. He continued his radio broadcasts from Singapore urging mainland Indians not to give up hope.

At Seremban, Malaya, at midnight on 10 August, Bose heard the news of Russia's declaration of war on Japan.[56] Hours later, on 11 August, he learned of Japan's impending surrender. Ayer, who observed his commander responding to this last serious change of circumstances, saw Bose 'laugh away the catastrophe. He was bubbling with scintillating humour. He cracked jokes and laughed like a child. It was the supreme moment of his life. He was not going to be crushed by the disaster.'[57] Bose ordered his closest advisers brought to Singapore from across Malaya for a conference the next evening. A long list of decisions remained. One that was uppermost in Bose's mind was the transfer to their homes of the Ranis still quartered at the Singapore Training Camp with sufficient money to help them get settled back in their communities.[58]

On 14 August, Bose, who was back in Singapore, knew that Japanese surrender was imminent. The Singapore Ranis were told to pack to break camp the next morning. As a farewell to their commander, to their comrades-in-arms and to their own time in the INA, they had staged one last drama – a play based on the life of Rani Lakshmibai of Jhansi. At 3 p.m., as the Supreme Commander of the Azad Hind Fauj, Bose sent a 'Special Order of the Day' to the officers and men of the INA, saying that all 'wild bazar rumours' to the effect that 'hostilities have ceased' were untrue and should be ignored. All personnel should continue 'like brave soldiers fighting for the freedom of their Motherland'.[59] Bose's determination to keep the news from his INA soldiers was somewhat mystifying, unless, of course, he wanted to prevent reality from ruining the Ranis' last grand performance. That evening Bose was the guest of honour at the play but arrived late, delayed by a tooth extraction; he was greeted by deafening applause from the audience of more than 3,000 members of the INA. The evening ended with the soldiers singing the national anthem of the prospective free India. In Washington DC, a few hours later, President Truman accepted Emperor Hirohito's surrender.

On the afternoon of 15 August 1945 after Tokyo had officially announced the Japanese capitulation, Bose and his inner circle understood that if he remained in Singapore he would be taken prisoner by the Allied forces. Bose at first insisted on staying, but was finally persuaded to leave for Moscow or at least Manchuria to continue the freedom fight. On 16 August Bose flew out of the Singapore aerodrome with three Indian advisers and a Japanese–English translator. In his last press release before departure, Bose repeated the same optimistic theme: 'In this unprecedented crisis in our history, I have only one word to say. Do not be depressed at our temporary failure. Be of good cheer and keep up your spirits. Above all, never for a moment falter in your faith in India's destiny. There is no power on earth that can keep India enslaved. India shall be free and before long.'[60]

The first stopover on his flight from Singapore was Bangkok. Here Bose met with INA officers and IIL officials, and he also invited the four Ranis, the Navarednam sisters and the girls returning to Burma who were still in the city, to attend the meeting and the dinner. Bose's second stop was Tourane [Da Nang], Vietnam. From there, the trip proved difficult because of a shortage of airplanes and a backlog of Japanese officers waiting for transport to Tokyo.[61] Only one seat was made available for Bose's group. After considerable pressure, the Japanese chief pilot, Aoyanagi, agreed to squeeze one more person into the overloaded bomber and Bose took off, accompanied by Colonel Habibur Rahman. Not even Ayer, who had accompanied Bose for all but the last leg of the trip, knew exactly where Bose was headed, but he guessed Manchuria.[62]

Bose's aircraft was a twin-engine 97-2 Japanese heavy bomber and the final destination was Tokyo.[63] On 18 August the plane took on fuel at Japanese-occupied Taipei, in Taiwan. Two hours later, after some repairs to the left engine and satisfactory retesting by the Japanese crew who declared it air-worthy, the heavy aircraft failed to gain altitude on takeoff. Habibur Rahman later told that he heard a loud explosion and then the plane crashed on to the airfield from a height of about 10 metres.[64] Bose was doused with gasoline and as the only exit from the wreckage was through flames, he was severely burned, especially on the face and chest.[65] He was taken to Nanmon Japanese military hospital at Taihoku, but his burns were so severe that he did not live through the night of 18-19 August 1945. At the age of forty-eight, Subhas Chandra Bose was dead. Habibur Rahman was less severely injured and recovered.

The unpublished 'Report on the Death of Subhas Chandra Bose' contains the transcripts of interrogations by British Intelligence of witnesses of Bose's last hours and the immediate aftermath.[66] Drawn from the British Library Asian and African Studies Collections, the United Kingdom Liaison Mission in Japan and the British embassy in Tokyo, this set of documents, together with the files from The National Archives of India in New Delhi, provide details of the cause of the crash, Bose's injuries and his death.

Lieutenant Colonel Nonogaki Shiro of Japan who was accompanying Bose on the last flight from Taipei survived and described the crash:

After pulling myself together, I got near the burning bomber. The fuselage was broken into pieces. [...] Mr. Bose and Mr. Rahman were in the passage near the tanks. One of the tanks was thrown forward and struck Lieutenant General Shidei. Another one broke and fell down. As a result, gasoline was poured over Mr. Bose. Though he ran out from a slit of the fuselage, his woolen jacket, soaked in gasoline, caught fire. It began to burn instantaneously.[67]

The reports of the sudden death, in a remote location, of a figure of such stature as Bose seemed beyond belief to many Indians. Politicians, critics, supporters, young and old all over India refused to accept that Bose had died. Unsubstantiated contrary accounts claimed that Bose survived the crash and made his way to Russia to escape British capture and trial as a war criminal. According to this scenario, he was to stay in Russia, awaiting India's independence, after which he would return in triumph.[68] Some imagined that the crash was staged with the help of Field Marshal Count Terauchi Hisaichi of Japan in order to allow Bose to cross over from Taipei into Manchuria without informing the Japanese government in Tokyo. Another popular legend had it that when the war ended Bose trekked into the Himalayas and lived out his life as a sadhu.

Shortly after the news of Bose's death broke in India, Gandhi added to the confusion with an announcement that 'his inner voice' told him that Bose was still alive; he later changed his mind. Bose's daughter, Anita Pfaff, doubts that the ashes in the urn returned from Japan are actually her father's remains; she, like many others, wants to see a DNA profile performed on the remaining bone fragments.[69] Every few years new assertions about the death of Bose surface in the press with claims of espionage and government cover-ups. Having examined the 2016 documentary evidence used to disprove the earliest reports of the accident on Formosa, I agree with Rani Mommata Gupta and Bose's daughter Anita Pfaff: Subhas Chandra Bose died on 18 August 1945.[70] In any case, Netaji's legacy still lives.

So goes the inspiring story of the courageous soldiers of the Rani of Jhansi Regiment. Surmounting extraordinary cultural, historical and religious barriers, they sought to take the fight for India's freedom to the enemy, to liberate a nation that virtually none of them had ever seen. That they did not succeed does not diminish their determination, their discipline, their bravery, their unending devotion to Mother India. Thus, these remarkable women serve as a beacon today for all those everywhere who demand liberty, and who continue the battle for genuine equality for women.

SIXTEEN

FINAL REFLECTIONS ON
SUBHAS CHANDRA BOSE AND THE RJR

THE RANI OF JHANSI Regiment of the Indian National Army existed for a scant two years, from October 1943 to August 1945. During its brief existence, awareness in India of the INA and the RJR was suppressed by the British military. Chiefly because of Dr Lakshmi Sahgal's persistent and effective publicity, the Ranis became more broadly known in India after the war. When Captain Lakshmi died in 2012, newspapers around the world revived the story of the Ranis, the courageous regiment of women combat soldiers that she had commanded. By then the embellished narrative included long marches by thousands of Ranis through malarial Burmese jungles, bloody engagements with the British Imperial Army and their Indian sepoys at the Battle of Imphal, successful rearguard actions as the Japanese withdrew, and the heroic rescue of their leader, the legendary Netaji Subhas Chandra Bose. This study has extracted and analysed the facts concerning the creation and strength of the Regiment and its wartime activities, presenting a more accurate account of the women's Regiment.

How could anyone in the early 1940s have conceived of a regiment of all-female Indian soldiers, given the traditional restrictions that rule the lives of Indian women? How could anyone have imagined sending young

Asian women into 'the most impenetrable and poisonous insects infested tropical forests' burdened with combat and survival gear?[1] Why would anyone risk a collaboration of Indian women with the brutal Japanese army that had captured thousands of foreign females to serve their soldiers as 'comfort women'? Why seek proximity with Japanese soldiers who had committed barbaric atrocities in every military action and to families in the Ranis' hometowns?

The answer to these questions rests with Subhas Chandra Bose. By any measure, Subhas Chandra Bose was a remarkable man. Spending his entire adulthood fighting to release India from its colonial yoke, he ultimately gave his life to that cause. Although he suffered the political consequences of standing against Mohandas Gandhi, a far more cunning politician than Bose, he was clearly one of the most important Indians in the first half of the twentieth century.

Raised into privilege in Cuttack, Orissa Division, Bengal Province, Bose exhibited early the taste and talent for leadership that were to characterize his career. His experience of and loathing for racial prejudice led him to challenge the immense power of the British Raj and to dedicate himself to the noblest of objectives: freedom for India, end to ethnic discrimination, elimination of illiteracy and equity for women. A devotee of the goddesses Kali and Durga, Bose saw India as a mother goddess in need of protection, protection he was determined to provide.

After his arrival in Singapore in June 1943, he rapidly and effectively rebuilt the INA and mobilized Indians of the diaspora behind his vision and his mission. Relentlessly hardworking, his brilliance was continually evident. His charisma was magnetic. He regularly drew massive crowds in India and, later, in the South-East Asian diaspora. In one-to-one encounters and in small groups, he both mesmerized and inspired. His appeal cut across religion, caste, class and gender, all important and divisive aspects of Indian society. He brought women into the mainstream of the armed struggle against the British with the establishment of the Rani of Jhansi Regiment.

Bose soon worked his way to the top of the Congress party, in part because ordinary, and especially young, Indians saw him as an advocate of their personal and nationalist agendas. In short, few questioned that Bose would play a major role in the independence struggle and in post-colonial India as a patriot, an Indian nationalist, for ages. One then asks, why did that positive destiny fail to materialize?

An element of the answer to this central question is that Bose, once past his youthful doubts about his worth in the world, developed an enormous ego. He solicited advice from friends and political associates, but in the end he followed only his own inclinations. Setting himself above the political process by insisting on a second term as Congress president in 1939, and then giving up this post despite the counsel of his staunchest supporters who urged him to ride out that political storm, he ended for all practical purposes his Indian political career. He asked about the propriety and utility of establishing the RJR. Most of his colleagues opposed the idea, but Bose went ahead.

As commander of the INA, Bose never doubted his tactical capabilities, even though he had no professional training. This arrogance led to INA catastrophes on the battlefields of north-west Burma. His insistence on wearing a military uniform like Hitler, Tojo and Mussolini in tropical Burma raises questions about the authenticity of his self-image. Moreover, while never acknowledging his own calamitous mistakes, he had no tolerance for those of others.

In addition, throughout his life Bose was curiously disconnected from the potentially disastrous consequences of his actions. From 1943 to 1945 he sent thousands of INA soldiers in Burma to their deaths, partly because of his military incompetence and partly because of his misplaced trust in the word of General Tojo. He insisted that INA soldiers with no food and no equipment stay behind to continue the campaign after the Japanese had surrendered, a sure recipe for their destruction. Possessing this draconian and authoritarian streak, completely at odds with his democratic and humanist rhetoric, makes one wonder what sort of political leader Bose would have become in an independent India.

As a leader he was capable of inspiring females, including the Ranis, to action. His political speeches expressed a view of women that was genuinely progressive for his era and which found expression in the Rani of Jhansi Regiment. Although Bose created the RJR and deployed its volunteers to Burma, he never fulfilled his promise to them to commit the Regiment to the battlefield. Moreover, despite his advocacy of feminist goals, Bose often evinced a paternalistic attitude regarding the Ranis, becoming preoccupied with their personal safety, most notably during the chaotic scramble to leave Rangoon. He wanted the RJR to project an image of fierce warriors, willing and able to engage in combat, while at the same time he saw the Ranis as defenseless females needing protection. In the end, Bose failed these courageous women by keeping them cloistered in Rangoon, as for generations Indian women have been protected by their fathers, husbands and sons.

Finally, there is Bose's most questionable and controversial action, the forging of an alliance with the heinous Nazi and Japanese regimes. Bose took enormous risks by joining the Axis, and this Machiavellian collaboration destroyed him and his movement. This decision developed out of Bose's distinctly un-Gandhian commitment to the use of violence in the struggle for Indian freedom. Bose's advocates argue that his 'deal with the devils' was a pragmatic choice, necessary for the liberation of India, and some contend that his actions had a long-term beneficial effect on India's quest for freedom. His critics assert that Bose never had any real influence in Berlin or Tokyo, and that if Japan had won the war an even more brutal Japanese oppression would have replaced the British yoke in India.

In any case, to the end of his life Bose seemed to have an affinity with the murderous Japanese regime. Well after it was clear that Japan was losing the war and as massive Japanese atrocities continued in China on 6 July 1944, Bose sent a message to Gandhi. In the radio broadcast calling Gandhi the creator of the present awakening in our country, Bose 'took the liberty', as he phrased it, to acquaint the Mahatma with the plans and activities of patriotic Indians outside India.[2] He asserted that Japan's attitude towards the world in general, and towards Asiatic nations in particular, had been completely revolutionized. 'After my visit to Japan and after establishing close contact with the present-day leaders of that country, I was fully satisfied that Japan's present policy towards Asia was no bluff, but was rooted in sincerity.[3] I have no objection personally to dictatorship, if it is for a righteous cause.'[4] Bose continued, 'In General

Tojo, Japan has a leader and a prime minister who is true to his word and whose actions are in full conformity with his declarations, and a leader, in moral stature, towers head and shoulders above contemporary statesmen.'[5]

It seems fair to say that not many of the people of Asia in the summer of 1944, terrorized by brutal Japanese occupation, shared Bose's admiration for the tyrants in Tokyo.

During the campaign in Burma and particularly on the retreat, Bose repeatedly exposed himself to danger, often refusing to take shelter during air attacks as if he were trying to get himself killed to avoid facing that his life's mission, his work and his sacrifice had all come to naught. If so, the airplane crash may have been tragically fortuitous. He avoided having to come to the Red Fort of Delhi, not as the conqueror as he had promised but instead to be tried as a traitor, and he evaded public acknowledgement that his failed quest had cost the lives of thousands of INA soldiers.

Milan Hauner, the German historian, saw Bose as 'the tragic hero of Asian nationalism, a Sisyphus-like figure, constantly overtaken by events and destined to lose the struggle'.[6] Perhaps a better Bose comparison might be drawn with Icarus, another Greek mortal who came to a bad end, but in his case because of his lofty aspirations rather than his sadistic crimes. An extraordinarily gifted man dedicated to bringing freedom to his people, Bose sacrificed everything and probably thought he had failed. However, year by year, India has moved closer to the destiny that Bose had envisioned for his beloved Motherland.

Subhas Chandra Bose's personal, political and moral goal throughout his life was to liberate India from British colonial rule. In this quest, he was determined to make it possible for Indians to live in freedom in a nation governed by Indians and not by white foreign oppressors who believed that they were genetically and culturally superior to Indians. Bose disregarded all other demands for his time and energy, abandoning Emilie Schenkl and his daughter for India.

During the time between the two world wars, the fight for Indian independence was carried on by many: famously by Mohandas Gandhi, Bose, Motilal Nehru and his son Jawaharlal. Of the leading Indian politicians, only Bose stood against Gandhi's passive resistance to advocate armed struggle. The reasons for Clement Attlee's Labour government to begin British withdrawal from India following the costly WWII victory were largely economic and had little to do with Gandhi's 'Quit India' movement, but it may have been aided by the weakening of the Indian Army because thousands of its soldiers had joined the INA. The fear in London was that the INA's nationalistic ideology had already influenced the Indian Army and thereby rendered it unreliable.

Emulating his heroes Garibaldi and Eamon de Valera, who had won independence for their countries against overwhelming opposition, Bose established his own fighting force, the Indian National Army, with more than 40,000 men and the Rani of Jhansi Regiment.

Bose inspired his soldiers, both men and women, and like all leaders of freedom fighters, as well as generals of any army, Bose accepted that many of his soldiers would die in the campaign. To some his ambition may have seemed overweening, bordering on fanaticism. Bose foresaw a necessary interim period of despotism as a necessary step on the way to full democracy for India. He was not alone in entering into foul wartime dealings. In the fight for his country, Winston Churchill, in a similar cold-blooded and pragmatic spirit observed, 'If Hitler invaded hell I would make at least a favourable reference to the devil in the House of Commons.' Churchill forged an alliance with Joseph Stalin who murdered tens of millions of his own citizens.

Comparing Bose's quest for freedom with those of Nelson Mandela or even George Washington, the chances of successful revolution in India looked reasonable, especially in 1943 when Japan's wartime conquests were still firmly controlled. As Mandela put it, 'It always seems impossible until it's done.' Certainly, Washington with his ragged, starving and disputatious force of colonists at Valley Forge could not have been certain of victory against the most powerful army in the world. Why should Bose think he could accomplish less?

With information from the British Intelligence documents, other archival records plus the personal papers and oral testimony of the surviving veterans of the RJR, a more definitive picture of the strength of the Regiment has emerged. The total number of soldiers was about 450, some of whom were nurses. They never got closer than 250 miles to the front lines, and no RJR member ever engaged the enemy in combat. Bose's stated intention for the Regiment was that the women would be fighters of equal training and competence as the men. Reality proved different. The women soldiers were smaller, younger and physically much weaker than their male colleagues, many of whom were professional soldiers, instructed by the British officer corps, and had served in the imperial military before they were captured and became Japanese POWs. They were experienced in jungle warfare, which was fought in small units, often hand to hand. They were skilled at reconnaissance and able to navigate in dense tropical rainforests.

None of the RJR members mentioned instruction in compass reading or communication. That their training in jungle navigation was inadequate was clearly demonstrated when Captain Lakshmi and her fighting group soldiers went out for a short walk through a jungle area during the monsoon. They were lost for hours and rescue teams had to be sent out to find them. The Ranis never stated that they had learned to purify water, or to identify what was edible in the bush if supplies did not arrive. In camp, cooks prepared their meals.

The Ranis worked hard to carry out their assignments and became much stronger than they were prior to enlistment, but the much acclaimed Rani training programme placed primary emphasis on marching through towns carrying rifles, looking smart in khaki uniforms and singing patriotic songs. The women did go on long night marches with full gear every two weeks or so; had an afternoon of target practice every fortnight; and enjoyed charging stuffed sacks with their bayonets. But much more of their time was spent learning the finer details of military parading and marching. As masters of half step, mark time, column half left and right according to shouted orders, they performed perfectly at the celebrations Bose so loved. Such ceremonial posturing was obviously not designed to mold soldiers for close and intense combat in the mountainous jungles on the Indo-Burmese border.

The Ranis were unaware, both during their service in Burma and at the time of the interviews, that their training would not have served them well in the jungle. They could not visualize themselves climbing mountains in torrential rains and monsoon mud with a full load of gear on their backs. When INA soldiers came back from the front in northern Burma, near-dead from wounds, malnutrition and malaria, the Ranis who treated them were shocked, but in interviews the women expressed no doubts that their training would have enabled them to engage the enemy had they served the same brutal tour of duty as the men.

Tellingly, the Ranis did not question the necessity for male guards around their camps and on trips outside the facility. Only Janaki Thevar mentioned the risk of rape, in the context of her early morning horseback rides from the Halpin Road camp to the hospital in Rangoon, two-and-a-half miles away.[7] The other women may have been aware of the typical horrific behaviour of Japanese soldiers without explicitly addressing the topic. One Rani stated that the most dangerous part of her experience in the Regiment was when Japanese soldiers bathed naked in front of the girls when they were travelling as guards for the RJR. No one voiced any fear that the taunts of the naked soldiers might have become more serious in the absence of their male INA escorts.

Unless further evidence materializes in the Bose papers held at the Netaji Research Bureau in Kolkata, it will never be known exactly what mission Bose had in mind for the RJR and why he wanted to spend precious materiel and limited time equipping and training young women who had no previous military experience. The overwhelming consensus of the citizens of Singapore regarding the uniformed women singing and marching through the streets of their war-torn city was that the RJR was simply a propaganda stunt. No one believed that these women would make real soldiers. General Kiani of the INA maintained that Bose had promised him that the Ranis would never fight. It is, therefore, possible that Bose never intended to send the Ranis into battle, although the Ranis repeatedly pointed out that their contract with Bose was that they serve in combat at the front line, shoulder by shoulder with their INA brothers.

A major rationale for fielding female soldiers, according to Bose, was that the spectacle of women taking responsibility for the liberation of the Motherland would strengthen the resolve of INA's male soldiers and change the hearts of Indian men fighting for the Allied forces. It is impossible to know if Bose actually believed that Allied Indian soldiers would end hostilities at the sight of Indian women adversaries, when reports asserted that they did not refrain from killing INA men from their own villages or even families. In that context, women dressed in men's khaki desert uniforms suddenly appearing in their gun sights would likely not have been recognized by the men of the Indian Army as their own compatriots. Bose never directly offered an alternative plan to his fantastic scenario of success should the tide of war not turn with the arrival of the RJR on the battlefield. What would have happened if Allied officers and sepoys had not put down their weapons as Bose hoped and had fired at the advancing Ranis?

This leads to a final theory, one that some Indian historians have claimed was Bose's plan from the beginning. It is that Bose created the Regiment so that the Ranis would become martyrs for the noble cause of India's liberation. In many of his speeches he struck the theme of Indian women's traditional willingness for self-sacrifice and that the price of freedom was blood.

In this framework, it is important to note that the RJR was never accorded a place in the regular INA chain of command; it began and remained under Bose's direct supervision, the only INA unit to be so. Because he considered each Rani to have been entrusted to him by her parents and families for the sacred cause of India's liberation, he might have thought it morally acceptable to sacrifice all of them if their deaths would help turn the Motherland against the colonial oppressors.

Ever fond of memorable tableaux and re-enactments, Bose may have wanted to stage a dramatic scene in which the Ranis, cast as reincarnations of the original Rani Lakshmibai, were slaughtered as martyrs on the battlefield. Bose may have hoped that a re-enactment on the hills of Manipur of the historical Rani's last stand would generate an emotional mass movement of outrage and indignation across India and the whole world, similar to the reaction to the Jallianwala Bagh massacre, igniting a revolt inside India and the ouster of the British Raj. In any event, many Ranis concurred with this view of their possible destiny, and several members of the Regiment in my interviews claimed to regret not having achieved martyrdom for India's freedom. But if Bose intended to send the Ranis into battle, why did he not do so? The answer may have been a matter of timing. The operational occasion for employing the RJR for tactical sacrifice never arrived. In March and April 1944, there was only a very short interval when the Japanese and the INA forces had invaded India and appeared to have a chance to win the battle for Imphal. At that time, the expected Rani contingent from Singapore was still lingering in Singapore and only twenty Burma-recruited Rani fighters were then stationed in Maymyo. Sending such a tiny number to Imphal to become martyrs would not have had the dramatic effect that Bose may have desired. Following the Allied victory at Imphal, the INA was in constant and chaotic flight during the next year retreating ever further from Indian soil. While the Allies pushed INA and Japanese troops southwards, the Ranis in Burma remained inside their guarded mansion on Halpin Road in Rangoon, begging Bose to send them into battle.

In any event, considering the demands on Bose during the Burma campaign, he spent a surprisingly great deal of his time on the RJR, the Regiment as a whole and also with the individual Ranis. General Shah Nawaz Khan who encountered the Ranis in Maymyo remarked: 'To all the Rani of Jhansi Girls he was like a father and was always concerned about their welfare and honour.'[8] No Rani in the interviews disagreed with this characterization of Bose's relationship with the members of the RJR. Every Rani who served in Burma told me her own story of Bose's kindness and her feelings that he had cared especially for her. Janaki Bai's father drowned while she was in the camp in Rangoon and Bose sent a car for her to bring her to his lodging so that he could comfort her.[9] Bose gave Labanya the loving care she needed when as a teenager she was widowed while serving in Burma. Shah Nawaz knew what had happened to the young woman and noted, Bose 'used to send for her and talk to her for hours consoling her like a father'.[10] Labanya later refused to believe that Bose had a biological daughter, Anita. That was not possible, she claimed, because 'Netaji loved his children in the INA, especially the members of the RJR'.[11] Labanya's theory, one she claimed that the entire INA agreed with, was that Bose's enemies had created the story of his relationship with the German woman as a plot to discredit his reputation.[12]

When a Rani had even a minor accident or illness, Bose visited her or sent candy. Aruna and other RJR soldiers received greetings from their families and friends that Bose met at meetings and on his trips. He loved the performances he worked on together with the Ranis and was proud and complimented them like a father when they did well. Shortly after Shanti and Anjuli Bhowmick had returned home from Burma, their uncle encountered Bose at a meeting in Seremban, Malaya. Bose asked why the girls were not there and Bhowmick told him that Shanti was ill. Bose sent greetings and urged Shanti's uncle to be sure that she received proper medical treatment. Shanti concluded, 'These words, apart from many others to us direct on former occasions, are clear indications of Netaji's filial [sic] affection and anxiety that he had for us and also the extent of close vigil he had always personally kept on even trivial matters concerning us.'[13] Shanti was right; Bose was a kind and caring father to the women in his Regiment.

When I asked the Ranis if parents, relatives or friends had alerted them that joining the RJR might cause future mothers-in-law to object to having a Regiment member as a daughter-in-law, not one Rani had been warned. Several women said that they had kept quiet at work and even to their husbands about their adventures during the war, because they feared social condemnation. Some Singapore citizens at the time assumed that the Ranis were 'loose' girls. In interviews, some Ranis mentioned that people on the street occasionally had taunted them with deprecatory remarks as they were driven through the city on military transport trucks.

Of the Ranis I interviewed, several reported that their parents, and one mother who was a widow, had hesitated to permit them to join the INA but were eventually persuaded to sign the papers. Why would parents who could well afford to safely feed and house their children entrust their daughters' lives in the Burmese jungle to Japanese soldiers who openly behaved with wanton cruelty and violence? Why would they agree to expose their innocent young girls to the brutal experiences of war and to possible death?

The answer is to be found in the political climates in Malaya and even more so in Burma after the humiliating British defeat in Singapore. Before that watershed event, Japanese Intelligence had worked hard to foster the expectation that Indian independence was imminent. When in July 1943 the energetic, optimistic and self-confident Subhas Chandra Bose arrived in Singapore, he was not only endorsed but also personally welcomed by Prime Minister Tojo of Japan. Indians in the diaspora saw this political alignment as a sign that time had come for a final communal effort to achieve independence, and many prosperous Indians donated all their property and considerable fortunes to the movement.

As this spirit of nationalism reached a fever pitch, parents let their children join the Regiment in exuberant pledges to fulfil the destiny of a new India. Although brought up in the conservative Indian culture of the diaspora communities, this relatively small group of young women seized the opportunity presented by the impassioned wartime atmosphere and by Bose's creation of the RJR to pursue their dream of fighting and dying for India, alongside the men.

The women and girls who signed up to become Ranis came from two dissimilar Indian communities in Malaya and Burma. The largest group were the daughters and wives Tamil labourers from Malayan rubber estates and tin mines, who were generally illiterate and spoke only Tamil. None of the older women were alive to be interviewed, and just two of the Tamil girls from the estates who joined when very young still lived in 2008. These young girls from the estates in Malaya served as sepoys in the Regiment. They were not politically active before enlisting in the Regiment.

The second, much smaller contingent of Ranis was composed of well-educated recruits, many Tamil and Sikh girls from Malaya, and fifty Indian girls from Burma, primarily Bengali Hindus. The Ranis formed two distinct groups: 'the not educated' and 'the educated'. All but two of the women I interviewed for this study were in the latter category, and except for one they all spoke fluent English. Their families were middle-class or wealthy and several of their relatives had been active in the freedom struggle and were strong Indians nationalists before the war. These recruits ranged from twelve to twenty-nine years of age, but most were between fifteen and nineteen years old. The few women over twenty were nurses and teachers before joining. All officers came from this group of educated girls and women.

If not strongly encouraged by their parents, almost all of these educated recruits enlisted to participate in the freedom struggle because they had heard and seen Bose speak and were captivated by his charisma and his message. Some of these girls joined because the Regiment also promised the possibility of wider horizons and a more exciting life or they saw the RJR as a means to get professional training not otherwise available.

A few Ranis declined to participate in this study because they regretted their membership of the RJR. One had come to believe that all killing is sinful, and another that she and her four sisters were too young when they joined, mere children, unaware of the political objectives of Bose and the INA. One said that she would not have agreed to the interview while her husband was alive because as an officer in the Indian Army he would have disapproved of her having supported the other side. In their many years of marriage, he did not know that his wife had spent two of her early teenage years as a Rani. As a widow she has decorated her comfortable Kolkata apartment with several large Bose portraits and RJR memorabilia. Another member of the Regiment had turned completely against Bose and his violent approach to liberation, and was now careful that her husband, who was still living in 2009, would not find out about her RJR membership.

But Ranis courageously joined the cause with great enthusiasm and dedicated themselves along with Bose to winning independence for their Motherland. Leaving their homes, these adventuresome young women wanted to end colonial oppression and they believed it was right to devote themselves to this sacred cause. Most of all, they trusted Bose absolutely and were convinced that he would, as he had promised, win freedom for India if they gave their blood.

More than sixty years later, the women of the RJR joyfully remembered their time in the Regiment and exclaimed, 'I loved myself as a Rani,' 'I am so proud of my country' and 'Netaji was like a god'. They agreed that those two years were the best of their lives. Many subsequently had happy marriages, good relationships with their children and satisfying jobs, but they nevertheless thought the experience of being in top physical shape and working together with other women for a noble common goal was more satisfying than any other life experience.

They always mentioned 'Netaji' with reverence, never using his name. They reaffirmed their happiness at having known him and their sorrow that he did not become the first leader of a free India. They also concurred that their only regret was that the Ranis were never employed in battle as Bose had promised each of them. These women felt deprived that they did not have the opportunity to win martyrdom for India, but not one in my many and lengthy interviews was able to find any flaw with Bose as the Supreme Commander of the INA or as a human being. Even after many years in which Bose was broadly criticized, ridiculed and rebuked in the Indian press, to the Ranis he remained a brilliant, kind and caring man with superhuman, even godlike qualities. In their minds, he could do no wrong.

While 80 per cent of Indians who had emigrated to Malaya before World War II had resettled in India by the time Malaysia became independent in 1957, of the twenty interviewed Ranis and their sisters who grew up in Malaya, only two Ranis, both Bengalis, besides Lakshmi moved to India before retirement age.[14] A few women indicated that because of their service in the war, they were denied jobs. One Rani wanted to join the Malaysian police force, but was told straightaway that they did not hire INA soldiers.

Two prominent Malaya-born Ranis, Rasammah Navarednam Bhupalan and Janaki Thevar Athinahappan, transferred their energy after the war to the struggle for Malaysian independence, and for equal rights and equal pay for women; they also became leaders in the movement against drug abuse and in several other social causes. For them the fight for the liberation of India was a cause that ignited their youthful sense of justice and moral right for the rest of their lives. The Motherland they fought for as adults was not India but Malaysia, the country where they were born and grew up, where their family and many relatives lived. After Burma achieved independence in 1948, discrimination against Indians prompted all Ranis in this study who had grown up in Burma to use their Indian citizenship and settle in India.

Subhas Chandra Bose continues to be seen by many Indians as a person whose ideas are important for India today, and his fight for equality for women may be the least controversial of his causes. The RJR was an important manifestation of the growing demand that Indians accept women as political persons with legal and moral rights and responsibilities. In her unpublished memoirs, Janaki Thevar Athinahappan enthused that the RJR brought about a moral and social revolution that thrilled all East Asia. This was certainly an overstatement and it is difficult, if not impossible, to calculate the impact of the RJR on the subsequent struggle for gender equity in India and on the Indian women's movement. Some Ranis told me that it had made no difference at all; the Regiment and all it stood for was too short-lived.

In his speech at the opening of the Singapore camp in October 1943, Bose stressed that the commitment of the assembled Ranis gave him hope for the future of Indian women. But despite improvements in the status of women over succeeding decades, gender equality issues remain conspicuous in contemporary India to even a casual observer. Such factors as the traditional assumption of male dominance, the archaic caste system and religious practices continue to pose barriers to Indian gender equity. More than seventy years ago, Bose instructed these spunky and determined Rani volunteers that such destructive attitudes were contrary to the ideals of the freedom struggle and to a free India. That lesson endures today as does the legend of the brave young girls of the Rani of Jhansi Regiment.

In the same spirit the Rani soldiers signed up to pursue their dream of liberty, not only for their Motherland and its citizens but also for all Indian women. They were not duped. Bose never misled them with respect to their mission, its difficulty or its dangers. From the outset, he stressed repeatedly that they would be risking their lives to bring freedom to their beloved India. As he put it, 'You give me your blood and I will give you independence.' Through their moral strength and commitment to liberate their country and their people, these pioneering women set an enduring example for succeeding generations of Indians. Their courage, their resolve, their loyalty to the cause and to one another have exemplary relevance for the women's movement today, indeed for the human race. The struggle for self-government, for political sovereignty and personal liberty, is universally respected as a positive moral quest. Despite the failure of their noble ambitions, the Ranis and their leader deserve to be honoured for their commitment to the highest of human aspirations – freedom.

LIST OF ABBREVIATIONS

BI	British Military Intelligence
BL-AAS	British Library – African and Asian Studies
BRM	Bengal Revolutionary Movement Papers
CSDIC(I)	Combined Services Detailed Interrogation Centre (India)
CWMG	Collected Works of Mahatma Gandhi
ICS	Indian Civil Service
IIL	Indian Independence League
INA	Indian National Army
IR	Interrogation Report
NAI	National Archives of India
NAS-OHC	National Archives of Singapore – Oral History Centre
NCW	Netaji: Collected Works
NRB	Netaji Research Bureau
RJR	Rani of Jhansi Regiment
SEAC	South East Asia Command

APPENDIX

RANI INTERVIEWS, PLACE AND DATES

Akilandam Vairavapillai, Kuala Lumpur, Selangor, Malaysia, 5 March 2008; 6 January 2009.

Amba Sen, Kasba, Kolkata, India, 11–12 December 2008.

Anjalai Ponnaswamy, Kuala Lumpur, Selangor, Malaysia, 6 March 2008.

Anjuli Bhowmick Ghosh, Kolkata, India, 9 January 2008.

Anjali Suppiah, George Town, Penang, Malaysia, 8 January 2009.

Aruna Ganguli Chatterjee, Kolkata, India, 8–10 January; 4 December 2008.

Asha Bharati Sahay Chaudhry, Jamshedpur, Jharkhand, India, 7–8 December 2008.

Dhanam Lakshmi Suppiah Ratnam, George Town, Penang, Malaysia, 8 January 2009.

Eva Jenny Murty Jothi, Tanjung Malim, Perak, Malaysia, 9 March 2008.

Janaki Bai, Rasah Jaya, Seremban, Negeri Sembilan, Malaysia, 7 March 2008.

Janaki Thevar Athinahappan, Kuala Lumpur, Selangor, Malaysia, 5–6 March 2008; 5–6 January 2009.

Jeeva Mudeliar, Singapore, 12 January 2009.

Karuna Ganguli Mukherjee, Kolkata, India, 10 December 2008.

Labanya Ganguli Chatterji, Kolkata, India, 9, 19, 26 December 2008.

Lakshmi Swaminathan Sahgal, Kanpur, India, 4–7 January 2008.

Manwati Panday Arya, Kanpur, India, 7 January 2008.

Mommata Gupta Mehta, New Delhi, India, 8 June; 21 November 2008; 15 February 2013.

Muniammah (Chinammah), Daughter of Eelavan Rengasamy, Kuala Lumpur, Selangor, Malaysia, 10 January 2009.

Ponnammah Esther Navarednam, Baldwin, Long Island, NY, USA, 5 April 2008; 2 November 2008; 15 December 2008.

Rama Mehta Khandwala, Mumbai, India, 28 April 2008; 24–26 November 2008.

Rasammah Navarednam Bhupalan, Petaling Jaya, Selangor, Malaysia, 10 March 2008.

Veesa Mudeliar, Singapore, 12 January 2009.

OTHER INTERVIEWS

Anisa Sahgal Puri, New Delhi, India, 10 June 2008.

Anita Schenkl Pfaff, Augsburg, Germany, 18 September 2012.

Kunizuka Ishiyo, Kobe, Japan, 7 June 2009.

Leonard Gordon, New York, USA, 27 August 2010.

S. S. Yagada, New Delhi, India, 5 June 2008.

Subhashini Sahgal Ali, Kanpur, India, 6 January 2008.

NOTES

INTRODUCTION: THE RANI OF JHANSI REGIMENT

1. Lakshmi Swaminathan Sahgal, interview, 5 January 2008.
2. *Netaji* is the Hindi word *neta,* 'leader', plus the suffix *ji* indicating respect. It is an honorific, meaning 'revered leader', a sobriquet which Bose adopted upon arrival in Singapore to take over command of the INA. This appellation is used by all supporters of Bose.
3. D'Ann Campbell, 'Women in Combat: The World War II Experience in the United States, Great Britain, Germany, and the Soviet Union', *The Journal of Military History* 57 (April 1993), 302.
4. Reina Pennington, *Wings, Women, &War: Soviet Airwomen in World War II Combat* (Lawrence, Kansas: University Press of Kansas, 2001), vii, 2. Svetlana Aleksijevitj, Kajsa Öberg Lindsten, trans. *Kriget Har Inget Kvinnligt Ansigte: Utopins Röster.* Stockholm, Sweden: Esatz, 2012. Original published in Russian in 2006.

ONE: SEARCHING FOR THE RANI OF JHANSI REGIMENT

1. Eva Jenny Murty, interview, 9 March 2008.
2. See Appendix for a list of names of the Ranis, and places and dates of the interviews.
3. Kunizuka Ishiyo, telephone interview by author, Kobe, Japan, 7 June 2009. INA Papers, BL-AAS, Mss Eur F275/9, 275/12. Kunizuka served as translator of Hindustani, but his English was also excellent. Interview with

Nobuo Ishikawa, another Japanese soldier, a Japanese-English translator, who accompanied the Ranis is included in Nobuko Nagasaki, Toshio Tanaka, Hisashi Nakamura and Shinya Ishizaka, eds, *Shiryoshu indo kokumingun kankeisha kikigaki (Refletions* [sic] *on the Indian National Army during the SecondWorldWar: A Collection of Interviews with Japanese Soldiers)* (Tokyo: Kenbun Shuppan, 2008), 38–46, did not yield any information on the RJR. INA Papers, BL-AAS, Mss Eur F275/9/275/12.

4. Interview with Captain S.S. Yadava, New Delhi, 5 June 2008.

5. Interview with Sheila Fernandez, maiden name P. K. Lakshmi Nair. Oral History Centre, National Archives of Singapore, Communities of Singapore, Part 2, Project Accession 000569, reel 4, 29 May 1985.

6. 'On April 22 1945 all branches of HQ Supreme command and all INA units in Rangoon were ordered by the chief of Staff (Habib-ur-Rehman) to burn or otherwise destroy all records.' INA Papers, BL-AAS, Mss Eur F275/6, 266, from IR of B985 Khushal Singh Rawat.

7. NAI, Letter from Lt Col. G. D. Andersson, Office of the Chief of the General Staff. GHQ (I), 20 March 1946.

8. A total of 990 files from 1943-45 on the INA and 130 items relating to the activities of the Indian Independence League.

9. BL-AAS, Mss Eur F275/1–27.

10. Peter Ward Fay, *The Forgotten Army: India's Armed Struggle for Independence; 1942-1945* (Ann Arbor: University of Michigan Press, 1995), 459: 35–59. Chandar Sundaram, Department of History, Lingnan University, Hong Kong. Personal communication, New Delhi, India, 8 January 2010.

11. BL-AAS, L/WS/1/1578, Letter from W. E. H. Condon to General Sir Geoffrey Scoones, Military Department, Commonwealth Relations Office, London, Simla, 25th November 1947.

12. BL-AAS, L/WS/1/1578 No. 1994/1/H, Letter from W E H Condon, Defence Department, Combined Inter-Services Historical Section India Command, Simla, 2nd December, 1947 to Lt Colonel J. Wilson, Clarence House, London.

13. BL-AAS, L/WS/1/1578.

14. Provenance information for the CSDIC(I) files is in permanent unrecoverable storage in British Library, Boston Spa, Wetherby, West Yorkshire, UK.

15. Leonard Gordon, telephone conversation with author, 27 August 2010.

16. The India Office at British Library, London, renamed Asian and African Studies.

17. Personal communication, British Library employee, 26 March 2010. The collection is now filed under British Library, Asian and African Studies, Mss Eur F 275/1–27.

18. Hugh Toye, 'Subhas Pasha', BL-AAS, Mss Eur D1228.

19. BL-AAS, Mss Eur F275/1, 4.

20. It is now known that the collection was placed with the British Library India Office by Hugh Toye in 1985 with the request that the documents not be made available for study until January 2008 or the January following one year after his death, whichever occurred later. Hugh Toye died on 15 April 2012, but as he had been confined to a nursing home for many years, the contents of the packages were made available for this study in September 2010.

21. Azad Hind government, the Government of Free India, the provisional government set up by Bose in 1943. Interview 172, 28 April 1972.

22. Nobuko Nagasaki, Toshio Tanaka, Hisashi Nakamura, and Shinya Ishizaka, eds, *Shiryo-shu- indo kokumingun kankeisha kikigaki* (Tokyo: Kenbun Shuppan, 2008).

23. Sugata Bose, *His Majesty's Opponent: Subhas Chandra Bose and India's Struggle against Empire* (Cambridge, MA: Belknap Press of Harvard University Press, 2011), 6. Sugata Bose is the elder son of Sisir Kumar Bose, son of Subhas Chandra Bose's elder brother, Sarat Chandra Bose.

24. Lakshmi Sahgal, 'The Rani of Jhansi Regiment', *The Oracle* 1, no. 2 (April 1979): 15–19. Manwati Arya, 'The Rani of Jhansi Regiment in Burma', *The Oracle* 2, no. 2 (April 1980): 16–20. Maya Banerjee, 'My Life with the Rani of Jhansi Regiment', *The Oracle* 2, no. 2 (April 1980): 21–24. Shanti Majumdar, 'Netaji's Rani of Jhansi Regiment', *The Oracle* 2, no. 3 (July 1980): 21–26. Janaki Athinahappan, 'The Rani of Jhansi Regiment', *The Oracle* 2, no. 1 (January 1980): 29–32. Originally presented at the Third International Netaji Seminar in Calcutta, January 1979.

25. Aruna Gopinath, *Footprints on the Sands of Time: Rasammah Bhupalan; A Life of Purpose* (Kuala Lumpur: Arkib Negara Malaysia, 2007), 49–104. Rasammah, interview, 10 March 2008, said that Chapter III, 'The Rani of Jhansi Regiment: A Will for Freedom' on her time in the RJR was written entirely by herself. All reference to that work below is to Rasammah, *Footprints*.

26. Manwati Arya, *Patriot: The Unique Indian Leader Netaji Subhas Chandra Bose; A New Personalised Biography by One Who Worked for Netaji* (New Delhi: Lotus Press, 2007).

27. Lakshmi Swaminathan and Prem Kumar Sahgal married in 1947, and for most of her writings and speeches she uses her married name.

28. Lakshmi Sahgal, *A Revolutionary Life – Memoirs of a Political Activist* (New Delhi: Kali for Women, 1997).

TWO: HISTORY OF INDIAN WOMEN IN INDIA AND THE DIASPORAS

1. Manmohan Kaur, *Women in India's Freedom Struggle* (New Delhi: Sterling Publishers, 1992), 1.

2. Jai Narain Sharma, foreword to *Women in Gandhi's Mass Movements,* by Bharti Thakur (New Delhi: Deep and Deep Publications, 2006), xi.

3. Ibid.

4. Bharati Ray, 'The Freedom Movement and Feminist Consciousness in Bengal, 1905-1929', in *From the Seams of History: Essays on Indian Women*, ed. Bharati Ray (Delhi: Oxford University Press, 1995), 178–79.

5. Kaur, *Women,* 18.

6. Uma Chrakravarti, 'Whatever Happened to the Vedic Dasi?' in *Recasting Women: Essays in Colonial History*, ed. Kumkum Sangari and Sudesh Vaid (New Delhi: Kali for Women, 1989), 27–87.

7. Kaur, *Women,* 23.

8. Mrs Marcus Fuller, 'The Wrongs of Indian Womanhood', in *Purdah: An Anthology*, ed. Eunice de Souza (Oxford: Oxford University Press, 2004), 69. *Purdah,* 'veil' or 'curtain' is an Urdu word.

9. Kaur, *Women,* 1–2. *Sati*, a Hindi or Sanskrit word meaning 'good woman'. In ancient Hindu culture a virtuous woman would not survive her husband. Instead, a widow would join her husband in death by jumping into his funeral pyre.

10. Anup Taneja, *Gandhi, Women, and the National Movement, 1920-47* (New Delhi: Har-Anand, 2005), 17.

11. Jawaharlal Nehru, *The Discovery of India* (New Delhi: Jawaharlal Nehru Memorial Fund, Oxford University Press, 2001), 118.

12. Wendy Doniger and Brian K. Smith, trans. *The Laws of Manu* (London: Penguin Books, 1991), xvii–xviii.

13. Ibid., 115.

14. Ibid., 208.

15. Jaya Sagade, *Child Marriage in India: Socio-legal and Human Rights Dimensions* (Delhi: Oxford University Press, 2005).

16. Sekhar Bandyopadhyay, 'Caste, Widow-remarriage and the Reform of Popular Culture in Colonial Bengal', in *From the Seams of History: Essays on Indian Women*, ed. Bharati Ray (Delhi: Oxford University Press, 1995), 8.

17. Kumkum Sangari and Sudesh Vaid, introduction to *Recasting Women,* 16.

18. Akilandam, interview, 5 March 2008.

19. Fuller, 'The Wrongs,' 69.

20. Kaur, *Women,* 22.

21. Mohandas K. Gandhi, 'Women's Education', *Indian Opinion*, Durban, South Africa, 19 January 1907, in *CWMG/6,* 282. Mohandas K. Gandhi, *An Autobiography: The Story of My Experiments with Truth* (Boston: Beacon Press, 1957), xxvi.

22. Chitra Ghosh, *Opening Closed Windows: The Role of Women in Indian Society – the Reality and Ideal as Envisaged by Subhas Chandra Bose* (Kolkata, Progressive Publishers, 2002), 27, 67.

23. Jana Matson Everett, *Women and Social Change in India* (New York: St Martin's Press, 1979), 44–45.

24. Ray, 'The Freedom Movement,' 176–77.

25. Everett, *Women,* 44–46.

26. Lakshmi, interview, 4 January 2008.

27. Everett, *Women,* 44.

28. *Satyagraha* is a word Gandhi created. It is a compound of the Hindi words for 'truth' and 'strength'. Gandhi, *Autobiography,* 318.

29. *CWMG/15,* 290.

30. Suruchi Thapar, 'Women as Activists: Women as Symbols: A Study of the Indian Nationalist Movement', *Feminist Review*, no. 44 (Summer 1993): 81–96.

31. *CWMG/ 22,* 21.

32. Geraldine Hancock Forbes, 'The Politics of Respectability: Indian Women and the Indian National Congress,' in *Women in Colonial India: Essays on Politics, Medicine, and Historiography* (New Delhi: Chronicle Book, 2005), 28.

33. Suruchi Thapar-Björkert, *Women in the Indian National Movement: Unseen Faces and Unheard Voices, 1930-42* (New Delhi: Sage Publications, 2006), 71–72.

34. Aparna Basu, 'The Role of Women in the Indian Struggle for Freedom', in *Indian Women from Purdah to Modernity,* ed. B. R. Nanda (New Delhi: Vikas Publishing House, 1976), 24.

35. Ibid., 25.

36. *CWMG/43*, 249.

37. Axel Michaels, *Hinduism: Past and Present,* trans. Barbara Harshav (Princeton, NJ: Princeton University Press, 2004), 153.

38. Leonard A. Gordon, 'Portrait of a Bengal Revolutionary', *The Journal of Asian Studies,* 27, no. 2, (February 1968): 197–216.

39. Ibid.

40. Ibid., 212. For further analysis, see Gordon, *Brothers against the Raj,* 113–16.

41. BRM, BL-AAS, Kalyani Bhattacharje, Mss Eur F341/169.

42. Ibid.

43. Manini Chatterjee, '1930: Turning Point in the Participation of Women in the Freedom Struggle', *Social Scientist* 29, no. 7/8 (Jul.–Aug. 2001): 39–47.

44. BL-AAS, Kalyani Bhattacharje.

45. Kalpana Dutt, *Chittagong Armoury Raiders: Reminiscences* (1945; repr. New Delhi: People's Publishing House, 1979); Bipan Chandra, *India's Struggle for Independence, 1857-1947* (New Delhi: Penguin Books, 1988), 251–53.

46. Basu, 'The Role of Women', 32.

47. Tirtha Mandal, *The Women Revolutionaries of Bengal, 1905-1939* (Calcutta: Minerva Associates, 1991), 40. A movie, *Ye Mothers,* based on Suniti and Shanti's life stories was released in 2009. In the film, Bose is given credit for having inspired the girls to carry out the assassination.

48. Ibid., 77.

49. Bose, *Chalo Delhi,* 123–27. Bose misremembered Shanti and Suniti's ages, saying that they were 16 and 17.

50. Forbes, *Women in Modern India,* 138–39.

51. Mandal, *Women Revolutionaries,* 4.

52. Chakravarti, *Indian Minority,* 1. Sandhu, *Indians in Malaya,* 2.

53. Sandhu, *Indians in Malaya,* viii. Chakravarti, *Indian Minority,* 199–200.

54. Ibid., 24.

55. Mahajani, *Role of Indian Minorities,* 103–04. Dancz, *Women and Party Politics,* 60. Sandhu, *Indians in Malaya,* 82. See also Chakravarti, *Indian Minority,* 24.

56. Mahajani, *Role of Indian Minorities*, 2.

57. Ibid., 3–6.

58. Ibid., 8.

59. Arya, 'Rani of Jhansi Regiment', 16–20.

60. Amarjit Kaur, 'Indian Labour, Labour Standards, and Workers' Health in Burma and Malaya, 1900-1940,' *Modern Asian Studies* 40, no. 2, (May 2006): 425–75.

61. Chakravarti, *Indian Minority*, xix.

62. Hugh Tinker, foreword to Chakravarti, *Indian Minority,* vi.

63. Chester L. Cooper, 'Moneylenders and the Economic Development of Lower Burma: An Exploratory Historical Study of the Role of the Indian Chettyars'. PhD diss., American University, Washington DC, 1959, 30.

64. Mirza M. Rafi, *The Problem of Indian Settlers in Burma* (New Delhi: The Indian Institute of International Affairs, 1946), 111–12.

65. Mahajani, *Role of Indian Minorities*, 96.

66. Ibid., 103–04.

67. *Kangani* means overseer or foreman in Tamil.

68. Heather Streets, *Martial Races: The Military Race and Masculinity in British Imperial Culture, 1857-1914* (Manchester: Manchester University Press, 2004), 18–20.

69. S.S. Yadava, *Forgotten Warriors of Indian War of Independence: 1941-1946; Indian National Army* (Delhi: All India INA Committee, 2005), 296-301.

70. Mahajani, *Role of Indian Minorities*, xxii.

71. Aruna Ganguli Chatterjee, unpublished memoir, 'Second World War in Burma, Netaji and Me'.

72. Mohammad Zaman Kiani, *India's Freedom Struggle and the Great INA* (New Delhi: Reliance Publishing House, 1994),150.

73. Hugh Toye, 'World War II: The Handling of "Suspects and Escapees" from Enemy Occupied Territory in India and S.E.A. Command'. INA Papers, BL-AAS, Mss Eur F275/1, 2, 1985. Hugh Tinker, 'A Forgotten Long March: The Indian Exodus from Burma, 1942', *Journal of Southeast Asian Studies* 6, no. 1 (March 1975): 1–15.

74. Shah Nawaz Khan, *My Memories of I.N.A. and Its Netaji*. Delhi: Rajkamal Publications, 1946, 51.

75. Tinker, 'Forgotten Long March.'

76. Manwati, interview, 7 January 2008.

77. Sharon M. Lee, 'Female Immigrants and Labor in Colonial Malaya: 1860-1947,' *International Migration Review* 23, no. 2 (Summer 1989): 309–31. Sandhu, *Indians in Malaya*, Appendix 1 to 4, 304–17. Of the 2,917,003 Indians who immigrated to Malaya between 1844 and 1940, 2,053,624 left Malaya and 863,379 remained.

78. Mahajani, *Role of Indian Minorities*, 25.

79. Ibid., vii.

80. N. Jayaram, 'Introduction: The Study of Indian Diaspora', in *The Indian Diaspora: Dynamics of Migration*, eds. N. Jayaram and Yogesh Atal (New Delhi: Sage Publications, 2004), 30.

81. Ibid., 16.

82. Hugh Tinker, foreword to *The Indian Minority in Burma: The Rise and Decline of an Immigrant Community*, by Nalini Ranjan Chakravarti (Oxford: Oxford University Press, 1971), vii.

83. Sagari Chhabra, 'The Heroes We Forgot,' *Sunday Times of India*, 28 May 2006, New Delhi edition.

84. Lakshmi, interview, 5 January 2008.

85. Dancz, *Women and Party Politics*, 70.

86. Akilandam, interview, 6 January 2009.

87. Janaki Bai, interview, 7 March 2008.

88. Arya, 'Rani of Jhansi Regiment,' 16–20.

89. Sandhu, *Indians in Malaya*, 245.

90. Chenchia Kondapi, *Indians Overseas, 1838-1949* (New Delhi: Indian Council of World Affairs, 1951) 63.

91. Dancz, *Women and Party Politics*, 60.

92. Aruna, 'Netaji and Me'.

93. Sandhu, *Indians in Malaya,* 259–60.

94. Ibid., 247.

95. Kondapi, *Indians Overseas,* 82–84.

96. Sandhu, *Indians in Malaya*, 99.

97. Dancz, *Women and Party Politics*, 62.

98. Sandhu, *Indians in Malaya*, 98.

99. Dancz, *Women and Party Politics*, 61–63.

100. Ibid., 66.

101. Sandhu, *Indians in Malaya*, 259-60.

102. Manwati, interview, 7 January 2008.

THREE: SUBHAS CHANDRA BOSE — A MAN NOT OF HIS TIME

1. Roy, *Subhash*, 17–19.
2. Shah Nawaz, *My Memories*, i.
3. Ayer, *Unto Him*, xxii.
4. Anjuli, interview, 9 January 2008.
5. A. C. Chatterji, *India's Struggle for Freedom* (Calcutta: Chakravarti, Chatterjee & Co., 1947), 81.
6. Bose, *Chalo Delhi*, 51–54.
7. Hindustani is a lingua franca being a mixture of Urdu and Hindi with some English words.
8. M. Sivaram, *The Road to Delhi* (Rutland, Vermont: Charles E. Tuttle, 1966), 140.
9. Nirad C. Chaudhuri, *Thy Hand, Great Anarch! India, 1921–1952* (London: Chatto and Windus, 1987), 473. Author's observation, January 2008.
10. Sahgal, *Revolutionary Life*, 49.
11. Ibid.
12. Goebbels' diary entry, 11 July 1943 in *Die Tagebücher von Joseph Goebbels*, ed. Elke Fröhlich (Munich: Bundesarchiv, Institut fur Zeitgeschichte, 1987), Vol. 9. 'Er organisiert seine Bewegung ganz nach nationalsozialistischem Muster und legt sich selbst den Titel "Führer" zu.' Author's translation.
13. Girija Mookerjee, 'Netaji the Great Resistance Leader', *The Oracle*, no. 8 (1986): 22–35. Bose thought Trott a friend, and several Indian historians mention their friendship. Mookerjee, probably erroneously, states that their relationship was so close that Bose knew about Trott's anti-Nazi activities.
14. Clarita von Trott zu Solz, *Adam von Trott zu Solz: Eine Lebensbeschreibung* (Berlin: Gedenkstätte Deutscher Widerstand, 1994), 158.
15. Chaudhuri, *Thy Hand*, 796–800.
16. Cuttack is now in the state of Odisha, but at the time of Bose's birth and youth Odisha (then Orissa) was part of the Bengal Presidency. Bose, *Indian Pilgrim*, 3.
17. Ibid., 7.
18. Gordon, *Brothers against the Raj*, 14.
19. Bose, *Indian Pilgrim*, 3.
20. Ibid., 4.

21. Ibid., 5.

22. Ibid.

23. As a postscript in two letters to his mother in 1912, Bose inquires, 'How is Sarada?' Sarada was a female servant in the Bose household, but no details about their relationship are available. Bose, *Indian Pilgrim,* 129, 141.

24. Ibid., 86.

25. Ibid.

26. Ibid., 23.

27. Ibid., 29.

28. Ibid.

29. Ibid., 30.

30. Ibid., 33.

31. Bengal Revolutionary Movement Papers (BRM), BL-AAS, Kalyani Bhattacharje, and her sister Bina Das. Mss Eur F341/169.

32. Bose, *Indian Pilgrim,* 257–58.

33. Ibid., 77.

34. Bose, *Indian Pilgrim,* 262. 'Appendix 5: Discipline in Presidency College; Report of the Enquiry Committee.' Bhola Nath Roy, *Oaten Incident, 1916: A Chapter in the Life of Netaji Subhas Bose* (Calcutta: S. C. Sarkar, 1975), 14.

35. Bose, *Indian Pilgrim,* 78.

36. Ibid., 77. One might, of course, understand Bose as saying that because he was a participant as well as an eyewitness he knew what happened.

37. Bose, *Indian Pilgrim,* 79.

38. Ibid., 80.

39. Ibid., 233.

40. The Bhagavadgita, part of the epic Mahabharata, is a Hindu scripture written in Sanskrit verse. Often just called the Gita, it is by many considered a guide to living as a good Hindu.

41. Bose, *Indian Pilgrim,* 83.

42. Ibid.

43. Ibid.

44. Bose, *Indian Pilgrim,* 190.

45. Ibid. Sarkar, Hemanta Kumar, *Subhaser Songe Baro Bochhor* [*Twelve Years with Subhas*]. 1946. http://subhaschandrabose.org/hks-withsubhas.php, 32, 5 of 12 (accessed on 3 August 2014).

46. Roy, *Subhash,* 48.

47. Bose, *Indian Pilgrim*, 94.

48. Ibid., 95.

49. Ibid., 114.

50. Ibid., 166.

51. Ibid., 111.

52. Ibid., 222–26.

FOUR: BOSE AND GANDHI AT ODDS OVER THE FREEDOM STRUGGLE

1. Subhas Chandra Bose, *The Indian Struggle: 1920-1942*, NCW/2, eds. Sisir K. Bose and Sugata Bose (New Delhi: Oxford University Press, 1997), 57.

2. Ibid., 58.

3. Ibid.

4. Ibid., 59.

5. Ibid., 78–82. *The Indian Struggle* in which Bose published his opinion of Gandhi, although available in Great Britain in 1935, was not published in India until 1948. See Sisir Kumar Bose and Sugata Bose, editors' introduction to *The Indian Struggle: 1920-1942*.

6. Subhas Chandra Bose, 'The pledge of the INA. Address to the Indian Legion in Europe and broadcast, June 1942,' in *Azad Hind: Writings and Speeches, 1941-1943*, NCW/11, eds. Sisir K. Bose and Sugata Bose (Calcutta: Netaji Research Bureau, 2002), 114.

7. David Kinsley, *Hindu Goddesses: Visions of the Divine Feminine in the Hindu Religious Tradition* (Delhi: Motilal Banarsidass, 1987), 181, 183–84.

8. Subhas Chandra Bose, 'Letter to Basanti Devi, July 27, 1927', in *NCW/4*, ed. Sisir K. Bose (Calcutta: Netaji Research Bureau, 1982), 232.

9. Roy, *Subhash*, 40.

10. The goddesses Kali and Durga have very similar functions and are both regarded as manifestations of the female cosmic energy, Shakti of the male god Shiva.

11. Kinsley, *Hindu Goddesses*, 126. Bankim Chandra Chattopadhyay, *Anandamath* (New York: Oxford University Press, 2005).

12. Bose, *Indian Pilgrim*, 7.

13. Ibid., 54, 63.

14. Sugata Bose, *His Majesty's Opponent*, 183, 187.

15. Bose, *Indian Pilgrim*, 143.

16. Bose, 'Letter to Bivabati Bose, December 16, 1925', in *In Burmese Prisons: Correspondence May 1923 – July 1926, NCW/3*, ed. Sisir K. Bose (Calcutta: Netaji Research Bureau, 2009), 170.

17. Gurbaksh Singh Dhillon, 'How Transparent!' in Subhas Chandra Bose, *Netaji Subhas Chandra Bose: CommemorationVolume:A Tribute in His CentenaryYear* (Calcutta: Scottish Church College, 1998), 10.

18. Bose, *Mission*, 202.

19. The ban in India on *The Indian Struggle* was lifted in or before April 1939. 'Letter to Emilie Schenkl, April 19, 1939', in Subhas Chandra Bose, *Letters to Emilie Schenkl: 1934-1942, NCW/7*, eds. Sisir Kumar Bose and Sugata Bose (Kolkata: Netaji Research Bureau, 2004), 208. Bose, *Indian Struggle,* 351.

20. Ibid.

21. Ibid., 128.

22. Ibid., 352.

23. Ibid.

24. Ibid., 398.

25. Ibid.

26. Ayer, *Unto Him*, 250–51.

27. Ibid.

28. Chaudhuri, *Thy Hand,* 500–29. Chaudhuri, employed as Sarat Bose's secretary, was privy to the correspondence and meetings between the Bose brothers and the other involved members of the INC; he devotes an entire chapter of his book to the 'Gandhi-Bose Feud'.

29. Bose, *Letters to Emilie*, 208.

30. Ibid., 55.

31. Bose, *Indian Struggle*, 372. Bose, *Letters to Emilie*, 211.

32. Rabindra Nath Tagore, 'Letter to Subhas Chandra Bose, April 2, 1939', in Subhas Chandra Bose, *Congress President: Speeches, Articles, and Letters; January 1938-May 1939, NCW/9*, eds. Sisir Kumar Bose and Sugata Bose (Calcutta: Netaji Research Bureau, 2004), 250.

33. Chaudhuri, *Thy Hand,* 524.

34. Bose, *Indian Struggle*, 373.

35. Ibid., 374–81.

36. Bose, 'A Word about Germany', Signed editorial in the *Forward Bloc*, 13 March 1940, in Subhas Chandra Bose, *The Alternative Leadership: Speeches, Articles,*

*Statements and Letters, June 1939-1941, NCW/*10, eds. Sisir Kumar Bose and Sugata Bose (Calcutta: Netaji Research Bureau, 1998), 82.

37. Bose, *Indian Struggle*, 379.
38. *CWMG/*72, 230.
39. Bose, *The Alternative Leadership,* 155.
40. Ibid.
41. Gordon, *Brothers against the Raj*, 417.
42. Bose, *Alternative Leadership*, 199.
43. Ibid., 197.
44. John A.Thivi, 'He Came, He Fought, He Conquered', in *Subhas Chandra Bose*, ed. Verinder Grover, Vol. 6 of *Political Thinkers of Modern India* (New Delhi: Deep and Deep Publications, 1991), 449. Thivi is sometimes also spelled Thivy.
45. Hauner, *India in Axis Strategy*, 254.
46. Rudolf Hartog, *The Sign of the Tiger: Subhas Chandra Bose and his Indian Legion in Germany, 1941-45* (New Delhi: Rupa and Company, 2001), i.
47. Hauner, *India in Axis Strategy*, 360.
48. Ibid., 592.
49. Hartog, *Sign of the Tiger*, iii.
50. Bose, *Azad Hind,* 114.
51. NRB gives the date of the meeting with Hitler as 29 May 1942.
52. Bose, *Azad Hind,* 102–08.
53. For further analysis, see Gordon, *Brothers against the Raj,* 113–16.

FIVE: SUBHAS CHANDRA BOSE AND WOMEN

1. Subhas Chandra Bose, 'Presidential address at the Maharashtra Provincial Conference, Poona, May 3, 1928', in *NCW/*5, ed. Sisir K. Bose (Calcutta: Netaji Research Bureau, 1985), 242–54.
2. Mrinalini Sinha, *Colonial Masculinity:The 'Manly Englishman' and the 'Effeminate Bengali' in the Late Nineteenth Century* (Manchester: Manchester University Press, 1995), 17. Meredith Borthwick, *The Changing Role of Women in Bengal 1849-1905* (Princeton: Princeton University Press, 1984), xi.
3. Bose, *Indian Pilgrim*, 11, 244.
4. Gordon, *Brothers against the Raj*, 15.
5. Ibid.

6. *Bhadramahila,* 'gentlewoman'.

7. Borthwick, *Changing Role,* xii–xiii.

8. Ibid., 65–66.

9. Gordon, *Brothers against the Raj,* 20.

10. Ibid., 11, 14.

11. Bose, *Indian Pilgrim,* 5.

12. Ibid.

13. Ibid., 159–60. Bose's salutations and closings are unfortunately not included in some of the letters to Hemanta, edited by the Netaji Research Bureau in Kolkata. The salutations addressed to other recipients are exuberant.

14. Ibid., 128–48.

15. Letter from Subhas Chandra Bose to Mrs J. Dharmavir, 7 May 1921, quoted in Gordon, *Brothers against the Raj,* 67.

16. Ibid., 327.

17. Krishna Bose, 'Important Women in Netaji's Life', *The Illustrated Weekly of India* 93 (13 August 1972): 35.

18. Bose, *NCW/4,* 271-72.

19. Krishna Bose, 'Important Women in Netaji's Life', 35.

20. Sisir Kumar Bose and Sugata Bose, Editors' introduction to Bose, *Indian Pilgrim,* xi–xvi. Bose, *Indian Pilgrim,* 36, 54–56.

21. Ibid., 68, 157.

22. Ibid., 27. Sarkar, *Twelve Years.*

23. Ibid.

24. Roy, *Subhash,* 19.

25. Ibid., 61.

26. Ibid., 55, 60.

27. Ibid., 52.

28. Ibid., 64.

29. Bose, *Indian Pilgrim,* 54.

30. Bose, *Indian Pilgrim,* 209.

31. Ibid., 54.

32. Ibid., 56, footnote 1.

33. Ibid.

34. Bose, *Letters to Emilie,* 228.

35. Aruna, interview, 9 January 2008.

36. Bose, *Letters, Articles,* 8–10. *Sadhana* is devotion to a spiritual task.

37. Anita Pfaff, telephone interview, 18 September 2012.
38. Gordon, *Brothers against the Raj,* 345. Nambiar, an Indian journalist and long-time resident of Germany before the war, became the first ambassador of independent India to the Federal Republic of Germany.
39. Leonard Gordon, telephone conversation with author, 27 August 2010. Sugata Bose, *His Majesty's Opponent,* 129. Sugata Bose states that the marriage occurred on 26 December 1937. However, Nambiar, who was with the couple in Badgastein on that visit, did not hear of a marriage taking place. Girija Mookerjee, 'Netaji the Great Resistance Leader,' *The Oracle,* no. 1 (1986): 22–35. Indian historian, Mookerjee claims to have seen a photocopy of the certificate of the marriage in civil court of Subhas Bose and Frl. Schenkl and mentions that 'the marriage certificate of Subhas Bose bears the signature of Herr von Trott as one of the two witnesses of the marriage'. As Adam von Trott zu Solz was posted to China in 1937-38 as a German diplomate, it seems unlikely that he would have been able to witness a marriage ceremony in Austria. Schenkl never claimed to have or have had a marriage certificate. Anita Pfaff, telephone interview, 18 September 2012.
40. Anita Pfaff, telephone interview, 18 September 2012.
41. NRB published the letter after the death of Sarat Bose, February 1950. Gordon, *Brothers against the Raj,* 604.
42. Subhas Chandra Bose, 'Letter to Emilie Schenkl, March 1936', in *The Essential Writings of Netaji Subhas Chandra Bose,* eds. Sisir Kumar Bose and Sugata Bose (Delhi: Oxford University Press, 1997), 160.
43. Anita Pfaff, telephone interview, 18 September 2012.
44. Sugata Bose, *His Majesty's Opponent,* 229.
45. Lakshmi, interview, 6 January 2008.
46. Bankim Chandra Chatterji, *Anandamath* (Delhi: Library South Asian Literature, Orient Paperbacks, Amazon Kindle Edition, 2012), Loc. 1496-1505 of 2779.
47. Asha, interview, 8 December 2008
48. Anita Pfaff, telephone interview, 18 September 2012.
49. Ibid.
50. In Bose, *Letters to Emilie,* 105.
51. Anita Pfaff, telephone interview, 18 September 2012.
52. Leonard Gordon, telephone conversation, 27 August 2010. Netajipapers. gov.in, Prime Minister's Office (PMO)/2(67)/56-71-PM | Netaji Subhas

Chandra Bose Papers, document 5 of 21.

53. Bose, *Indian Struggle,* 70–71.

54. Bose, *Indian Pilgrim*, 201–02.

55. Ibid.

56. Subhas Chandra Bose, *NCW*/6, eds. Sisir K. Bose and Sugata Bose (Calcutta: Netaji Research Bureau, 1987), 92–94.

57. Ibid., 10–13.

58. BRM, BL-AAS, Leela Roy, Mss Eur F341/158.

59. Forbes, 'Netaji Oration 1980.'

60. Ibid., 7.

61. BRM, BL-AAS, Lotika Ghose, Mss Eur F341/140.

62. Ibid.

63. Ibid.

64. Sugata Bose, *His Majesty's Opponent*, 43.

65. BRM, BL-AAS, Lotika Ghose, Mss Eur F341/140.

66. Bose, *NCW*/4, 231-32.

67. Gordon, *Brothers against the Raj*, 160.

68. Bose, *Congress President*, 270–71.

69. *CWMG*/13, 31.

70. See Gordon, *Brothers against the Raj,* 160–61.

71. M.K. Gandhi, *Birth Control,* ed. Anand T. Hingorani (Bombay: Bharatiya Vidya Bhavan, 1962), 1.

72. Bose, *Letters, Articles,* 209–10.

73. Ibid.

74. Ibid., 210.

75. Damodar Rao was five years old in 1852 when he was adopted by the Raja and Rani of Jhansi.

76. Bose, *NCW*/5, 242–54.

SIX: THE INDIAN FREEDOM MOVEMENT IN MALAYA AND BURMA PRIOR TO THE ARRIVAL OF BOSE

1. Mohan Singh, *Soldiers' Contribution to Indian Independence: The Epic of the Indian National Army* (New Delhi: Army Educational Stores, 1974), 109.

2. Tilak Raj Sareen, *Indian National Army: A Documentary Study* (New Delhi: Gyan, 2004), 170. 'British Assessment of the Indian National Army after

NOTES 261

Its Expansion and Formation in the Light of Bangkok Conference. Weekly Intelligence Summary, General Headquarters, India F. No 6017688 – Historical Section Ministry of Defence, New Delhi'.

3. Manwati, interview, 7 January 2008. Aruna, interview, 4 December 2008. Aruna mentioned that she grew up right near the Insein jail where Bose was kept prisoner.

4. Rama, interview, 28 April 2008. Gandhi, *Autobiography,* 473–74.

5. Rama, interview, 25 November 2008.

6. Hugh Toye, 'The First Indian National Army, 1941-1942', *Journal of Southeast Asian Studies,* 15, no. 2 (September 1984): 365–81.

7. Dancz, *Women and Party Politics,* 70.

8. Paul H. Kratoska, *The Japanese Occupation of Malaya: A Social and Economic History* (London: Hurst and Company, 1998), 28–9.

9. Joyce C. Lebra, *Japanese-Trained Armies in Southeast Asia* (New York: Columbia University Press, 1977), 6.

10. Mohan Singh, *Soldiers' Contribution,* 144.

11. Iwaichi Fujiwara, Keynote Address, 'Reminiscences and Cherished Wishes', The Third International Netaji Seminar, Calcutta, 23 January 1979. *The Oracle* 1, no. 2 (April 1979): 58–66.

12. Ibid., 59.

13. Lebra, *Japanese-Trained Armies,* 6.

14. Ibid., 8.

15. Ibid., 2.

16. Aruna, 'Netaji and Me'.

17. Damodaran, son of K. Kesevan, interview, NAS-OHC, Japanese Occupation of Singapore Project, reel 3, 19 November 1981.

18. Damodaran, ibid. Fay, *Forgotten Army,* 92.

19. Not a relative of Subhas Chandra Bose.

20. Mohan Singh, *Soldiers' Contribution,* 65.

21. Ibid.

22. Ibid., 67.

23. BL-AAS, INA, Mss Eur F275/2, IR B47 Abdul Hayat Khan, 28 December 28 1942.

24. Shah Nawaz, *My Memories,* 17–18.

25. Ibid., 18.

26. Ibid., 20–21.

27. Ibid., 22.

28. NAI, 244/INA, Rani of Jhansi Regt., IIR L3719 Dr Lakshmi Swaminathan, dated August 4, 1945, 7

29. Joyce C. Lebra. *The Indian National Army and Japan* (Singapore: Institute of Southeast Asian Studies, 2008), 41.

30. Ibid.

31. Ibid., 40.

32. Ibid., 42.

33. Mehervan Singh, interview, NAS-OHC, Communities of Singapore Project, Part 2, reel 19, 24 May, 1985.

34. Damodaran, interview, NAS-OHC, reel 3, 19 November 1981.

35. Lebra, *Indian National Army,* 66.

36. Mohan Singh, *Soldiers' Contribution,* 78.

37. Ibid., 112. Historians disagree about the exact numbers of soldiers who joined the INA and who chose to remain prisoners of war. Mohan Singh says that 42,000 volunteered. Sugata Bose, *His Majesty's Opponent,* 242. Sugata Bose quotes Fujiwara who believes that he had persuaded 50,000 soldiers to switch sides.

38. Shah Nawaz, *My Memories,* 21.

39. Ibid., 42.

40. Mohan Singh, *Soldiers' Contribution,* 143–44.

41. A. C. Chatterji, *India's Struggle,* 49–50.

42. Mohan Singh, *Soldiers' Contribution,* 211.

SEVEN: BOSE IN SOUTH-EAST ASIA

1. Hartog, *Sign of the Tiger,* 108–09. Alexander Werth, 'Planning for Revolution: 1941-1943', in Sisir Bose, *Beacon,* 121. Alexander Werth gives the departure date as 8 February but most historians agree that it was 9 February 1943. Abid Hasan's original name was Zain-ul-Abideen Hasan. Subsequently he wanted to be known as Abid Hasan and finally as Abid Hasan Safrani.

2. For examples of this theme see Bose, *Azad Hind,* 119 and Bose, *Chalo Delhi,* 57.

3. Shah Nawaz, *My Memories,* 65.

4. Bose, *Chalo Delhi,* 30. Lebra, *Indian National Army,* 116.

5. Shah Nawaz, *My Memories,* iii.

6. Roy, *Subhash*, 190.
7. Ibid., 193.
8. Ibid.
9. After Bose took over command of the INA, that army became known as the Second INA, while the army commanded by Mohan Singh was referred to as the First INA.
10. Bose, *Chalo Delhi,* 39. A film available at NRB shows Bose giving his acceptance speech.
11. Lebra, *Indian National Army,* 134–35.
12. Toye, *Springing Tiger,* 100. Toye quotes 'Oppenheimers's [sic] *International Law*, Vol. II, 341'. Those rules are found in L. Oppenheim, *International Law: A Treatise* (Longmans, Green and Company, 1920–21), 376–77.
13. Bose, *Chalo Delhi,* 53. The exact numbers of Indians in Singapore, Malaya and Burma are reported variously by historians and by Bose. In 1943 Bose says that there are three million Indians in Burma and Malaya. Sugata Bose, *His Majesty's Opponent,* 239. Sugata Bose believes: '[Subhas Chandra] Bose probably overestimated by about one third.' Other historians agree with Sugata Bose that the resident Indian population in the region was probably close to two million. Toye, *Springing Tiger,* 84. Toye, a British Intelligence officer, finds even that number inflated, as it does not take into account the Indian exodus from Burma in 1942. INA Papers, BL-AAS, Mss Eur F275/13, 99 shows the British Intelligence breakdown of the 1931 Malaya census: Total population of Malaya was 4,385,346; of these 624,009 were Indians. Tinker, 'Forgotten Long March'. Tinker cites the last complete Burma census from 1931, which reports 1,017,825 Indians, of whom between 400,000 and 500,000 either fled or were killed fleeing in early 1942.
14. Bose, *Chalo Delhi,* 53.
15. Ibid., 141–43.
16. Shah Nawaz, *My Memories,* ix.
17. Ibid.
18. Bose, *Chalo Delhi,* 120. Toye, *Springing Tiger,* 94.
19. INA Papers, BL-AAS, Mss Eur F275/10, 126.
20. NAI, 244/INA, Rani of Jhansi Regt., IR L3719 Dr Lakshmi Swaminathan, 9. INA Papers, BL-AAS, Mss Eur F275/10, 126.
21. IR L3719 Dr Lakshmi Swaminathan, 9.
22. INA Papers, BL-AAS, Mss Eur F275/12, Appendix 'C'. Précis of Siva Ram's

Book, produced by Rai Bahadar, Deputy Supt. of Police. F309 Siva Ram worked for Bose and the Azad Hind in several positions of trust until 16 September 1944 when he resigned because he disapproved of Bose's goals and his methods for achieving them. He was allowed to resign only by promising to keep his resignation secret.

23. Toye, *Springing Tiger*, 115.

24. Sugata Bose, introduction to Bose, *Chalo Delhi,* 6. No census was carried out in Singapore and Malaya between 1931 and 1947. On the basis of figures given by Charles Hirschman, 'Trends in Peninsular Malaysia, 1947-75', *Population and Development Review* 6, no. 1 (March 1980), 103–25, who disagrees with earlier estimates of the size of the Indian population of Malaya in 1942, Sugata Bose sets the Indian population in Malaya at the time of the Japanese occupation at roughly 450,000.

25. Bose, *Chalo Delhi,* 252.

26. Ibid., 45.

27. Ibid., 46. *Jawan,* 'young man', is an Urdu word that in this context denotes the military rank of private.

28. Kiani, *India's Freedom Struggle*, 76.

29. Ibid., 108–130. Major General Mohammad Zaman Kiani commanded the first division of the INA that took part in the devastating Imphal campaign. Kiani's sober account and analysis of the military decisions made by both the Japanese and Bose show that Kiani disagreed fundamentally with the plans and was proven right. Also Ayer and Shah Nawaz report instances of unnecessarily dangerous and counterproductive military decisions by Bose.

30. Ibid., 76.

31. Bose, *Indian Pilgrim*, 89.

32. Ibid., 90.

33. Ibid., 92.

34. Ibid.

35. Ibid., 233.

36. Emilie Schenkl interviewed by B.R. Nanda, 1971 Oral History Transcript No. 178, Oral History Section, Nehru Memorial Museum and Library, New Delhi, quoted in H.N. Pandit, *Netaji Subhas Chandra Bose, from Kabul to Battle of Imphal* (New Delhi: Sterling Publishers, 1988), 140. See also A. C. Chatterji, *India's Struggle,* 105.

37. Bose, *Congress President*, 252.

38. Lakshmi, interview, 6 January 2008. Lebra, *Indian National Army*, 135.
39. A. C. Chatterji, *India's Struggle*, 59. Sugata Bose, *His Majesty's Opponent*, 251. Sugata Bose sets the initial strength of the Second INA at 12,000 men.
40. A. C. Chatterji, *India's Struggle*, 52.
41. Kiani, *India's Freedom Struggle*, 72.
42. A. C. Chatterji, *India's Struggle*, 93.
43. Ibid.
44. Ibid. Lakshmi, interview, 6 January 2008. Lakshmi argues that the total strength was 60,000: 30,000 soldiers from the Indian Army who joined instead of remaining prisoners of war and 30,000 civilian Indian volunteers from Malaya.
45. Shah Nawaz Khan, Gurbaksh Singh Dhillon, Prem Kumar Sahgal, the three INA officers who were put on trial at the Red Fort, were all graduates of the Indian Military Academy at Dehradun, Uttarakhand. The highest-ranking officer in the INA, General J. K. Bhonsle graduated from both Dehradun and Sandhurst.
46. Toye, *Springing Tiger*, 122–23.
47. Some INA brigades were named the Gandhi Brigade, Subhas Brigade, Azad Brigade and Nehru Brigade. The rest were numbered.
48. INA Papers, BL-AAS, Mss Eur F275/9. The South Indian Ranis were dubbed 'Madrassi girls' by the British after the capital Madras, now Chennai, of Tamil Nadu.
49. Toye, *Springing Tiger*, 122–23.
50. Mohan Singh, *Soldiers' Contribution*, 266.
51. Ibid.
52. Ibid.
53. Shah Nawaz, *My Memories*, 70.
54. Katakura Tadashi, *Inparu Sakusen hishi* [Secret History of the Imphal Operation]. Quoted in Louis Allen, *Burma: The Longest War, 1941-45* (London: Phoenix Press, 2000), 159–67.
55. Several different dates for the transfer of the Azad Hind headquarters to Maymyo have been given. Sugata Bose, *His Majesty's Opponent*, 273. Sugata Bose gives the same date, 7 April 1944, as Hugh Toye for Bose's transfer to Maymyo; Sahgal, *Revolutionary Life*, 76. Lakshmi gives 29 February 1944 as the date of the transfer.

56. Bose, *Alternative Leadership*, 81–82. Sugata Bose, *His Majesty's Opponent*, 275. Sugata Bose claims that Bose was against Mutaguchi's strategy and made 'a virtue out of necessity'. The INA generals do, however, not support that assertion.

57. Santimoy Ganguli et al., 'Netaji's Underground in India during World War II: An Account by participants in a Daring and Historic Undertaking', *The Oracle*, 1, (April 1979): 7–14. Ganguli was a member of the Bengal Volunteer Group.

58. A. C. Chatterji, *India's Struggle*, 158. Shah Nawaz, *My Memories*, 70-71.

59. Toye, *Springing Tiger*, 104.

60. Shah Nawaz, *My Memories*, 77.

61. Toye, *Springing Tiger*, 104.

62. Ibid., 178.

63. William Joseph Slim, *Defeat into Victory: Battling Japan in Burma and India, 1942-1945* (New York: David McKay Company, 1961), 248.

64. Allen, *Burma*, 266. Tilak Raj Sareen, *Japan and the Indian National Army* (Delhi: Agam Prakashan, 1986), 134–39. See also Kiani, *India's Freedom Struggle*, 127–30.

65. Shah Nawaz, *My Memories*, 112–13.

66. Ibid., 113.

67. Ibid., 114.

68. Allen, *Burma*, 310. Allen quotes Kawabe, *Inparu sakusen*, II, [The Imphal Operation] in the account of the Japanese High Command, *Dai Honei Rikigunbu* [Imperial General Headquarters], Department of the Army, Vol. 1–10.

69. Quoted in Allen, *Burma*, 310. Allen is quoting OCH, *Inparu Sakusen*, II, 156.

70. Shah Nawaz, *My Memories*, 85-6.

EIGHT: CREATION AND MISSIONS OF THE RANI OF JHANSI REGIMENT

1. BRM, BL-AAS, Lotika Ghose, Mss Eur F341/140.

2. Mandal, *Women Revolutionaries*, 19. Gordon, *Brothers against the Raj*, 90. Forbes, 'Netaji Oration 1980', 9.

3. BRM, BL-AAS, Kalyani Bhattacharje, and her sister Bina Das, Mss Eur

F341/169. BRM, BL-AAS, Santa Ganguli, Mss Eur F341/139.

4. BRM, BL-AAS, Lotika Ghose, Mss Eur F341/140.

5. Sahgal, *Revolutionary Life,* 48-9. Lakshmi, interview, 7 January 2008.

6. Gordon, *Brothers against the Raj,* 194. Forbes, 'Netaji Oration 1980.'

7. Sahgal, *Revolutionary Life,* 49.

8. Gordon, *Brothers against the Raj,* 189-91. Chaudhuri, *Thy Hand,* 317.

9. Abid Hasan Safrani, *The Men from Imphal* (Calcutta: Netaji Research Bureau, 1971), 17–18.

10. Ibid., 17–19.

11. Ibid.

12. Safrani, 'A Soldier Remembers', *The Oracle,* 1, (January 1984): 24–65.

13. Safrani, *Men from Imphal* , 19.

14. Chrakravarti, 'Whatever Happened', 27.

15. Subhadra Kumari Chauhan's (1904–48) eighteen-stanza ballad, *'Jhansi Ki Rani'.*

16. Bose, *Chalo Delhi,* 54.

17. Sahgal, *Revolutionary Life,* 56. Lakshmi, interview, 4 January 2008.

18. Bose, *Chalo Delhi,* 55–59.

19. INA Papers, BL-AAS, Mss Eur F275/16, 249.

20. NAI, IR H1152 Dr Nasira Kiani. 380/INA.

21. INA Papers, BL-AAS, Mss Eur F275/16, 249.

22. A. C. Chatterji, *India's Struggle,* 120–24.

23. Mehervan Singh, interview, NAS-OHC, reel 21, 7 June 1985.

24. Ibid.

25. Yadava, interview, 5 June 2008.

26. NAI, 244/INA, 18. Rani of Jhansi Regt. Extract from Report No. 897 on 5 INA Staff Officers.

27. Dr Kanichat Raghava Menon, interview, NAS-OHC, Japanese Occupation of Singapore Project, reel 7, 27 May 1982.

28. Ibid., 80–81.

29. M. S. Varma, interview, NAS-OHC, Japanese Occupation of Singapore Project, reels 22–23, 18 November and 8 December 2003.

30. Vilasini Perumbulavil, interview, NAS-OHC, Civil Service Project, reel 2, 28 September 2000.

31. Dr Tan Ban Cheng, interview, NAS-OHC, Japanese Occupation of Singapore Project, reel 5, 15 February 1984.

32. Bose, *Chalo Delhi*, 211.
33. Ibid., 58.
34. Ibid., 56. *Young India* 1, no. 20 (18 July 2603 [1943]), 7.
35. Janaki, interviews, 5 and 6 March 2008; 5 and 7 January 2009.
36. NAI, 244/INA, 28, IIL Papers, IR L2243 Rahmat Bibi Ma Khin U.
37. Pandit, *Netaji*, 194–95.
38. Rasammah, interview, 10 March 2008.
39. Janaki, interview, 5 March 2008.
40. Manwati, interview, 7 January 2008.
41. Mommata, interview, 21 November 2008.
42. *Young India* 1, no. 20 (18 July 2603 [1943]), 8.
43. *Syonan Sinbun*, 2 August 2603 [1943]. Quoted in Kratoska, *Japanese Occupation*, 107.
44. Bose, *Chalo Delhi*, 423.
45. Lakshmi Nair [Sheila Fernandez], interview, 5 June 1985, NAS-OHC, Communities of Singapore Project, Part 2, reel 4, 29 May 1985.
46. Amba Sen, telephone interview, 12 December 2008.
47. Abdealli K. Motiwalla, interview, NAS-OHC, Japanese Occupation of Singapore Project, reel 2, 19 August 1982.
48. *Bahadur* is 'brave' in Hindi.
49. INA Papers, BL-AAS, F275/10, 170. 'Propaganda' Bahadur Group, Interrogation of M1899 Mohd Sayeed.
50. IR L3719 Dr Lakshmi Swaminathan, 10. Toye, *Springing Tiger*, 114.
51. Bose, *Chalo Delhi*, 422.
52. Dhanam, interview, 8 January 2009.
53. Anjali, interview, 8 January 2009.
54. The term 'educated' most likely means that no only-Tamil speakers were included.
55. Majumdar, 'Netaji's Rani.'
56. Anjuli, interview, 9 January 2008. Ponnammah, interview, 2 November 2008.
57. Ibid.
58. Ibid.
59. Rama, interview, 24 November 2008. Pratima Sen and Maya Ganguli died several years before this study began.
60. Ibid.

61. Anjuli, interview, 9 January 2008.
62. Mommata, interview, 21 November 2008.
63. INA Papers, BL-AAS, Mss Eur F275/6, 307. IR B978 Ehsan Qadir. L3158
    Biren Roy was later suspected of trying to poison Bose and his closest aides.
64. Rama, interview, 28 April 2008. After the war, Mommata and Rama's elder
    brother married.
65. IR L3719 Dr Lakshmi Swaminathan, 6.
66. Janaki Bai, interview, 7 March 2008.
67. Ponnammah, interview, 5 April 2008.
68. Mommata, interview, 21 November 2008.
69. Sahgal, *Revolutionary Life*, 78.
70. Eva Jenny, interview, 9 March 2008.

NINE: CAPTAIN LAKSHMI, BOSE AND THE RECRUITMENT OF THE RJR

1. Sahgal, *Revolutionary Life*, 62.
2. The information in the following segment is based on the interviews with
   Lakshmi, 4–7 January 2008.
3. Vilasini Perumbulavil, interview, NAS-OHC, reel 2, 28 September 2000.
4. Harvard University confirms Captain Lakshmi's proud story that Subbarama
   Swaminathan spent one year at Harvard, 1899–1900 to earn his PhD degree.
5. http://bombayhighcourt.nic.in/libweb/historicalcases/cases/De_La_
   Haye_Murder_Case_-1920.html. (accessed on 29 August 2012).
6. Note the similarity to the widely published 1916 attack on Professor Oaten
   for which Bose was expelled from Presidency College, Calcutta.
7. Sahgal, *Revolutionary Life*, 4–5.
8. Ibid., 8–9.
9. Margaret Cousins (1878-1954) was an Irish suffragist who helped establish
   the Indian women's movement.
10. Lakshmi, interview, 6 January 2008.
11. Saqui, *Facts*, 52.
12. Lakshmi, interview, 6 January 2008.
13. Subhashini Sahgal Ali, daughter of Prem and Lakshmi Sahgal, interview, 7
    January 2008. Anisa Sahgal Puri, daughter of Prem and Lakshmi Sahgal,

interview, 10 June 2008. IR L3719 Dr Lakshmi Swaminathan. Captain Lakshmi stated that her husband Rao divorced her after two years of marriage for having an affair with Dr Abraham.

14. Sahgal, *Revolutionary Life*, 17.

15. Ibid., 21, 25.

16. Anisa Sahgal Puri, interview, 10 June 2008.

17. Lakshmi, interview, 6 January 2008.

18. Akilandam, Anjalai and Janaki, interview, 6 March 2008.

19. Amba, interview, 12 December 2008.

20. Gawankar, *Woman's Regiment*, 293.

21. Rama, interview, 25 November 2008.

22. Janaki, interview, 6 March 2008.

23. Ibid.

24. Rasammah, interview, 10 March 2008. Ponnammah, interview, 5 April 2008.

25. Anjali, interview, 8 January 2009.

26. Dhanam, 'Memoir'. Dhanam, interview, 8 January 2009.

27. Ibid.

28. Aruna, 'Netaji and Me'. Banerjee, 'My Life', 21.

29. Aruna, 'Netaji and Me'.

30. Ibid. Aruna, interview, 8 January 2008.

31. INA Papers, BL-AAS, Mss Eur F275/10, 156.

32. Sahgal, *Revolutionary Life*, 59.

33. Aruna, 'Netaji and Me'.

34. INA Papers, BL-AAS Mss Eur F275/21, 75.

35. Sahgal, *Revolutionary Life*, 59.

36. Ibid., 169. Lakshmi, interview, 4 January 2008. IR Dr Lakshmi Swaminathan. Other reports repeat Captain Lakshmi's numbers.

37. Ibid.

38. Mehervan Singh, interview, NAS-OHC, reel 21, 7 June, 1985.

39. Yadava, *Forgotten Warriors*, 132, 266, 296–315. Yadava's list includes forty-three Kaurs out of 199 names.

40. Janaki Bai, who grew up on a plantation where her father was a manager, was Rajput, not South Indian.

41. Yadava, *Forgotten Warriors*, 296–315.

42. Janaki, interview, 7 January 2009.

43. Ibid., 67.
44. Labanya Ganguli Chatterji, telephone interview, 19 December 2008.
45. Lakshmi, interview, 4 January 2008.
46. Akilandam, interview, 5 March 2008.
47. Anjuli, interview, 9 January 2008. Muniammah, daughter of Eelavan, interview, 10 January 2009.
48. Lakshmi Nair [Sheila Fernandez], interview, NAS-OHC, reel 6, 5 June 1985.
49. Eva Jenny, interview, 9 March 2008.
50. Rasammah, *Footprints*, 50.
51. Aruna, interview, 9 January 2008. Aruna's first word to describe Bose was that he was 'fair', meaning light-skinned.
52. Karuna, interview, 10 December 2008.
53. Rama, interview, 24 November 2008.
54. Lakshmi, interview, 6 January 2008.
55. Asha, interview, 8 December 2008.
56. Anjuli, interview, 9 January 2008.
57. Majumdar, 'Netaji's Rani'.
58. Rama, interview, 28 April 2008.
59. Ibid.
60. Ibid.
61. Eva Jenny, interview, 9 March 2008.
62. Ibid.
63. Labanya, interview, 9 December 2008. INA Papers, BL-AAS, Mss Eur F275/21, 39.
64. Aruna, 'Netaji and Me'.
65. INA Papers, BL-AAS, Mss Eur F275/21, 39. Eva Jenny, interview, 9 March 2008.
66. Kratoska, *Japanese Occupation*, 247, 262.
67. Muniammah, interview, 10 January 2009.
68. Ibid.
69. Eva Jenny, 'Unpublished Memoir'.
70. Kratoska, *Japanese Occupation*, 277.
71. Aruna, 'Netaji and Me'.
72. Muniammah, interview, 10 January 2009. Lakshmi Nair [Sheila Fernandez], interview, NAS-OHC, reel 4, 29 May 1985.
73. Ponnammah, interview, 2 November 2008.

74. Lakshmi, interview, 5 January 2008.
75. NAI, 380/INA, 26.
76. Janaki Bai, interview, 7 March 2008.
77. Rasammah, interview, 10 March 2008.

TEN: SINGAPORE — THE RANIS PREPARE FOR WAR

1. Sahgal, *Revolutionary Life*, 170.
2. Ibid., 60.
3. Fay, *Forgotten Army*, 220–21.
4. A. C. Chatterji, *India's Struggle,* 125.
5. Sahgal, *Revolutionary Life,* 60. Captain Lakshmi and several Ranis mentioned that 22 October was the birthday of Rani Lakshmibai. Some scholars set it in November, but the exact date is not known.
6. Fay, *Forgotten Army,* 221. Sahgal, *Revolutionary Life,* 62–3. Bose, *Chalo Delhi,* 127.
7. Ibid., 124.
8. Ibid., 125.
9. Ibid. Lotika Ghose and other women, who volunteered for the corps in 1928, say that they were about 250 women.
10. Ibid., 127.
11. Janaki Bai, interview, 7 March 2008.
12. Vilasini Perumbulavil, interview, NAS-OHC, reel 2–3, 28 September, 2000. A Nissen hut is a prefabricated semicircular steel structure used to house soldiers.
13. Anjali, interview, 8 January 2009.
14. Gita is the abbreviated name commonly used for the Bhagavadgita, a part of the Hindu scripture, the Mahabharata.
15. Janaki Thevar's maiden last name is spelled in several ways (Devar being one such) in the reports, histories and even by herself.
16. Janaki, 'Memoir,' 10.
17. Sahgal, *Revolutionary Life*, 60.
18. Janaki, interview, 7 March 2008.
19. Bose, *Chalo Delhi,* 418, 431.
20. Rasammah, interview, 10 March 2008.
21. Bose, *Chalo Delhi,* 419, 422.

22. Ibid., 423.
23. Rasammah, interview, 10 March 2008.
24. Bose, *Chalo Delhi*, 432.
25. Eva Jenny, interview, 9 March 2008.
26. Ponnammah, interview, 2 November 2008.
27. Rasammah, interview, 10 March 2008.
28. Bose, *Chalo Delhi,* 428, 432.
29. Ponnammah, interview, 2 November 2008.
30. Rama, interview, 28 April 2008.
31. Janaki Bai, interview, 7 March 2008.
32. Mommata, interview, 8 June 2008.
33. Lakshmi Sahgal, 'Speech at The Third International Netaji Seminar, Calcutta, 23 January 1979', in *The Oracle* 1, no. 2 (April 1979): 69–70.
34. NAI, British Intelligence, DIC No. 2 Section Report No. 770, Rani of Jhansi Regt., 22. Jan 1945.
35. Bose, *Chalo Delhi,* 419.
36. Lakshmi, interview, 5 January 2008.
37. Mommata, interview, 21 November 2008.
38. Sahgal, *Revolutionary Life*, 66–67.
39. Ibid., 67.
40. Mehervan Singh, interview, NAS-OHC, reel 21, 7 June 1985.
41. Rasammah, interview, 10 March 2008.
42. Janaki, 'Memoir', 8. *Ragi Dosa* is a millet pancake, a common breakfast dish.
43. Lakshmi, 'My Days in the Indian National Army', http://www.ndtv.com/article/india/my-days-in-the-indian-national-army-by-lakshmi-sahgal-246587, 2 (Updated on 23 July 2012, 15:10 IST).
44. Manwati, interview, 7 January 2008.
45. A. C. Chatterji, *India's Struggle,* 126.
46. Ibid. The Dutch rifles, M-95, designed in 1895 were outdated and needed 6.5 mm ammunition, not the 8 mm used by most rifles in WWII. The 'Dutch' rifle, alluded to by General Chatterji is probably the M-95.
47. Ibid.
48. Ibid.
49. '303' usually refers to the Lee-Enfield rifle, but 303 is the rifle bullet calibre, and the Rosses were chambered with the same rounds as the Lee-Enfields.
50. Akilandam, interview, 6 January 2009.

51. Aruna, 'Netaji and Me.'

52. Janaki Bai, interview, 7 March 2008.

53. Lakshmi, interview, 6 January 2008.

ELEVEN: DAILY RANI ROUTINES IN CAMP

1. Kaur, *Women*, 230.

2. *Bande Mataram* or *Vande Mataram* is Hindi or Sanskrit meaning 'Hail Mother.' The mother is India as the war goddess Durga, personified as the sacred mother of all Indians.

3. Janaki, 'Memoir', 10.

4. Janaki Bai, interview, 7 March 2008.

5. Spoken Urdu and Hindi are mutually intelligible, but the scripts are completely different.

6. Lakshmi, interview, 4 January 2008.

7. Ibid.

8. Rasammah, interview, 10 March 2008. Dhanam, interview, 8 January 2009.

9. Lakshmi, interview, 4 January 2008.

10. IR L3719 Dr Lakshmi Swaminathan, section 3, 4 August 1945..

11. INA Papers, BL-AAS, Mss Eur F275/21, 39. L 3968 Gian Kaur.

12. Bose, *Chalo Delhi*, 419.

13. Lakshmi, interview, 5 January 2008.

14. Janaki Bai, interview, 7 March 2008.

15. Aruna, 'Netaji and Me'.

16. Mss Eur F 275/21, 147, subsection 26, IR M2734 Captain Sayed Munawar Hussain,.

17. Ibid.

18. Janaki Bai, interview, 7 March 2008.

19. Rasammah, interview, 10 March 2008. Datuk is a high federal title in Malaysia held for life and granted for exceptional service to the country. Only two hundred recipients hold the title at any one time.

20. Shah Nawaz, *My Memories*, 261.

21. Ibid., 71.

22. Sahgal, *Revolutionary Life*, 77. Lakshmi, interview, 5 January 2008.

23. Apparently, a sub-officer is not an NCO, but she has not either reached the level of second lieutenant, the lowest rank of commissioned officers.

24. Bose, *Chalo Delhi,* 431.

25. INA Papers, BL-AAS, Mss Eur F275/21, 39-40.

26. Toye, *Springing Tiger,* 122.

27. Sahgal, *Revolutionary Life,* 77.

28. Bose, *Indian Pilgrim*, 91–92.

29. Shah Nawaz, *My Memories*, 261.

30. Anjalai, interview, 6 March 2008.

31. Akilandam, interview, 5 March 2008.

32. Janaki Bai, interview, 7 March 2008.

33. One woman requested not to be mentioned by name, because she has never told her husband that she was a Rani.

34. Veesa Mudeliar, conversation, Singapore, 12 January 2009.

35. Eva Jenny, interview, 9 March 2008.

36. A. C. Chatterji, *India's Struggle,* 96. Shah Nawaz, *My Memories,* 261.

37. Anjali, interview, 8 January 2009.

38. Dhanam, interview, 8 January 2009.

39. Janaki Bai, interview, 7 March 2008.

40. Aruna, interview, 9 January 2008.

41. Sahgal, *Revolutionary Life,* 169. Lakshmi, interview, 5 January 2008.

42. Sahgal, *Revolutionary Life,* 64. Lakshmi, interview, 5 January 2008.

43. Asha, 'Diary.'

44. Ponnammah, interview, 5 April 2008.

45. Janaki Bai, interview, 7 March 2008.

46. Ibid.

47. Athinahappan, 'Rani of Jhansi Regiment', 30.

48. Sahgal, *Revolutionary Life*, 171. Lakshmi, interview, 5 January 2008.

49. Ibid.

50. Ibid.

51. Bose, *Indian Pilgrim,* 55–56.

52. Ponnammah, interview, 2 November 2008.

53. Ibid., Janaki Bai, interview, 7 March 2008. Janaki Thevar, interview, 5 March 2008.

54. Ponnammah, interview, 2 November 2008.

55. Ibid.

56. Karuna, interview, 10 December 2008.

57. Rama, interview, 25 November 2008. Janaki Bai, interview, 7 March 2008.

58. At the time of the interview, 7 January 2008, Manwati was married to Krishnachandra Arya and did not volunteer information about an earlier marriage and divorce. NAI, 244/INA, 18. Rani of Jhansi Regt. Extract from Report No. 897 on 5 INA Staff Officers.

59. Ponnammah, interview, 15 December 2009.

60. Janaki, 'Memoir', 18.

61. Ibid., 24.

62. NAI, 244/INA, 18. Rani of Jhansi Regt. Extract from Report No. 897 on 5 INA Staff Officers.

63. NAI, 244/INA, Appendix 'B', Names of Members of Rani of Jhansi Regiment in Rangoon in 1944.

64. NAI, 244/INA, 18, Rani of Jhansi Regt.

65. INA Papers, BL-AAS, Mss Eur F275/6, 317. IR B978 Ehsan Qadir. Qadir was known in the INA for his lampooning. The translation is also part of the interrogation report and its quality is not known.

66. Asha, 'Diary'.

67. Asha, 'Diary', 17 June 1945. Gordon, *Brothers against the Raj,* 447.

68. Hasan's original name was Zain-ul-Abideen Hasan. Subsequently he wanted to be known as Abid Hasan and finally as Abid Hasan Safrani.

69. Shah Nawaz, *My Memories,* 102.

70. Ibid., 103.

71. Toye, *Springing Tiger,* 123. INA Papers, BL-AAS, Mss Eur F275/22,1. 'The capitulation of 5,000 JIFCs in Rangoon as reported in W.L. No. 41 is now confirmed. In fact, the total of INA prisoners captured there now exceeds 5,000.'

72. Toye, *Springing Tiger*, 123.

73. Rama, interview, 24 November 2008.

74. INA Papers, BL-AAS, Mss Eur F275/20, 28.

75. Manwati, interview, 7 January 2008.

TWELVE: THE RJR IN RANGOON AND MAYMYO

1. Aruna, 'Netaji and Me'. Banerjee, 'My Life', 21.

2. IR L3719 Dr Lakshmi Swaminathan, 11, 4 August 1945.

3. Sahgal, *Revolutionary Life*, 72.

4. Arya, 'Rani of Jhansi Regiment', 16–20.
5. Manwati, interview, 7 January 2008.
6. Sahgal, *Revolutionary Life*, 72.
7. Ibid.
8. NAI, 244/INA, Rani of Jhansi Regt., Rep. 948 on B961 Lieutenant Saleem, 8 June, 1945. As soldiers with Indian Army experience were rapidly promoted in the INA, their rank changed quick. Saleem/Salim is mentioned as Lieutenant, Captain and Major.
9. NAI, 244/INA, 18. Rani of Jhansi Regt. Extract from Report No. 897 on 5 INA Staff Officers. NAI, 244/INA, Appendix 'B', Names of Members of Rani of Jhansi Regt. in Rangoon in 1944.
10. Mommata, interview, 21 November 2008. Amba, interview, 11 December 2008. Banerjee, 'My Life'.
11. Mommata, interview, 21 November 2008.
12. Rama, interview, 28 April 2008.
13. Aruna, interview, 9 January 2008.
14. Karuna, interview, 10 December 2008. Aruna, 'Netaji and Me'.
15. Mommata, interview, 21 November 2008. Rasammah, *Footprints*, 77. NAI, New Delhi, 244/INA, Rani of Jhansi Regiment, January 22, 1945.
16. Rasammah, interview, 10 March 2008.
17. Bose, *Chalo Delhi*, 419.
18. Ibid., 428.
19. Sahgal, *Revolutionary Life*, 76, 83. Captain Lakshmi had left Singapore for Burma two months before the Ranis' departure but she specifies that the group of Ranis consisted of eight officers, ten NCOs, eighty jawans plus fifteen Rani nurses, a total of one hundred and fifteen women. Lebra, *Women*, 91. Lebra claims incorrectly that two groups of Ranis were sent to Burma.
20. Dhanam, interview, 8 January 2009.
21. Rasammah, *Footprints*, 71-72. Lakshmi Swaminadhan [sic], 'The Rani of Jhansi Regiment', *Roshni: Journal of the All-India Women's Conference* 2, no.4 (May 1947): 33–42.
22. Rasammah, *Footprints*, 71.
23. Anjuli, interview, 9 January 2008.
24. Rasammah, *Footprints*, 71.
25. Ibid., 72.

26. Bose, *Chalo Delhi,* 428.
27. Rasammah, *Footprints*, 72–73.
28. Ibid., 73.
29. Ibid.
30. Ponnammah, interview, 15 December 2009.
31. Aruna, interview, 10 January 2008.
32. Rama, interview, 26 November 2008.
33. Aruna, 'Netaji and Me'.
34. Ibid.
35. Ponnammah, interview, 2 November 2008.
36. Aruna, interview, 10 January 2008. Ponnammah, interview, 2 November 2008.
37. Ibid.
38. Aruna, 'Netaji and Me'.
39. Majumdar, 'Netaji's Rani'.
40. Banerjee, 'My Life'. NAI, 244/INA, Rani of Jhansi Regiment, 22 January 1945.
41. NAI, 244/INA, Preliminary Examination Report Y199/1, 32. Recruiting of Women.
42. Banerjee, 'My Life'.
43. Ponnammah, interview, 15 December 2009.
44. NAI, 244/INA, 'Rani of Jhansi Regt.', HQSC No. R693 Chajju Ram, 31.
45. Ibid.
46. NAI, 244/INA, Rani of Jhansi Regiment, 22 January 1945.
47. Lakshmi Nair [Sheila Fernandez], interview, NAS-OHC, reel 6, 5 June 1985.
48. Banerjee, 'My Life'.
49. Bose, *Chalo Delhi,* 418. Rama, interview, 28 April 2008.
50. Mommata, interview, 21 November 2008. Janaki 'Memoir', 18.
51. Janaki, interview, 7 January 2009. Janaki 'Memoir', 19.
52. Banerjee, 'My Life'.
53. Aruna, interview, 4 December 2008. Banerjee, 'My Life'.
54. Ibid.
55. Ibid.
56. Aruna, 'Netaji and Me'.
57. Toye, *Springing Tiger*, 108. Sugata Bose, *His Majesty's Opponent,* 272–73.

58. Toye, *Springing Tiger*, 273. Banerjee, 'My Life'.
59. Sahgal, *Revolutionary Life*, 77–78. NAI, 244/INA, Extract Report, no. 856 on B956, paragraph 29.
60. INA Papers, BL-AAS, Mss Eur F275/21, 39. IR L3968 Captain Gian Kaur. NAI, 244/INA, Rani of Jhansi Regt., Extract from Report no. 956 on B956, section 29. Aruna, interview, 10 January 2008.
60. Banerjee, 'My Life'. Sahgal, *Revolutionary Life*, 77–78.
62. Aruna, 'Netaji and Me'.
63. Ibid.
64. Sahgal, *Revolutionary Life*, 80.
65. Aruna, interview, 4 December 2008.
66. Fay, *Forgotten Army*, 262.
67. Shah Nawaz, *My Memories*, 89.
68. Banerjee, 'My Life'. Sahgal, *Revolutionary Life*, 80.
69. Ibid.
70. Aruna, 'Netaji and Me'.
71. Ibid.
72. Banerjee, 'My Life'.
73. INA Papers, BL-AAS, Mss Eur F275/21, 39. IR L3968 Captain Gian Kaur.
74. Aruna, 'Netaji and Me'.
75. INA Papers, BL-AAS, Mss Eur F275/21, 39. IR L3968 Captain Gian Kaur.
76. NAI, 244/INA, 28, IIL Papers, IR L2243 Rahmat Bibi Ma Khin U.
77. Sahgal, *Revolutionary Life*, 88.
78. Aruna, 'Netaji and Me'.
79. Labanya, interview, 19 December 2008.
80. Ibid.
81. Manwati, interview, 7 January 2008. Sahgal, *Revolutionary Life*, 87. Rama, interview, 24 November 2008. Mommata, interview, 21 November 2008. Aruna, 'Netaji and Me'.
82. Sahgal, *Revolutionary Life*, 87.
83. Labanya, interview, 19 December 2008.
84. Toye, *Springing Tiger*, 120.
85. Kiani, *India's Freedom Struggle*, 132.
86. Toye, *Springing Tiger*, 126.
87. Shah Nawaz, *My Memories*, 127.

88. Aruna, 'Netaji and Me'.

89. Ibid.

90. Shah Nawaz, *My Memories*, 127.

91. Sahgal, *Revolutionary Life*, 88–89.

92. Aruna, 'Netaji and Me'.

93. Ibid.

94. Ibid.

95. Ibid.

96. Ponnammah, interview, 2 November 2008.

97. NAI, 244/INA, The Bahadur Shah Corps, 105.

98. NAI, 244/INA, Rep. 1004 on B1052, Suicide Party, 101.

99. INA Papers, BL-AAS, Mss Eur F275/6, IR B1021 Captain Asiruddin Jehangir, 23. NAI, 244/INA, Report 1001 on B1021, Bose's Birthday Celebration and 'Blood Sealing' Ceremony of Suicide Squad, 102.

100.NAI, 244/INA, Report No. 985 on B985 Khushal Singh Rawat, Janbaz BN, Suicide Squad, 26. NAI, 244/INA, Report No. 956 on B956, Bose's Birthday, 103.

101.Rasammah, interview, 10 March 2008. Also on YouTube: www.youtube.com/watch?v=9uRg_QD24s4. In her biography, Rasammah does not mention having volunteered for the Janbaz, nor Bose's reason for not letting her join.

102.Dhanam, interview, 8 January 2009.

103.Lebra, *Women*, 64.

104.Meenachi Perumal, www.youtube.com/watch?v=FUqQ5nzDn-Q.

105.Janaki, interview, 5 January 2009. Several requests for appointments with Meenachi Perumal for this study remained unanswered.

106.Janaki Bai, interview, 7 March 2008. INA Papers, BL-AAS, Mss Eur F275/6, IR B1021 Captain Asiruddin Jehangir, 23. NAI, 244/INA, Report 1001 on B1021, Bose's Birthday Celebration and 'Blood Sealing' Ceremony of Suicide Squad, 102. Aruna, interview, 4 December 2008.

107.INA Papers, BL-AAS, Mss Eur F275/6, IR B1021 Captain Asiruddin Jehangir, 23.

108.Lebra, *Indian National Army*, 181.

109.Ibid.

THIRTEEN: RJR RETREATS FROM RANGOON

1. NAI, 244/INA, Extract from Report 956 on B956, paragraph 43, Rani of Jhansi Regt.
2. Ibid.
3. A. C. Chatterji, *India's Struggle*, 259. Every Rani, who had been in Burma, expressed the same disappointment and feeling of having been cheated.
4. Ponnammah, interview, November 2, 2008.
5. Rasammah, *Footprints*, 80.
6. Bose, *Chalo Delhi*, 314.
7. Kiani, *India's Freedom Struggle*, 76. Shah Nawaz, *My Memories*, 200.
8. Slim, *Defeat into Victory*, 498.
9. Kiani, *India's Freedom Struggle*, 130.
10. Ibid.
11. Hugh Toye, 'Subhas Pasha', BL-AAS, Mss Eur D1228, 459. Toye is quoting from Prem Sahgal's impounded diary.
12. Ibid., 463.
13. Ibid., 142.
14. Ibid., 459.
15. NAI, 244/INA, Extract from Report 956 on B956, paragraph 43, Rani of Jhansi Regt. Toye, 'Subhas Pasha', 475.
16. NAI, 244/INA, Rani of Jhansi Regt., 17, Rep. No. 985 on B985, 24, IR B985 Khushal Singh Rawat.
17. Rasammah, *Footprints*, 84. Four women, Rasammah, Ponnammah, Janaki Bai and Muniammah, of this group were interviewed for this study.
18. Ibid. NAI, 244/INA, Extract from Report 956 on B956, paragraph 43, Rani of Jhansi Regt. Toye, 'Subhas Pasha', 475.
19. Rasammah, *Footprints*, 84.
20. Janaki Bai, interview, 7 March 2008.
21. In the interviews Rasammah, Ponnammah and Janaki Bai told about this event, all agreeing on almost every detail.
22. Janaki Bai, interview, 7 March 2008.
23. Rasammah, interview, 10 March 2008. Rasammah was not among the Ranis attacked in Maymyo.
24. Janaki Bai, interview, 7 March 2008.
25. Ibid.

26. Ponnammah, interview, 5 April 2008.
27. Janaki Bai, interview, 7 March 2008. When not found on maps, the names of villages and other locations are written the way the Ranis spelled them and may not all be correct, e.g. Chambpoori.
28. Ibid.
29. Majumdar, 'Netaji's Rani'.
30. Rasammah, *Footprints*, 84.
31. Lebra, *Women*, 64.
32. Rasammah, *Footprints*, 86.
33. Janaki Bai, interview, 7 March 2008.
34. Shah Nawaz, *My Memories,* 200.
35. Ibid.
36. Aruna, interview, 10 January 2008.
37. Aruna, 'Netaji and Me'.
38. INA Papers, BL-AAS, Mss Eur F275/21, Rani of Jhansi Regt.
39. NAI, 244/INA, Rep. No. 985 on B985 Khushal Singh Rawat, Rani of Jhansi Regt., 17.
40. Aruna, 'Netaji and Me'.
41. Ibid.
42. Ayer, *Unto Him*, 14.
43. Toye, 'Subhas Pasha', 475–76.
44. A. C. Chatterji, *India's Struggle*, 264. INA papers, BL-AAS, F275/20, 5,000/6,000 INA troops were found in the city. Shah Nawaz, *My Memories,* 203.
45. Toye, 'Subhas Pasha', 478.
46. Ayer, Interview 172, Centre of South Asian Studies, Cambridge University, UK. 28 April 1972.
47. NAI, 244/INA, Rani of Jhansi Regt., 76. 'B978 Ordered to Accompany Rani of Jhansi Regt from Rangoon.' INA Papers, BL-AAS, Mss Eur F275/6, 313. IR B978 Ehsan Qadir. Toye, 'Subhas Pasha', 476.
48. NAI, 244/INA, Rani of Jhansi Regt., 76. 'B978's [Ehsan Qadir's] last meeting with Bose'.
49. Toye, 'Subhas Pasha', 476.
50. Ibid.
51. NAI, CSDIC (India), Red Fort, Delhi, No. 2 Section Report NO 957 [Abdul Rashid] Dated 14 June 1945, 13.

52. NAI, 244/INA, Rani of Jhansi Regt., No. L3719, IR Dr Lakshmi Swaminathan, 7

53. Janaki, 'Memoir', 22.

54. Toye, *Springing Tiger,* 223–24.

55. Shanti Majumdar, 'Netaji's Rani of Jhansi Regiment,' *The Oracle* 2, no. 3 (July 1980): 21–26.

56. NAI, 244/INA, Rani of Jhansi Regt., 17, Rep. No. 985 on B985 Khushal Singh Rawat, 24. BL-AAS, Mss Eur F275/6, 313. NAI, 244/INA, Rani of Jhansi Regt., Extract from Report no. 956 on B956, paragraph 29. Ayer, *Unto Him,* 17.

57. Toye, 'Subhas Pasha', 503. Ayer, *Unto Him,* 17.

58. Majumdar, 'Netaji's Rani', 24.

59. Ibid.

60. Ibid., 18. A. C. Chatterji, *India's Struggle,* 264. Toye, 'Subhas Pasha', 503.

61. Shah Nawaz, *My Memories,* 204.

62. Janaki Thevar Athinahappan, speech at Netaji Golden Jubilee Celebrations, NRB, Kolkata, 23 January 2007 and unpublished memoirs. No other source mentions an attack at the Rangoon railway station or any Rani casualties among this group of retreating Ranis. Janaki gives no details, no names and no information as to how the Ranis were buried.

63. Ibid.

64. Ibid.

65. Ibid.

66. Ibid.

67. Ayer, *Unto Him,* 18.

68. Janaki, quoted in Shah Nawaz, *My Memories,* 205.

69. Ibid.

70. Ayer, *Unto Him,* 19–20.

71. Janaki, quoted in Shah Nawaz, *My Memories,* 205.

72. Majumdar, 'Netaji's Rani', 24.

73. Janaki, quoted in Shah Nawaz, *My Memories,* 206. Majumdar, 'Netaji's Rani', 24.

74. Ayer, *Unto Him,* 20 Janaki, quoted in Shah Nawaz, *My Memories,* 206.

75. Ayer, *Unto Him,* 21. Janaki, quoted in Shah Nawaz, *My Memories,* 207.

76. Ayer, *Unto Him,* 23.

77. Janaki, 'Memoir', 21. At the time of the year the Ranis crossed the Sittang,

the river was at least half a mile wide.

78. Ayer, *Unto Him*, 24.
79. Ibid., 25–26. Janaki, quoted in Shah Nawaz, *My Memories*, 207.
80. Ibid.
81. Ibid., 208. Ayer, *Unto Him*, 28.
82. Majumdar, 'Netaji's Rani', 25.
83. Ayer, *Unto Him*, 28.
84. Janaki, quoted in Shah Nawaz, *My Memories*, 208.
85. Ayer, *Unto Him*, 29.
86. Ibid., 30.
87. A. C. Chatterji, *India's Struggle*, 268.
88. Janaki, quoted in Shah Nawaz, *My Memories*, 209.
89. Ibid.
90. A. C. Chatterji, *India's Struggle*, 268. Toye, 'Subhas Pasha', 504.
91. Janaki, quoted in Shah Nawaz, *My Memories*, 209.
92. Ibid.
93. Ibid.
94. NAI, 244/INA, Rani of Jhansi Regt., 17, Rep. No. 985 on B985 Khushal Singh Rawat. Rani of Jhansi Regt. Rasammah, *Footprints*, 50.
95. Majumdar, 'Netaji's Rani', 25.
96. A. C. Chatterji, *India's Struggle*, 270.
97. Janaki, 'Memoir', 23.
98. Ibid., 24.
99. Rasammah, interview, 10 March 2008. Rasammah, *Footprints*, 85. Ponnammah, interview, 2 November 2008
100. Ibid.
101. Ponnammah, interview, 15 December 2009.
102. Rasammah, interview, 10 March 2008.
103. Ponnammah, interview, 15 December 2009.
104. Ibid.
105. Rasammah, interview, 10 March 2008.
106. Ponnammah, interview, 5 April 2008.
107. INA Papers, BL-AAS, Mss Eur F275/10. Report by Col. Sheodatt Singh CSDIC(I) on INA Thailand up to 23 October 1945. A Strengths in Thailand' 'Rannee Jhansi Girls 7'. Point 2. Rannee Jhansi Girls.'
108. Asha, interview, 8 December 2008. INA Papers, BL-AAS, Mss Eur F275/10.

'Report by Col. Sheodatt Singh CSDIC (I) on INA Thailand up to 23 October 1945.

109. It is not possible to say exactly how many Ranis were quartered in the main training camp in Singapore in August 1945.

110. Dhanam, interview, 8 January 2009.

111. Ibid.

112. Ibid.

FOURTEEN: VARYING ACCOUNTS OF THE RJR

1. Amritlal Seth, *Jai-Hind: The Diary of a Rebel Daughter of India with the Rani of Jhansi Regiment* (Bombay: Janmabhoomi Prakashan Mandir, 1945).

2. Sahgal, *Revolutionary Life*, 109.

3. Ibid.

4. Amritlal Seth, *Jai-Hind*, 84.

5. Sahgal, 'The Rani of Jhansi Regiment', *The Oracle* 1, no. 2 (April 1979): 15–19.

6. Ibid.

7. Sahgal, *Revolutionary Life,* 78. Aruna, 'Netaji and Me'.

8. NAI, 244/INA, Rani of Jhansi Regt., IR L3719 Dr Lakshmi Swaminathan, 3-4. 'Two sections of the Burma company were stationed at Maymyo.' There were eight or nine Ranis in each section.

9. Sahgal, 'The Rani of Jhansi Regiment'.

10. Ibid.

11. Lakshmi, interview, 5 January 2008.

12. Nair, *The Story of I.N.A.,* 29.

13. Roma Banerjee, 'The Rani of Jhansi Regiment and Women Empowerment', in *Netaji Subhas Chandra Bose and Indian Freedom Struggle: Netaji and Indian National Army (INA),* ed. Ratna Ghosh, Vol. 2 (New Delhi: Deep and Deep, 2006), 139–41.

14. Ibid.

15. NAI, 244/INA, 28, IIL Papers, IR L2243 Rahmat Bibi Ma Khin U.

16. Aruna, 'Netaji and Me'.

17. Bose, *Chalo Delhi,* 124.

18. Gordon, *Brothers against the Raj,* 496. Quoting from a recorded interview with Dr (Mrs) Lakshmi Sahgal, 15 April 1977, Nehru Memorial Museum

and Library, Oral History Interview, 11.

19. INA Papers, BL-AAS, Mss Eur F275/21, 75, A, Captain R. Yusuf Ali.

20. Bose, *Chalo Delhi*, 418.

21. NAI, 244/INA, IR L3719 Dr Lakshmi Swaminathan, 244/INA, sections 16 and 17.

22. Sahgal, 'The Rani of Jhansi Regiment'.

23. Lakshmi, 'Speech', 70.

24. Ritu Menon and Kamla Bhasin, 'An Interview with Lakshmi Sahgal', March 1989, in Sahgal, *Revolutionary Life*, 169.

25. Lakshmi, interview, 4 January 2008.

26. Yadava, *Forgotten Warriors*, 132, 266, 296-315.

27. Ibid., 266, 301.

28. Ayer, *Unto Him*, xviii.

29. Prem Kumar Sahgal, 'My I.N.A. Odyssey', *The Oracle* 7, no. 2 (April 1985): 1–22.

30. Ayer, *Unto Him*, 22.

31. Shah Nawaz, *My Memories*, 261.

32. Ibid., 198–99.

33. A. C. Chatterji, *India's Struggle*, 128.

34. INA Papers, BL-AAS, Mss Eur F275/4, 101r-101v.

35. INA Papers, BL-AAS, Mss Eur F275/22, 26.

36. INA Papers, BL-AAS, Mss Eur F275/21, 75.

37. INA Papers, BL-AAS, Mss Eur F275/21, 75, A, Captain R. Yusuf Ali.

38. Sugata Bose, *His Majesty's Opponent*, 246. Som, *Subhas Chandra Bose*, 8.

39. Sugata Bose, *His Majesty's Opponent*, 267.

40. Gordon, *Brothers against the Raj*, 497.

41. Forbes, *Women in Modern India*, 213.

42. Hills and Silverman, 'Nationalism and Feminism', 741.

43. Kalyan Kumar Ghosh, *Indian National Army*, 157.

44. Pandit, *Netaji*, 194.

45. Sahgal, *Revolutionary Life*, 169.

46. Ibid. Ponnammah, interview, 5 April 2008.

47. Shanti Majumdar, 'Netaji's Rani of Jhansi Regiment', The Oracle 2, no. 3 (July 1980): 21–26.

48. Janaki Bai, interview, 7 March 2008.

49. NAI, 244/INA, Rani of Jhansi Regt., 17, B1156 Corporal Badr-ud-din.

50. Eva Jenny, interview, 9 March 2008.

51. Dhanam, interview, 8 January 2009.

52. Dhanam, Memoirs, 3.

53. Dhanam, interview, 8 January 2009. Anjali, interview, 8 January 2009.

54. Lakshmi Nair [Sheila Fernandez], interview, NAS-OHC, reel 6, 5 June 1985.

55. Ponnammah, interview, 5 April 2008.

56. Ibid.

57. NAI, 244/INA, Rani of Jhansi Regt., Rep. 948 on B961 Lieutenant Saleem [Salim], 8 June, 1945. Aruna, 'Netaji and Me'. NAI, 244/INA, Appendix 'B', Names of Members of Rani of Jhansi Regt. in Rangoon in 1944. The list contains the names of thirty-one Ranis in residence'.

58. Aruna, interview, 8 January 2008.

59. Athinahappan, 'Rani of Jhansi Regiment', 29.

60. Ibid., 30.

61. Shah Nawaz, My Memories, 70.

62. Bose, Chalo Delhi, 428.

FIFTEEN: THE END OF THE QUEST

1. INA Papers, BL-AAS, Mss Eur F275/21, 39. IR L3968, Captain Gian Kaur.

2. Sahgal, Revolutionary Life, 84.

3. NAI, 244/INA, Extract from SEAC and India Command WSIS no. 192, July 6, 1945.

4. Ibid.

5. NAI, 244/INA, Report No. 956 on B956.

6. Ibid.

7. Lakshmi, interview, 6 January 2008.

8. Ibid. A. C. Chatterji, India's Struggle, 258.

9. Sahgal, Revolutionary Life, 96–101.

10. Ibid., 101.

11. Lakshmi, interview, 6 January 2008.

12. Ibid.

13. Sahgal, Revolutionary Life, 101–02.

14. Mss Eur F275/22, 41, 'Weekly letter no. 46, (Produced by GSI(B)(iii), Adv. HQ, ALFSEA), Review of I.N.A. activities during period 9 May – 15 May 1945.

15. NAI, 244/INA, Rani of Jhansi Regt., IR L3719 Dr Lakshmi Swaminathan, Aug 4, 1945.

16. INA Papers, BL-AAS, Mss Eur F275/20, 21.

17. Lakshmi, interview, 6 January 2008.

18. Sahgal, *Revolutionary Life*, 105.

19. Ibid., 106.

20. INA Papers, BL-AAS, Mss Eur F275/20, *Fortnightly Digest*, 13, August 9, 1945.

21. NAI, 244/INA, Rani of Jhansi Regt., IR L3719 Dr Lakshmi Swaminathan, 4 August 1945. The following information is all extracted from this Interrogation Report on Captain Lakshmi.

22. Mss. Eur F275/20, Twelfth Army, Fortnightly Digest No. 13, 25 July to 7 August 1945.

23. Sahgal, *Revolutionary Life*, 107.

24. Lakshmi, interview, 6 January 2008.

25. Ibid.

26. Ibid.

27. Fay, *Forgotten Army*, 395.

28. Ibid.

29. BL-AAS, L/WS/1/1578.

30. INA Papers, BL-AAS, Mss Eur F275/1, 3. Hugh Toye, 5 September 1985. 'World War II: The handling of "Suspects and Escapees" from enemy occupied territory in India and S.E.A. Command'.

31. NAI, 244/INA, Rani of Jhansi Regt., IR L3719 Dr Lakshmi Swaminathan, 4 August 1945.

32. Ibid.

33. NAI, 244/INA, Rani of Jhansi Regt., IR L3719 Dr Lakshmi Swaminathan, 3, 4 August 1945.

34. In the summary of the rating of Ranis, L3719 Lakshmi Swaminathan is classified as 'Black'. INA Papers, BL-AAS, Mss Eur F275/21. NAI, 244/INA, Rani of Jhansi Regt., IR L3719 Dr Lakshmi Swaminathan, 3, 4 August 1945.

35. Fay, *Forgotten Army*, 401. INA Papers, BL-AAS, Mss Eur F275/21.

36. INA Papers, BL-AAS, Mss Eur F275/20, 21r. IR L3719 Dr Lakshmi Swaminathan, 5, and Appendix 'A', Personalities in the movement

37. Sahgal, *Revolutionary Life*, 108-11.

38. Lakshmi, interview, 5 January 2008.

39. Ibid.

40. NAI, 244/INA, Rani of Jhansi Regt., IR L3719 Dr Lakshmi Swaminathan, 4 August 1945..

41. INA Papers, BL-AAS, Mss Eur F275/21, 74–75. Sahgal, *Revolutionary Life,* 108. Captain Lakshmi states that British intelligence officers interrogated most of the RJR. In fact, the CSDIC(I) interviewed only a few of the officers, and none of the sepoys.

42. INA Papers, BL-AAS, Mss Eur F275/21, 74.

43. Ibid.

44. INA Papers, BL-AAS, Mss Eur F275/21,75, 2 October 1945. Gauri Bhattacharya's [Gori Bhattacharji] names are spelled in several different ways in the various reports, diaries and memoirs. INA Papers, BL-AAS, Mss Eur F275/20, HQ Twelfth Army for GSI. Review of Information received from interrogations, for the period 25 July to 7 August 1945. L3945 Latta Bharadwaja, a secretary at the IIL office in Rangoon, was also interrogated because the British assumed she was a Rani.

45. INA Papers, BL-AAS, Mss Eur F275/1, 4, 5 September 1985.

46. Janaki, 'Memoir', 26.

47. Majumdar, 'Netaji's Rani', 26.

48. Ibid.

49. Rama, interview, 28 April 2008.

50. INA Papers, BL-AAS, Mss Eur F275/20, *Fortnightly Digest,* 9, 13 June 1945.

51. Ibid.

52. INA Papers, BL-AAS, Mss Eur, F 275/21, 74.

53. Ayer, *Unto Him,* 40.

54. Bose, *Chalo Delhi,* 321, 324.

55. Ibid., 324–25.

56. Ayer, *Unto Him,* 48.

57. Ibid., 52.

58. Ibid., 56–57. Ayer gives the number of Ranis in Singapore as 500.

59. BL-AAS, Mss Eur F275/1. 'Special Order of the Day', signed by Subhas Chandra Bose, 14 August 1945 at 1500 Hours.

60. Bose, *Chalo Delhi,* 410.

61. NAI, No. C-5. Intelligence Bureau, (H.D.), New Delhi 3. 19 February 1946.

62. Ayer, *Unto Him,* 69.

63. NAI, No. C-5. Intelligence Bureau, (H.D.), New Delhi 3. 19 February 1946.
64. Taiwan was called Formosa during World War II and Taipei was Taihoku. The Intelligence reports use both sets of names: Taihoku and Formosa; Taipei and Taiwan. 'Extract from Allied Land Forces South East Asia Weekly Intelligence Review, No. 57 for week ending 2nd November 1945', NAI. Another more formal version of this report contains the same information, except in this version the height reached by the airplane before the crash was 200 metres. Since the plane was still within the perimeter of the airfield, the height of 10 metres is probably the more accurate height.
65. Gordon, *Brothers against the Raj*, 538. Ayer, *Unto Him*, 66–92.
66. BL-AAS, Mss Eur C785/1-4. 25 July 1946, Report on the Death of Subhas Chandra Bose.
67. Ibid. [BI] Note on Subhas Chandra Bose. No. C-5, Intelligence Bureau, New Delhi, 19 May 1946.
68. The expectation that Bose would return might have been sustained because when he escaped house arrest in January 1941, it was rumored that he had died in an airplane crash, until he surfaced in Berlin a few months later.
69. Anita Pfaff, telephone interview, 18 September 2012.
70. Amitabha Bhattasali, 'Subhas Chandra Bose: Secret Files on Independence Hero'. BBC, News India, 21 November 2013. Anuj Dhar, *India's Biggest Cover-up*. (New Delhi: Vitasta, 2012). Momta [Mommata Gupta]Mehta, YouTube, *Times Now*, 14 October 2015. Anita Pfaff, YouTube, *Times Now*, 14 October 2015.

SIXTEEN: FINAL REFLECTIONS ON SUBHAS CHANDRA BOSE AND THE RJR

1. Shah Nawaz, *My Memories,* 266.
2. Bose, Chalo Delhi, 212
3. Ibid., 217-18
4. Ibid., 219
5. Ibid., 219-220.
6. Hauner, *India in Axis Strategy,* 244.
7. Janaki, Memoir, 18.
8. Shah Nawaz, *My Memories,* v.

9. Janaki Bai, interview, 7 March 2008.
10. Shah Nawaz, *My Memories*, v.
11. Labanya, interview, 26 December 2008.
12. Ibid.
13. Majumdar, 'Netaji's Rani', 25.
14. Dancz, *Women and Party Politics*, 70.

BIBLIOGRAPHY

UNPUBLISHED SOURCES

British Library, Oriental and India Office Collections, United Kingdom Liaison Mission in Japan, British Embassy, Tokyo.
'Report on the Death of Subhas Chandra Bose'. Interrogations of individual witnesses into the death of Bose.

National Archives of Singapore, Oral History Centre, Singapore Civil Service Project interviews:
Vilasini Perumbulavil. Interview, Reel 2-3, 28 September 2000.

Communities of Singapore Project, Part 2, interviews:
Sheila Fernandez [P.K. Lakshmi Nair]. Interview, Reel 4, 29 May 1985; Reel 6, 5 June 1985.
Mehervan Singh. Interview, Reel 18–19, 24 May 1985; Reel 20–21, 7 June 1985.

Japanese Occupation of Singapore Project interviews:
Abdealli K. Motiwalla. Interview, Reel 2, 19 August 1982.
Damodaran, Son of K. Kesevan. Interview, Reel 3, 19 November 1981.
Dr Kanichat Raghava Menon. Interview, Reel 7, 27 May 1982.
Dr Tan Ban Cheng. Interview, Reel 5, 15 February 1984.
M. S. Varma. Interview, Reel 22, 18 November 2003; Reel 23, 8 December 2003.

Centre of South Asian Studies, Oral History Collection, Cambridge University, Cambridge, UK.
Subbier Appadurai Ayer. Interview number 172, April 28, 1972.

British Library - Asian and African Studies (BL-AAS), London, UK.

'Subhas Chandra Bose'. Investigation into the Death of Bose in an Airplane Crash.

Bengal Revolutionary Movement Papers

Mss Eur F341/139, Santa Ganguli.

Mss Eur F341/140, Lotika Ghose.

Mss Eur F341/158, Leela Roy.

Mss Eur F341/169, Kalyani Bhattacharje and her sister Bina Das.

Indian National Army (INA) Papers

Mss Eur F275/1, 2.

Mss Eur F275/1, 3, 5 September 1985. 'World War II: The handling of "Suspects and Escapees" from enemy occupied territory in India and S.E.A. Command'.

Mss Eur F275/1, 4, 5 September 1985.

Mss Eur F275/2, Intelligence Report B47 Abdul Hayat Khan, 28 December 1942.

Mss Eur F275/2, 30 Hugh Toye, Investigating the INA.

Mss Eur F275/2, CSDIC (I) No.2 Section Report No. 82, 13 January 1943. Intelligence Report B46 Nur Mohd.

Mss Eur F275/4, 101r-101v.

Mss Eur F275/6, 307. Intelligence Report B978 Ehsan Qadir.

Mss Eur F275/6, 317. Intelligence Report B978 Ehsan Qadir.

Mss Eur F275/6, Intelligence Report B1021 Capt. Asiruddin Jehangir, 23.

Mss Eur F275/9, 139. The INA February 1942-April 1944, Administration and Organisation.

Mss Eur F275/10, 126.

Mss Eur F275/10, 156.

Mss Eur F275/10. Report by Col. Sheodatt Singh CSDIC(I) on INA Thailand up to 23 October 1945, 'INA Strengths in Thailand', 'Rannee Jhansi Girls 7'. Point 2. Rannee Jhansi Girls.'

Mss Eur F275/10, 170. 'Propaganda' Bahadur Group, Intelligence Report M1899 Mohd Sayeed.

Mss Eur F275/12, Appendix 'C.'

Mss Eur F275/16, 249.

Mss Eur F275/16, CSDIC(I), Report no. 1103, 28 Nov 1945, Intelligence Report H1152 Mrs [Dr Nasira] M.Z. Kiani.

Mss Eur F275/20, 28, Rani of Jhansi Regt. L3242 Bhattacharya and L3239 Mukherji.

Mss Eur F275/20, 21, Lakshmi 'Comes in.'

Mss Eur F275/20, Report no. F309.

Mss Eur F275/20, Fortnightly Digest, 9, 13 June 1945.

Mss Eur F275/20, Fortnightly Digest, 13, 9 August 1945.

Mss Eur F275/20, HQ Twelfth Army for GSI. Review of information from interrogations, for the period 25 July to 7 August 1945.

Mss Eur F275/21, Rani of Jhansi Regt.

Mss Eur F275/21, No. 2 Forwarding Unit, Selected Reports.

Mss Eur F275/21, 21r.

Mss Eur F275/21, Intelligence report L3698 Kannappa Muthia.

Mss Eur F275/21, 39. Intelligence Report L3968, Capt. Gian Kaur.

Mss Eur F275/21, 74.

Mss Eur F275/21, 74-75.

Mss Eur F275/21, 75, A, Capt. R. Yusuf Ali.

Mss Eur F275/21,75, 2 October 1945. Rani of Jhansi Regt.

Mss Eur F275/22, 1.

Mss Eur F275/22, 26.

Mss Eur F275/22, 41, 'Weekly letter no. 46, (Produced by GSI[B][iii], Adv. HQ, ALFSEA), Review of I.N.A. activities during period 9 May – 15 May 1945.

Mss Eur C785/1-4. 25 July 1946, Report on the Death of Subhas Chandra Bose.

Note on Subhas Chandra Bose. No. C-5, Intelligence Bureau, New Delhi, 19 May 1946.

Mss Eur C785, 'The Death of Subhas Chandra Bose'. Tokyo, 25 July 1946.

Mss Eur 397, 145-147. No.63/2/10/GSI(b), 'Subhas Chandra Bose'. Saigon, 18 October 1945.

Mss Eur 397, 152-54, 'Army Doctor Describes Bose's Death', n.d.; 'Was Headed for Russia', n.d.; 'Netaji' No Longer Waits for His Hour', Early October 1956.

Mss Eur D1228. Toye, Hugh. 'Subhas Pasha'.

L/WS/1/1578.

L/PJ/12/771, File 2188/45, Secret report from Intelligence Bureau (Home Department) on the Indian National Army. Date Nov – Dec 1945, 20 November 1945.

National Archives of India (NAI), New Delhi

244/INA, Intelligence Report L3719, Dr Lakshmi Swaminathan, 4 August 1945.

244/INA, 28, IIL Papers, Intelligence Report L2243 Rahmat Bibi Ma Khin U.

244/INA, IIL Papers, Intelligence Report L3945 Latta Bharadwaja.

244/INA, The Bahadur Shah Corps, 105.

244/INA, Preliminary Examination Report Y199/1, 32. Recruiting of Women.

244/INA British Intelligence, DIC No. 2 Sec Report No. 770, RJR, 22 January 1945.

244/INA, Appendix 'B', Names of 31 Members of RJR in residence in Rangoon in 1944.

244/INA, 'Rani of Jhansi Regt.,' HQSC No. R693 Chajju Ram, 31.

244/INA, Report No. 770, Rani of Jhansi Regt.

244/INA, 18. Rani of Jhansi Regt. Extract from Report No. 897 on 5 INA Staff Officers.

244/INA, Rani of Jhansi Regt., Rep. 948 on B 961, Lt. Saleem, 8 June 1945.

244/INA, Rani of Jhansi Regt., Extract from Report no. 956 on B956, paragraph 29.

244/INA, Report No. 956 on B956, Bose's Birthday, 103.

244/INA, Extract from Report 956 on B956, paragraph 43, Rani of Jhansi Regt.

244/INA, Report No. 956 on B956, Dr Lakshmi.

244/INA, Report 978 on B978, B978 Ordered to Accompany RJR from Rangoon.

244/INA NAI, CSDIC (India), Red Fort, Delhi, No. 2 Section Report NO 957 [Abdul Rashid], 14 June 1945, 13.

244/INA, 77. B978's Last Meeting with Bose.

244/INA, Report No. 985 on B985, Rani of Jhansi Regt., 17.

244/INA, Report No. 985 on B985, Janbaz BN, Suicide Squad, 26.

244/INA, Report 1001 on B1021, Bose's Birthday Celebration and 'Blood Sealing' Ceremony of Suicide Squad, 102.

244/INA, Report 1004 on B1052, Suicide Party, 101.

244/INA, 18. Rani of Jhansi Regt. Report on B1156.

244/INA, Extract from SEAC and India Command WSIS no. 192, 6 July 1945. RJR.

380/INA, 26.

380/INA, Intelligence Report H1152 Dr Nasira Kiani.

PUBLISHED SOURCES

Ahluwalia, Bhupinder Kumar, and Shashi Ahluwalia. eds. *Netaji and Indian Independence*. New Delhi: Harnam Publications, 1983.

Aleksijevitj, Svetlana, and Kajsa Öberg Lindsten. *Kriget Har Inget Kvinnligt Ansigte: Utopins Röster*. Stockholm: Esatz, 2012.

Ali, T. 'The Untold and Alternate Story of the Indian Subcontinent's War of Independence'. *African and Asian Studies* 2 (2003): 37–61.

Ali, Tahseen H. 'Revolutionary Violence and Subversion: Re-examining the Role of Subhas Chandra Bose and Armed Struggle against the British Raj in India'. PhD diss., University of Houston, 2008.

Allen, Louis. *Burma: The Longest War, 1941–45*. New York: St Martin's Press, 1984.

———. 'The Image of Netaji: A Study in Mythology.' *The Oracle* 1 (1979): 20–25.

Arya, Manwati. *Patriot: The Unique Indian Leader Netaji Subhas Chandra Bose; A New Personalised Biography by One Who Worked for Netaji*. New Delhi: Lotus Press, 2007.

———. 'The Rani of Jhansi Regiment in Burma'. *The Oracle* 2 (1980): 16–20.

Asaf Ali, Aruna. *Resurgence of Indian Women*. New Delhi: Radiant, 1991.

Athinahappan, Janaki. 'The Rani of Jhansi Regiment'. *The Oracle* 2, (1980): 29–32.

Ayer, Subbier Appadurai. *Unto Him a Witness: The Story of Netaji Subhas Chandra Bose in East Asia*. Bombay: Thacker and Co., 1951.

———. 'The Indian Independence Movement in East Asia'. *The Oracle* 3 (1981): 6–17.

Bala, Usha, and Anshu Sharma. *Indian Women Freedom Fighters, 1857–1947*. New Delhi: Manohar, 1986.

Bandyopadhyay, Sekhar. 'Caste, Widow-Remarriage and the Reform of Popular Culture in Colonial Bengal'. In *From the Seams of History: Essays on Indian Women*, ed. B. Ray. Delhi: Oxford University Press, 1995: 8–36.

Banerjee, Maya. 'My Life with the Rani of Jhansi Regiment'. *The Oracle* 2 (1980): 20–24.

Banerjee, Tapan. *Mystery of Death of Subhash Chandra Bose*. New Delhi: Rajat Publications, 2002.

Barkawi, Tarak. 'Culture and Combat in the Colonies: The Indian Army in the Second World War'. *Journal of Contemporary History* 41 (2006): 325–355.

Basu, Aparna. 'The Role of Women in the Indian Struggle for Freedom'. In

Indian Women from Purdah to Modernity, ed. B. R. Nanda, New Delhi: Vikas Pub. House, 1976: 16–40.

Basu, Subho, and Sikata Banerjee. 'The Quest for Manhood: Masculine Hinduism and Nation in Bengal'. *Comparative Studies of South Asia, Africa and the Middle East* 26 (2006): 476–90.

Bawa, Anand Singh. *Netaji Subhas Chandra Bose and Germany*. New Delhi: Mosaic Books, 2013.

Bayly, Christopher Alan, and Tim Harper. *Forgotten Armies: The Fall of British Asia, 1941–1945*. Cambridge, MA: Belknap Press of Harvard University Press, 2005.

Bhattacharya, Sanjoy. 'British Military Information Management Techniques and the South Asian Soldier: Eastern India during the Second World War'. *Modern Asian Studies* 34 (May 2000): 483–510.

Bhupalan, Rasammah. 'The Rani of Jhansi Regiment: A Will for Freedom'. In *Footprints on the Sands of Time: Rasammah Bhupalan; A Life of Purpose, ed.* Aruna Gopinath. Kuala Lumpur: Arkib Negara Malaysia, 2007: 49–104.

Bose, Krishna. 'Important Women in Netaji's Life'. *The Illustrated Weekly of India* 93 (1972): 34–35, 48–49.

Bose, Sisir Kumar, Alexander Werth, and Subbier Appadurai Ayer. eds. *A Beacon Across Asia: A Biography of Subhas Chandra Bose*. Hyderabad: Orient Black Swan, 2008.

Bose, Subhas Chandra. *The Alternative Leadership: Speeches, Articles, Statements and Letters, June 1939–January 1941*. eds. Sisir Kumar Bose and Sugata Bose. Calcutta: Netaji Research Bureau, 1998.

————. *Azad Hind: Writings and Speeches, 1941–43*. eds. Sisir Kumar Bose and Sugata Bose. Calcutta: Netaji Research Bureau, 2002.

————. *Chalo Delhi: Writings and Speeches, 1943–1945*. eds. Sisir Kumar Bose and Sugata Bose. Calcutta: Netaji Research Bureau, 2007.

————. *Congress President: Speeches, Articles and Letters, January 1938–May 1939*. eds. Sisir Kumar Bose and Sugata Bose. Kolkata: Netaji Research Bureau, 2004.

————. *Crossroads, Being the Works of Subhas Chandra Bose, 1938–1940*. ed. Sisir Kumar Bose. London: Asia Publishing House, 1962.

————. *The Essential Writings of Netaji Subhas Chandra Bose*. eds. Sisir Kumar Bose and Sugata Bose. Delhi: Oxford University Press, 1997.

————. *Fundamental Questions of Indian Revolution*. ed. Sisir Kumar Bose. Calcutta: Netaji Research Bureau, 1970.

————. *In Burmese Prisons: Correspondence May 1923 – July 1926.* ed. Sisir K. Bose Calcutta: Netaji Research Bureau, 2009.

————. *An Indian Pilgrim: An Unfinished Autobiography and Collected Letters, 1897–1921.* eds. Sisir K. Bose and Sugata Bose. New Delhi: Oxford University Press, 1997.

————. *The Indian Struggle, 1920–1942.* eds. Sisir Kumar Bose and Sugata Bose. Delhi: Oxford University Press, 1997.

————. *Letters to Emilie Schenkl, 1934–1942.* eds. Sisir Kumar Bose and Sugata Bose. Delhi: Oxford University Press, 1994.

————. *Letters, Articles, Speeches and Statements, 1933–1937.* eds. Sisir Kumar Bose and Sugata Bose. Delhi: Oxford University Press, 1994.

————. *The Mission of Life,* ed. Gopallal Sanyal. Calcutta: Thacker, Spink and Company, 1953.

Bose, Sugata. *His Majesty's Opponent: Subhas Chandra Bose and India's Struggle against Empire.* Cambridge, MA: The Belknap Press of Harvard University Press, 2011.

Campbell, D'Ann. 'Women in Combat: The World War II Experience in the United States, Great Britain, Germany, and the Soviet Union'. *The Journal of Military History* 57, 2 (1993): 301–23.

Chakrabarty, Bidyut. *Subhas Chandra Bose and Middle-Class Radicalism: A Study in Indian Nationalism, 1928–1940.* London: London School of Economics and Political Science and I. B. Tauris, 1990.

Chakravarti, Nalini Ranjan. *The Indian Minority in Burma: The Rise and Decline of an Immigrant Community.* Oxford: Oxford University Press, 1971.

Chakravarti, Uma. 'Whatever Happened to the Vedic *Dasi?*'. In *Recasting Women: Essays in Colonial History.* ed. Kumkum Sangari and Sudesh Vaid. New Delhi: Kali for Women, 1989: 27–87.

Chanana, Karuna. 'Social Change or Social Reform: The Education of Women in Pre-Independence India'. In *Socialisation, Education and Women: Explorations in Gender Identity.* ed. Karuna Chanana. New Delhi: Orient Longman, 1988: 96–128.

Chandra, Bipan. *India's Struggle for Independence, 1857–1947.* New Delhi: Penguin Books, 1988.

Chatterjee, Manini. '1930: Turning Point in the Participation of Women in the Freedom Struggle'. *Social Scientist* 29, no. 7/8 (2001): 39–47.

Chatterjee, Partha. 'The Nationalist Resolution of the Women's Question'. In *Recasting Women: Essays in Colonial History.* eds. K. Sangari and S. Vaid. New

Delhi: Kali for Women, 1989: 233–53.

Chatterji, Amal Chandra. *India's Struggle for Freedom*. Calcutta: Chakravarti, Chatterjee & Co., 1947.

Chattopadhyay, Bankim Chandra. *Anandamath*. New York: Oxford University Press, 2005.

Chaudhuri, Nirad C. *Thy Hand, Great Anarch! India, 1921–1952*. London: Chatto and Windus, 1987.

———. 'Subhas Chandra Bose - His Legacy and Legend'. *Pacific Affairs* 26 (1953): 349–57.

Chowdhury, Indira. *The Frail Hero and Virile History: Gender and the Politics of Culture in Colonial Bengal*. Delhi: Oxford University Press, 1998.

Cohen, Stephen P. 'Subhas Chandra Bose and the Indian National Army'. *Pacific Affairs* 36, 4 (1963): 411–29.

Cooper, Chester L. 'Moneylenders and the Economic Development of Lower Burma: An Exploratory Historical Study of the Role of the Indian Chettyars'. PhD diss., American University, Washington DC, 1959.

Dancz, Virginia H. *Women and Party Politics in Peninsular Malaysia*. Oxford: Oxford University Press, 1987.

Das Gupta, Hemendranath. *Subhas Chandra*. Calcutta: Jyoti Prokasalaya, 1946.

Dhar, Anuj. *Back from Dead. Inside the Subhas Bose Mystery*. New Delhi: Manas Publications, 2005.

———. *India's Biggest Cover-up*. New Delhi: Vitasta Publishing, 2012.

Dhillon, Gurbaksh Singh. 'How Transparent!'. In *Netaji Subhas Chandra Bose Commemoration Volume: A Tribute in His Centenary Year*. Edited by Anonymous. Calcutta: Scottish Church College, 1998: 9–14

Doniger, Wendy, and Brian K. Smith, trans. *The Laws of Manu*. London: Penguin Books, 1991.

Dube, Leela. 'On the Construction of Gender: Hindu Girls in Patrilineal India'. In *Socialisation, Education and Women: Explorations in Gender Identity,* ed. K. Chanana. New Delhi: Orient Longman, 1988: 166–192.

Dubey, Muchkund. ed. *Subhas Chandra Bose: The Man and His Vision*. New Delhi: Har-Anand, 1998.

Dutt, Kalpana. *Chittagong Armoury Raiders: Reminiscences*. New Delhi: People's Publishing House, 1979.

Dutta, Krishna, and Andrew Robinson. *Rabindranath Tagore: The Myriad-Minded Man*. New York: St. Martin's Press, 1996.

Elsbree, Willard H. *Japan's Role in South-East Asian Nationalist Movements, 1940 to 1945*. Cambridge, MA: Harvard University Press, 1953.

Everett, Jana Matson. *Women and Social Change in India*. New York: St Martin's Press, 1979.

Fay, Peter Ward. *The Forgotten Army: India's Armed Struggle for Independence, 1942–1945*. Ann Arbor, MI: University of Michigan Press, 1993.

Forbes, Geraldine. *Women in Modern India*. eds. Gordon Johnson, Christopher Alan Bayly and John F. Richards. The New Cambridge History of India. Vol. 4.2. New Delhi: Cambridge University Press, 1996.

————. 'Mothers and Sisters: Feminism and Nationalism in the Thought of Subhas Chandra Bose'. *Asian Studies* 2 (1984): 23–30.

————. 'Netaji Oration 1980: Goddesses or Rebels? The Women Revolutionaries of Bengal'. *The Oracle* 2 (1980): 1–15.

Forbes, Geraldine Hancock. *Women in Colonial India: Essays on Politics, Medicine, and Historiography*. New Delhi: Chronicle Books, 2005.

Fruzzetti, Lina. 'Kinship Identity and Issues of Nationalism: Female Abandonment in Calcutta'. In *Culture, Power, and Agency: Gender in Indian Ethnography*. ed. Lina Fruzzetti and Sirpa Tenhunen. Kolkata: Stree, 2006: 1–20.

Fujiwara Iwaichi. *F. Kikan. Japanese Army Intelligence Operations in South East Asia during World War II*. Singapore: Heinemann Asia, 1983.

Fuller, Marcus. 'The Wrongs of Indian Womanhood'. In *Purdah: An Anthology*. ed. Eunice de Souza. Oxford: Oxford University Press, 2004: 69.

Gandhi, Mohandas K. *An Autobiography: The Story of My Experiments with Truth*. Boston: Beacon Press, 1957.

————. *Collected Works of Mahatma Gandhi*. New Delhi: Publications Division, Ministry of Information and Broadcasting, Govt. of India, 1958.

Ganguli, Santimoy, Sudhir Ranjan Baksi, Dhiren Saha Roy, Ratul Roy Chowdhury, and Sisir Kumar Bose. 'Netaji's Underground in India during World War II: An Account by Participants in a Daring and Historic Undertaking'. *The Oracle* 1 (1979): 7–14.

Gawankar, Rohini. *The Women's Regiment and Captain Lakshmi of INA: An Untold Episode of NRI Women's Contribution to India's Freedom Struggle*. New Delhi: Devika Publications, 2003.

Getz, Marshall J. *Subhas Chandra Bose: A Biography*. Jefferson, NC: McFarland and Company, 2002.

Ghosh, Chitra. *Opening the Closed Windows: The Role of Women in Indian Society – the*

Reality and Ideal as Envisaged by Subhas Chandra Bose. eds. Some Ray and Chandni Chande. Kolkata: Progressive Publishers, 2002.

———. 'Subhas Chandra Bose: His Contribution to Women's Movement in India'. In *Subhas Chandra Bose: The Man and His Vision*. ed. M. Dubey. New Delhi: Har-Anand, 1998: 106–15.

Ghosh, Jitendra Nath. *Netaji Subhas Chandra: Political Philosophy of Netaji; History of Azad Hind Government, I.N.A. and International Law*. Calcutta: Orient Book Company, 1946.

Ghosh, Kalyan Kumar. *The Indian National Army: Motives, Problems and Significance*. Kuala Lumpur: Dept. of History, University of Malaya, 1968.

———. *The Indian National Army: Second Front of the Indian Independence Movement*. Meerut, UP: Meenakshi Prakashan, 1969.

Ghosh, Ratna. ed. *Netaji Subhas Chandra Bose and Indian Freedom Struggle: Netaji and Indian National Army (INA)*. New Delhi: Deep & Deep, 2006.

———. *Netaji Subhas Chandra Bose and Indian Freedom Struggle: Subhas Chandra Bose; His Ideas and Vision*. New Delhi: Deep & Deep, 2006.

Goebbels, Joseph. *Die Tagebücher von Joseph Goebbels*. ed. Elke Fröhlich. Vol. 9. Munich: Bundesarchiv, Institut für Zeitgeschichte, 1987.

Gopinath, Aruna. *Footprints on the Sands of Time: Rasammah Bhupalan; A Life of Purpose*. ed. P. C. Shivadas. Kuala Lumpur: Arkib Negara Malaysia, 2007.

Gordon, Leonard A. *Brothers against the Raj: A Biography of Indian Nationalists Sarat and Subhas Chandra Bose*. New Delhi: Rupa and Co., 1997.

———. 'Portrait of a Bengali Revolutionary'. *The Journal of Asian Studies* 27 (1968): 197–216.

Green, Leslie Claude. 'The Indian National Army Trials'. *The Modern Law Review* 11 (1948): 47–69.

Gupta, Amit Kumar. *Myth and Reality: The Struggle for Freedom in India, 1945–47*. New Delhi: Manohar, 1987.

Gupta, Samjukta Gombrich. 'The Goddess, Women, and their Rituals in Hinduism'. In *Faces of the Feminine in Ancient, Medieval, and Modern India*. ed. M. Bose. Oxford: Oxford University Press, 2000: 87–106.

Hartog, Rudolf. *The Sign of the Tiger: Subhas Chandra Bose and His Indian Legion in Germany, 1941–45*. New Delhi: Rupa & Co., 2001.

Hauner, Milan. *India in Axis Strategy: Germany, Japan, and Indian Nationalists in the Second World War*. Stuttgart: Klett-Cotta, 1981.

Hayes, Romain. *Subhas Chandra Bose in Nazi Germany: Politics, Intelligence and*

Propaganda, 1941–43. London: Hurst and Company, 2011.

Heehs, Peter. 'India's Divided Loyalties?'. *History Today* 45 (1995): 16–23.

Heimsath, Charles Herman. *Indian Nationalism and Hindu Social Reform.* Princeton, NJ: Princeton University Press, 1964.

Hills, Carol, and Daniel C. Silverman. 'Nationalism and Feminism in Late Colonial India: The Rani of Jhansi Regiment, 1943–45'. *Modern Asian Studies* 27 (1993): 741–60.

Jayaram, N., and Yogesh Atal. eds. *The Indian Diaspora: Dynamics of Migration.* New Delhi: Sage Publications, 2004.

Jog, Narayan Gopal. *In Freedom's Quest: A Biography of Netaji Subhas Chandra Bose.* Bombay: Orient Longmans, 1969.

Kasturi, Leela, and Vina Mazumdar. *Women and Indian Nationalism.* New Delhi: Vikas Pub. House, 1994.

Kaur, Amarjit. 'Indian Labour, Labour Standards, and Workers' Health in Burma and Malaya, 1900–1940'. *Modern Asian Studies* 40 (2006): 425–75.

Kaur, Manmohan. *Women in India's Freedom Struggle.* New Delhi: Sterling, 1992.

Khan, Shah Nawaz. *My Memories of I.N.A. and Its Netaji.* Delhi: Rajkamal Publications, 1946.

Khan, Shah Nawaz, Prem Kumar Sahgal, and Gurbax Singh Dhillon. *The I.N.A. Heroes: Autobiographies of Maj. Gen. Shahnawaz, Col. Prem K. Sahgal, Col. Gurbax Singh Dhillon of the Azad Hind Fauj.* Lahore: Hero Publications, 1946.

Khosla, G. D. *Last Days of Netaji.* Delhi: Thomson Press (India), Publication Division, 1974.

Kiani, Mohammad Zaman. *India's Freedom Struggle and the Great INA: Memoirs.* New Delhi: Reliance Publishing House, 1994.

Kinsley, David R. *Hindu Goddesses: Visions of the Divine Feminine in the Hindu Religious Tradition.* Delhi: Motilal Banarsidass, 1987.

Kinvig, Clifford. 'Allied POWs and the Burma-Thailand Railway'. In *Japanese Prisoners of War.* eds. P. Towle, M. Kosuge and Y. Kibata. London: Hambledon and London, 2000: 37–57.

Kondapi, Chenchia. *Indians Overseas: 1838–1949.* New Delhi: Indian Council of World Affairs, 1951.

Kratoska, Paul H. *The Japanese Occupation of Malaya: A Social and Economic History.* London: Hurst, 1998.

Kuhlmann, Jan. *Subhas Chandra Bose und die Indienpolitik der Achsenmächte.* Berlin: Hans Schiler, 2003.

————. *Netaji in Europe*. New Delhi: Rainlight, 2012.

Kulkarni,V. S., and K. S. N. Murty. *First Indian National Army Trial*. Poona: Mangal Sahitya Prakashan, 1946.

Kumar, Rai, Rameshwari Devi, and Romila Pruthi. eds. *Women's Role in Indian National Movement*. Jaipur: Pointer, 2003.

Kurti, Kitty. *Subhas Chandra Bose as I Knew Him*. Calcutta: Mukhopadhyay, 1966.

Lambert-Hurley, Siobhan. 'Fostering Sisterhood: Muslim Women and the All-India Ladies' Association'. *Journal of Women's History* 16 (2004): 40–65.

Lebra, Joyce Chapman. *The Indian National Army and Japan*. Singapore: Institute of Southeast Asian Studies, 2008.

————. *Japanese-Trained Armies in Southeast Asia: Independence and Volunteer Forces in World War II*. New York: Columbia University Press, 1977.

————. *Jungle Alliance: Japan and the Indian National Army*. Singapore: Donald Moore for Asia Pacific Press, 1971.

————. *The Rani of Jhansi: A Study in Female Heroism in India*. Honolulu: University of Hawaii Press, 1986.

————. *Women Against the Raj: The Rani of Jhansi Regiment*. Singapore: Institute of Southeast Asian Studies, 2008.

Lee, Sharon M. 'Female Immigrants and Labor in Colonial Malaya, 1860–1947'. *International Migration Review* 23 (1989): 309–31.

Legg, Stephen. 'Gendered Politics and Nationalised Homes: Women and the Anti-Colonial Struggle in Delhi, 1930–47'. *Gender, Place and Culture* 10 (2003): 7–27.

Liddle, Joanna, and Rama Joshi. *Daughters of Independence: Gender, Caste, and Class in India*. New Brunswick, NJ: Rutgers University Press, 1986.

Mahajani, Usha. *The Role of Indian Minorities in Burma and Malaya*. Bombay: Vora and Co., 1960.

Maikap, Satish Chandra. *Netaji Subhas Chandra Bose and Indian War of Independence*. Calcutta: Punascha, 1998.

Majumdar, Shanti Bhowmick. 'Netaji's Rani of Jhansi Regiment. Reminiscenses.' *The Oracle* 2 (1980): 21–26.

Mandal, Tirtha. *The Women Revolutionaries of Bengal, 1905–1939*. Calcutta: Minerva Associates, 1991.

Mangat, Gurbachan Singh. *Indian National Army: Role in India's Struggle for Freedom*. Ludhiana, Punjab: Gagan Publishers, 1991.

Manu. *The Laws of Manu.* Wendy Doniger and Brian Smith, eds. and trans. London: Penguin Books, 1991.

Mookerjee, Girija K. 'Netaji the Great Resistance Leader'. *The Oracle* 8 (1986): 22–35.

Mookerjee, Nanda. *Subhas Chandra Bose: The British Press, Intelligence and Parliament.* Calcutta: Jayasree Prakashan, 1981.

Mukherjee, Hirendranath. *Bow of Burning Gold: A Study of Subhas Chandra Bose.* New Delhi: People's Pub. House, 1977.

Nair, Kusum. *The Story of I.N.A.* Bombay: Padma Publications, 1946.

Nanda, Bal Ram. *Indian Women from Purdah to Modernity.* New Delhi: Vikas Pub. House, 1976.

Nehru, Jawaharlal. *The Discovery of India.* New Delhi: Jawaharlal Nehru Memorial Fund, Oxford University Press, 2001.

Olivelle, Patrick, ed. *The Law Code of Manu.* Oxford: Oxford University Press, 2004.

Palta, Krishan Raj. *My Adventures with the I.N.A.* Lahore: Lion Press, 1946.

Pandit, H. N. *The Last Days of Netaji.* Delhi: All India INA Committee, 1993.

———. *Netaji Subhas Chandra Bose, from Kabul to Battle of Imphal.* New Delhi: Sterling, 1988.

Pelinka, Anton. *Democracy Indian Style: Subhas Chandra Bose and the Creation of India's Political Culture.* New Brunswick, NJ: Transaction Publishers, 2003.

Pennington, Reina. *Wings, Women, and War: Soviet Airwomen in World War II Combat.* Lawrence, Kansas: University Press of Kansas, 2001.

Pruthi, Rai K. *Subhas Chandra Bose: His Dream of Free India.* New Delhi: Rajat Publications, 2005.

Rafi, Mirza M. *The Problem of Indian Settlers in Burma.* New Delhi: The Indian Institute of International Affairs, 1946.

Ray, Bharati. ed. *From the Seams of History: Essays on Indian Women.* Delhi: Oxford University Press, 1995.

Ray, Raka. *Fields of Protest: Women's Movements in India.* Minneapolis, MN: University of Minnesota Press, 1999.

Roy, Bhola Nath. *Oaten Incident, 1916: A Chapter in the Life of Netaji Subhas Bose.* Calcutta: S. C. Sarkar & Sons, 1975.

Roy, Dilip Kumar. *The Subhash I Knew.* Bombay: Nalanda Publications, 1946.

Safrani, Abid Hasan. *The Men from Imphal.* Calcutta: Netaji Research Bureau, 1971.

_____, 'A Soldier Remembers', *The Oracle* 6 (1984): 24–65.

Sagade, Jaya. *Child Marriage in India: Socio-legal and Human Rights Dimensions.* New Delhi: Oxford Univeristy Press, 2005.

Sahgal, Lakshmi. 'INA and the Role of Subhas Chandra Bose'. In *Netaji Subhas Chandra Bose Commemoration Volume: A Tribute in His Centenary Year,* edited by Anonymous. Calcutta: Scottish Church College, 1998: 1–8.

_____. 'Netaji's Ideology'. In *Subhas Chandra Bose: The Man and His Vision,* ed. M. Dubey. New Delhi: Har-Anand, 1998: 21–24.

_____. 'The Rani of Jhansi Regiment'. *The Oracle* 1 (1979): 15–19.

_____. *A Revolutionary Life – Memoirs of a Political Activist.* New Delhi: Kali for Women, 1997.

Sahoo, Shridhar Charan. *Subhas Chandra Bose: Political Philosophy.* New Delhi: APH Publishing, 1997.

Sandhu, Kernial Singh. *Indians in Malaya: Some Aspects of Their Immigration and Settlement, 1786–1957.* Cambridge, UK: Cambridge University Press, 1969.

Sangari, Kumkum, and Sudesh Vaid. eds. *Recasting Women: Essays in Colonial History.* New Delhi: Kali for Women, 1989.

Saqui, A. B. *The Facts about the I.N.A.* Lahore: The National Book Society of India, 1946.

Sareen, Tilak Rai. *Japan and the Indian National Army.* Delhi: Agam Prakashan, 1986.

_____. *Select Documents on Indian National Army.* Delhi: Agam Prakashan, 1988.

Sarkar, Hemanta Kumar. *Subhaser Songe Baro Bochhor* [*Twelve Years with Subhas*]. Calcutta: Sarkar and Co. 1946. http://subhaschandrabose.org/hks-withsubhas.php

Sarkar, Jayabrata. 'Power, Hegemony and Politics: Leadership Struggle in Congress in the 1930s'. *Modern Asian Studies* 40 (2006): 333–70.

Seth, Amritlal. *Jai-Hind: The Diary of a Rebel Daughter of India with the Rani of Jhansi Regiment.* ed. Vithalbhai K. Jhaveri and Soli S. Batliwala. Bombay: Janmabhoomi Prakashan Mandir, 1945.

Seth, Hira Lal. *Personality and Political Ideals of Subhas Chandra Bose: Is He Fascist?* Lahore: Hero Pubs., 1946.

Singh, Durlab. *Formation and Growth of the Indian National Army.* Lahore: Hero Pubs., 1946.

Singh, Mohan. *Soldiers' Contribution to Indian Independence: The Epic of the Indian National Army.* New Delhi: Army Educational Stores, 1974.

Sinha, Mrinalini. *Colonial Masculinity: The 'Manly Englishman' and the 'Effeminate Bengali' in the Late Nineteenth Century.* Manchester: Manchester University Press, 1995.

Sivaram, M. *The Road to Delhi.* Rutland, VT: Charles E. Tuttle, 1966.

Slim, William. *Defeat into Victory: Battling Japan in Burma and India, 1942-45.* New York: Cooper Square Press, 2000.

Som, Reba. *Gandhi, Bose, Nehru: And the Making of the Modern Indian Mind.* New Delhi: Penguin, 2004.

————. *Subhas Chandra Bose and the Resolution of the Women's Question.* New Delhi: Centre for Women's Development Studies, 2002.

Souza, Eunice de. ed. *Purdah: An Anthology.* Oxford: Oxford University Press, 2004.

Streets, Heather. *Martial Races: The Military Race and Masculinity in British Imperial Culture, 1857–1914.* Manchester: Manchester University Press, 2004.

Subbamma, Malladi. *Hinduism and Women.* Delhi: Ajanta Books International, 1992.

Sundaram, Chandar S. 'A Paper Tiger: The Indian National Army in Battle, 1944–1945'. *War and Society* 13 (1995): 35-60.

Tamayama, Kazuo. ed., and John Nunneley, trans. *Tales by Japanese Soldiers of the Burma Campaign, 1942–1945.* London: Cassell and Co., 2000.

Taneja, Anup. *Gandhi, Women, and the National Movement, 1920–47.* New Delhi: Har-Anand, 2005.

Thakur, Bharti. *Women in Gandhi's Mass Movements.* New Delhi: Deep and Deep Publ., 2006.

Thapar, Suruchi. 'Women as Activists; Women as Symbols: A Study of the Indian Nationalist Movement'. *Feminist Review* 44 (1993): 81–96.

Thapar-Björkert, Suruchi. *Women in the Indian National Movement: Unseen Faces and Unheard Voices, 1930–42.* New Delhi: Sage Publications, 2006.

Thivi, John A. 'He Came, He Fought, He Conquered.' In *Subhas Chandra Bose.* ed. Verinder Grover, *Political Thinkers of Modern India.* New Delhi: Deep and Deep Publications, 1991.

Tinker, Hugh. 'A Forgotten Long March: The Indian Exodus from Burma, 1942'. *Journal of Southeast Asian Studies* 6 (1975): 1–15.

Toye, Hugh. 'The First Indian National Army, 1941–42'. *Journal of Southeast Asian Studies* 15 (1984): 365–81.

————. *Subhash Chandra Bose: The Springing Tiger; A Study of a Revolution.* Bombay: Jaico Publishing House, 1959.

Trott zu Solz, Clarita von. *Adam von Trott zu Solz: Eine Lebensbeschreibung.* Berlin: Gedenkstätte Deutscher Widerstand, 1994.

Voight, Johannes H. *Indien im Zweiten Weltkrieg.* Stuttgart: Deutsche Verlags-Anstalt, 1978.

Webster, Donovan. *The Burma Road: The Epic Story of the China-Burma-India Theater in World War II.* New York: Farrar, Straus and Giroux, 2003.

Yadav, Kripal Chandra, and Akiko Seti. *Adventure into the Unknown: The Last Days of Netaji Subhas Chandra Bose.* Gurgaon, Haryana: Hope India Publ., 1996.

Yadava, S. S. *Forgotten Warriors of Indian War of Independence, 1941–1946: Indian National Army.* Gurgaon, Haryana: All India INA Committee, Hope India Publ. 2004.

INDEX

Vishpala, Queen, 3
Vivekananda, Swami, 59, 147

Waddedar, Preetilata, 24, 25–26
Washington, George, 231
Widow remarriage, 18, 123
Women, arrested for civil disobedience, 22, 25, 64; Bose's friendship with, 57, 58, 64, 65; exclusion from ground combat of, 4; legal standing of, 17–19; in Soviet Air Force, 4; as violent revolutionaries, 23, 24, 25–26, 39; women's movements, 20, 23, 56, 64–65, 71, 91–92, 93, 94, 107, 112, 126, 240, 241

World War II, 1, 4, 5, 6, 11, 12, 14, 30, 31, 51, 53, 69, 78, 122, 124, 210, 231

Xavier, Rani Emily, 192

Yadava, Captain S.S., 9, 96, 113–14, 201
Yellappa, Attavar, 94, 126, 197, 210–11, 216
Yoneo Ishii, 14
Young Men's Indian Association, 71

Zai, Colonel, 149
Zenanas, 19

ACKNOWLEDGEMENTS

My deepest appreciation goes to the remarkable members of the Rani of Jhansi Regiment, who spent many hours sharing their experiences of World War II with me.

Subhashini Sahgal Ali, Anisa Sahgal Puri and Anita Schenkl Pfaff took time to tell me about their parents. Anuradha Bhattacharjee in Mumbai and P.J. Kaur in New Delhi helped me locate of some of the Ranis. Shilpi and Yadav Rai invited me to join their family and gave me a home the many times I spent weeks in the National Archives in New Delhi. Antonia Moon and 'Freulein X' at the British Library went out of their way to help and succeeded in locating the documents I hoped still existed.

Shankar Bajpai, S. Jaishankar, Shyam Sarin and Namita Gokhale in New Delhi; Hiroshi Hirabayashi, Yoneo Ishii and Yukio Sato in Tokyo; Nagasaki Nobuko in Kyoto; Ashley Tellis in Washington, DC; Leonard Gordon in New York, and Claus Hjort Frederiksen in Copenhagen gave welcome advice, useful information and much needed help. Robert Blackwill, Henk Bos, Lina Fruzetti, Seth Sicroff and Anders Uhrskov read, reread and commented on several drafts of the manuscript. At the last moment, IT wizard Kevin McLean recovered photos of the Ranis from my old, dead computer; and my editor at HarperCollins, Arcopol Chaudhuri, was a delight to work with throughout as we scoured the text together.

To all I send my warmest thanks and deepest gratitude for their generous contribution to this study that means so much to me.